Virtue Ethics

Virtue Ethics

An Introduction, a Proposal, and a Case

ROBERT CAMPBELL ROBERTS

OXFORD
UNIVERSITY PRESS

OXFORD

UNIVERSITY PRESS

Oxford University Press is a department of the University of Oxford.
It furthers the University's objective of excellence in research, scholarship,
and education by publishing worldwide. Oxford is a registered trade mark of
Oxford University Press in the UK and in certain other countries.

Published in the United States of America by Oxford University Press
198 Madison Avenue, New York, NY 10016, United States of America.

© Robert Campbell Roberts 2026

CIP data is on file at the Library of Congress

ISBN 9780197847978 (pbk.)
ISBN 9780197847961 (hbk.)

DOI: 10.1093/9780197848005.001.0001

Paperback printed by Marquis Book Printing, Canada
Hardback printed by Lightning Source, Inc., United States of America

The manufacturer's authorized representative in the EU for product safety is
Oxford University Press España S.A. of Parque Empresarial San Fernando de Henares,
Avenida de Castilla, 2 – 28830 Madrid (www.oup.es/en or product.safety@oup.com).
OUP España S.A. also acts as importer into Spain of products made by the manufacturer.

Contents

PART 2. CHRISTIAN VIRTUE ETHICS

Introduction

In the fall of 1973, with my PhD almost in hand, I took a job teaching philosophy at Western Kentucky University. I regarded ethics as a focus of my work in the university and hoped that teaching it would have a healthy effect both on me and on the students in my care. The potential for human improvement seemed natural to the discipline of ethics and was one of its attractions. I taught my courses in the usual way, introducing students to Kant and Mill and Hume and the debates about the foundations of ethics and the factions' "isms": rationalism, utilitarianism, sentimentalism, social contractarianism. In short, I taught ethical theory. I tried to be fair, giving the arguments for and against each "position."

This went on for a while, and I learned alongside my students. I became clearer about the debates and also thought about the significance of the whole enterprise of ethics as I was teaching it. As these thoughts and questions percolated, I became increasingly uneasy about my "vocation." Was ethics doing what I supposed ethics should do? Was anybody, including me, acquiring any wisdom or other improvement from the exercises in which I was leading my students? Were we becoming better, wiser people? Was ethics seeping into us through our faculties of reflection? We certainly weren't securing the foundations of ethics: The debates among the theories always ended in a draw or at least didn't establish the kind of solidity that befits a foundation. In fact, the exercise seemed to engender a certain skepticism: Morality needs a foundation, but our efforts, and those of the very smart thinkers we were studying, all seemed to end in frustration. And suppose we did once and for all establish, say, that Kantian ethics was right and the competing theories inferior and flawed. What would we have gained? Would we be ethically better positioned than if we had never heard of Kant and the debates?

Virtue Ethics. Robert Campbell Roberts, Oxford University Press.
© Robert Campbell Roberts 2026. DOI: 10.1093/9780197848005.003.0001

One afternoon, as I jogged laps on the university track, reflections like these came together in an impression: *I'm in the wrong business*. The crisis was mostly unspoken and played out in the theater of my uneasy conscience. The inertia of having a decent income, a pleasant situation, and not knowing what else to do carried me along, however, and I continued teaching ethics for the next forty years.

In the meantime, the "movement" of virtue ethics was groping for something new (and something old). Already in 1958, Elizabeth Anscombe, in a protest against modern ethical theory, had hinted at proposing something like a "return to virtue" and the ethics of Aristotle. In 1981, Alasdair MacIntyre's *After Virtue* made a splash, creating a wave that continues lapping to this day. And many a lesser dinghy has been riding the wave.

This development encouraged me. At least virtue sounded like something in the neighborhood of ethical improvement. And isn't wisdom a virtue? I noticed, along with many others, that Kant and Mill and Hume all nodded to virtues, though in ways that subordinated these excellences in their more fundamental foundational projects and gave little detailed attention to the virtues. So, without abandoning the modern ethical theories, I gradually gave more and more space and time in my courses to the ethical concept of a virtue and the concepts of the virtues. The virtue ethicists, old and new, eventually took over my courses altogether.

I noticed, too, that the virtue ethicists of the twentieth and twenty-first centuries tended to differ from those of the ancient world in their purpose of studying the virtues. Socrates, Aristotle, the Stoics, and the writers of the New Testament, as well as the prophets and wise persons of ancient Israel, aimed quite explicitly at the virtuous formation of persons and communities, while the more recent virtue ethicists suffered from a hangover: The latter saw the study as continuous with establishing the foundations of ethics, or at least as somehow mixed up in that modern project and as only remotely connected with the actual formation of people.

This book is an *introduction* to virtue ethics, a *proposal* about how it is best practiced, and an extended *illustration* of that proposed practice. Let me explain each aspect.

It is an intermediate[1] introduction, partly conceptual and partly historical. Chapter 1 introduces the enterprise of modern ethical theory as a way of solving a problem: That ethical pluralism (which is obviously our situation) can devolve into ethical relativism or skepticism, both of which are toxic to morality. As a proposed solution to this problem, ethical theory is preventive medicine. Whether in Thomas Hobbes, David Hume, Immanuel Kant, or J. S. Mill, the modern strategy is foundationalist: Find a humanly indisputable and universal ethical or pre-ethical commitment on which to secure ethics—"ethics" here being principles of right action, obligations, ideas of good and evil, and conceptions of virtue and vice. Then, by sound logic, bolt this ethical "content" with lock-washers to that irresistible and universally accepted commitment. In ethics, as in all of philosophy, the bolts, nuts, washers, and screws, the mortises, tenons, and dovetails—in short, the connectors—are *conceptual* (we philosophers are thinkers, after all!). Just as the bolts connect the frame of a house firmly to its foundation, so the conceptual connection between, say, the greatest happiness of the greatest number of people (Mill's candidate for the unavoidable, universally accepted, and compelling commitment) and the virtue of justice or compassion, or parents' obligation to feed and nurture their children, holds those dimensions of ethics firmly to the ethical foundation. The strong conceptual connection of those principles, virtues, and so forth, to that immovable foundation is the ethics-guarding theory that will keep it from blowing away or collapsing, under the floods and tremors of pluralism, into relativism or skepticism, and from there into nihilism.

I introduce this idea in Chapter 1, thereby introducing contemporary virtue ethics because virtue ethics as pursued by most practitioners today is another iteration of modern ethical theory, as I argue in Chapter 3. Turning to recent history, Chapter 2 expounds the early and instigating contributions of Elizabeth Anscombe and Alasdair MacIntyre to virtue ethics as it is known today. Neither of these instigators is as outright foundationalist as the more recent virtue ethicists, which Michael Slote indicates by calling his variety

---

[1] For a briefer introduction, tailored more for beginning students and more casual readers, see my *Virtue Ethics in Christian Perspective* (Eugene: Cascade, 2025).

"pure virtue ethics." Pure virtue ethics is a late-coming modern ethical theory. Continuing the introduction in Chapter 4, I contrast "pure" virtue ethics with ancient virtue ethics, which I take to be a model; and so we begin the proposal: *Let's retrieve the ancient practice.* In that chapter, my chief illustrative examples are Socrates, Seneca the Stoic, and Aristotle. These thinkers weren't trying to keep ethics from blowing away by anchoring it to a foundation but were seeking to become wise and to foster wisdom, virtue, and human flourishing in their communities. They did so by conceptual exploration of the ethical domain as they construed it, with special interest in the ethical formation of people.

Being philosophers, they, like the modern theorists, were tracing conceptual connections, now not in the interest of fixing ethical concepts to a foundational one, but in pursuit of a kind of understanding that was itself wisdom and so would enhance the humanity of their souls. If the ancients are our model, virtue ethics can and should be, not a theoretical enterprise as conceived in modern theories, but a practical-analytical-contemplative activity of exploring the concepts of the virtues, aimed at the formation of good people and good communities. Such exploration will, as Elizabeth Anscombe anticipated, involve exploring the psychology of motivation, thought, and self-managing skill, of which the virtues are particular kinds of formation.

The ancient philosophers explored the ethical domain *as they construed it*, and they didn't all construe it the same way. Pluralism prevailed in their case, as it does in ours. The ancient world was populated by Aristotelians, Stoics, Platonists, Skeptics, and Epicureans, not to speak of Zoroastrians and Jews and later Christians, among other outlooks, each with a variant domain of exploration, a somewhat different map of the virtuous personality, and so a distinct "virtue ethics."[2] Following this feature of the ancient world, my proposal assumes that outlooks on life and human flourishing come in a

---

[2] For excellent expositions, see Martha Nussbaum, *The Therapy of Desire: Theory and Practice in Hellenistic Ethics* (Princeton: Princeton University Press, 1994) and Pierre Hadot, *Philosophy as a Way of Life: Spiritual Exercises from Socrates to Foucault,* trans. Michael Chase (Oxford: Blackwell, 1995).

variety of traditions, and that to explore the virtues in depth is to honor and plumb the peculiarities of those traditions. Among the ancient outlooks that seek to promote the formation of souls and communities is the Hebrew tradition of the prophets and wise thinkers about the law of God, which is extended and developed in the teachings and actions of Jesus of Nazareth and his followers. A distinctive feature of this book among books about virtue ethics is the "case" that is its central illustration. The chief example of the whole book is the virtue ethics that is embodied in the Bible considered as two Testaments, an "old" one and a "new" one.

The book is nevertheless philosophical. It defends the idea that philosophy can be a source of wisdom, where wisdom is a full-fledged human virtue and not just an ability to make astute observations. It also attempts to illustrate how philosophy can have this function. It defends the idea that philosophy can make a distinctive contribution to Christian ethics, an important contribution beyond what biblical exploration alone can afford. Philosophy can contribute to the inculcation of biblical wisdom and the virtues of Christian character. But the book also makes a case that any kind of virtue ethics, including the most ardently secular, might learn something from the pastoral temper of Christian theology.

I agree with the later MacIntyre in pressing (1) the need for an overall fundamental conception of human nature (a metaphysical biology, if you will) for any adequate account of the virtues and the practical wisdom that infuses and shapes them; and (2) that that conception of human nature will give a central role to human dependency. Thomas Aquinas satisfies those conditions, but in doing so, he draws on the Bible and especially the New Testament and the traditions it spawned. Without minimizing the importance of that more elaborate project, in this book, I attempt to simplify the task and the result by appealing directly to the source.

Bible quotations are from the New Revised Standard Version unless otherwise indicated.

PART 1
VIRTUE ETHICS

1
Modern Ethical Theory

Introduction

This book is about a philosophical activity called "virtue ethics." In Chapters 2 and 3, I will try to say what many philosophers today understand virtue ethics to be. The present chapter will help prepare us to understand how it works. As we'll see in the fourth chapter, philosophers have been thinking about the virtues for a long time. The activity the ancients pursued differs from what most people today call virtue ethics. But virtue ethics today has one thing in common with what the earlier philosophers of virtue did. And that is to give the human virtues—character traits like fairness, generosity, and courage—a prominent place in their thinking.

A big difference between what the earlier philosophers did and what is called virtue ethics today is the *particular* places in ethical thinking that the different generations of philosophers give to the virtues. What is the function or purpose of thinking hard about the virtues? Virtue ethicists today tend to make the virtues the "foundation" of an ethical theory. The earlier philosophers didn't place the virtues there. They had a different goal in thinking hard about the virtues. They wanted to be virtuous and help others be so, because they thought it was required for living the best possible life for a human being. They considered philosophy a discipline in becoming more fully human. It was an exercise in personal and communal maturity.

They tended to think of living a human life as an activity comparable to such activities as building a house and playing a violin. Doing such activities well requires being fit for them. To build a house, you have to have strengths and skills and understanding; otherwise, you'll do a bad job of it. To play a violin well, you need hard-won skills and

Virtue Ethics. Robert Campbell Roberts, Oxford University Press.
© Robert Campbell Roberts 2026. DOI: 10.1093/9780197848005.003.0003

understanding and developed taste: years of practice. Otherwise, you'll do it poorly. To varying extents, many people make a mess of their lives, and the older virtue ethics was designed to help us avoid failure and make a success of ours. This wasn't the same as being a professional success, becoming famous, having good ratings, or making a lot of money before you die. Many are the ways to make lots of money, but being a success at living a human life requires that you become generous, grateful, truthful, just, kind, and brave. That's the basic reason that the ancient philosophers gave the virtues the central place in their ethical thinking. They wanted to know what the virtues are so they could practice them and so have a good life.

In this book, I will use the term "virtue ethics" for any philosophy that gives the virtues a central place, including that of the ancient philosophers, even though they didn't use the term.

The Question of Modern Ethics

We're getting ahead of (or perhaps behind!) ourselves in talking about the earlier virtue ethicists. We want first to consider contemporary practitioners of virtue ethics. But to understand what contemporary virtue ethicists are up to, we need a sketch of what modern ethical theorists are up to, and that will be our task in the present chapter.

As I said, virtue ethicists today tend to be primarily interested in the foundation of ethics. In this, they are like other kinds of ethical theorists—sentimentalists, Kantians, and utilitarians. Why would anybody worry about the foundation of ethics? We worry about foundations when there's some danger of a structure falling down or coming apart as a result of stresses like hurricanes and earthquakes or just the normal gradual shifting of the earth's surface. A good foundation is something like a guarantee that what's built on it will have integrity and be reliable and stay put. On June 25, 2021, the Champlain Towers South condo building in Surfside, Florida, collapsed, killing ninety-eight people. An extensively investigated report by *USA Today* that was published on October 14, 2021, says that "even before developers sold off the 136 condominiums to their first owners, the construction had been botched and the building had been set on a course to rot from the foundation up."[1] The whole building rested on the foundation, and faults in the foundation threatened and doomed everything that was being held up by it.

The dangers that are thought to threaten ethics if it isn't firmly fixed to a solid foundation are pluralism, relativism, and skepticism. What are these "isms"?

Moral Disagreement and Argument

Moral disagreement is a familiar fact of everyday life. Republicans disagree with Democrats about taxing the rich to support the poor. The Christian disagrees with the Muslim about the consumption of pork and port. A father disagrees with his daughter about whether it's morally substandard to have sleepovers with the boy she's been dating for three weeks. People dispute about a woman's moral right to abort her "pregnancy."

We argue about some of these things. We offer reasons for rejecting moral practices and beliefs that contradict our own. The Christian appeals to the authority of the Holy Spirit and the apostles in relaxing the Mosaic law, and the Muslim appeals to the authority of Mohammed and the Qur'an in extending it to alcohol. The father appeals to his daughter by pointing out that the purpose of sexual intercourse is the permanent moral–spiritual union of two persons in a context of possible procreation, and the daughter defends her view with references to the importance of physical expressions of love. The choice advocate appeals to a woman's right to control her body, and the advocate for fetal life appeals to a baby's right to live.

In some cases, the dispute may be resolved by argument. Perhaps the daughter has picked up her ideas about physical expression of "love" quite casually from television and schoolmates, but more deeply does accept her father's vision of marriage. When she hears his argument, it touches this latent moral premise, and she gives up the idea of sleepovers. The dispute about abortion seems to turn on a factual

---

[1] https://www.wsws.org/en/articles/2021/10/18/surf-o18.html.

question: Is a fetus a baby, or is it just a piece of the mother's body? So we can imagine a person changing sides as a result of learning that the fetus is, in fact, a complete and genetically unique human organism. But these and the other moral disagreements are, in many cases, much more resistant than this to resolution by argument. In one degree or another, they may result from a confrontation of different moral *outlooks*—that is, different *systems* of moral commitments and different fundamental starting points for moral deliberation.

Pluralism and Relativism

A situation in which some important moral disagreements aren't resolvable by appeal to commonly acknowledged facts and commonly held moral premises is a *moral pluralism*. The cultural anthropologists have shown us that the earth is such a situation, and it's clear that European and American societies are also such a situation.

From the indisputable fact of *moral pluralism*, people often infer the disputable thesis of *moral relativism*. Ruth Benedict, an anthropologist of fifty years ago, is famous for this fallacy: "We do not any longer make the mistake of deriving the morality of our own locality and decade directly from the inevitable constitution of human nature. We do not elevate it to the dignity of a first principle. We recognize that morality differs in every society, and is a convenient term for socially approved habits. Mankind has always preferred to say, 'It is morally good,' rather than 'It is habitual,' and the fact of this preference is matter enough for a critical science of ethics. But historically the two phrases are synonymous."[2] Relativism can be formulated in either of the following ways. (A) Ethical propositions such as *Abortion is usually wrong* and *The rich may be taxed to support the poor* and *Humility is a vice* are not true or false. Instead, they express habits or attitudes of social groups or even individuals. For example, within the moral

---

[2] Ruth Benedict, "Anthropology and the Abnormal," *Journal of General Psychology* 10 (1934): 59–80. Reprinted in Joel Feinberg, *Reason and Responsibility: Readings in Some Basic Problems of Philosophy*, sixth edition (Belmont, CA: Wadsworth Publishing Company, 1985), 472.

outlook to which Friedrich Nietzsche appeals, humility is a vice and a disposition to dominate others is a virtue, whereas many of our contemporaries believe the reverse. According to this version of relativism, 'believe' is not quite the right word for the way the relativist adheres to the ethical propositions, since she doesn't think they're true or false. This would be Ruth Benedict's version of relativism. (B) Truth and falsity do apply in ethics, but only within one outlook or another. In this version, while truth and falsity apply to ethical propositions, they don't apply *between ethical outlooks.* "Humility is a virtue" is true in, say, Christianity, but it's false in Nietzsche's framework. It would be like saying that double negatives are bad grammar: It's bad grammar to say, "I don't never do that," but it's not bad grammar to say, "Je ne fais jamais ça." It all depends on which language you're speaking. Similarly, an action that amounts to killing a human fetus (which is wrong and bad) in a Christian framework is reproductive health care (which is right and good) in a secular framework. The attempt to criticize people occupying a different outlook violates the relativist principle that such judgments can be made only from within the outlook whose members' actions are being evaluated.

The second formulation of relativism has some advantages: The moral attitude of people occupying a moral framework is antagonistic to the proposition, *My moral judgments aren't true or false, but merely expressions of my habits and attitudes.* This is why Benedict's suggestion that we might substitute "It is habitual" for "It is morally good" sounds implausible. It sounds implausible to say, "I know that the head-hunters of Nueva Viscaya think it's OK to chop off your uncle's head as a trophy, but my church and I are just in the habit of taking a dim view of it." By supplying a sense of 'true' and 'false,' the second formulation honors, in a way the first doesn't, people's inclination to attribute truth and falsity to ethical propositions. The second version also offers an explanation of why some ethical disagreements are endless: The disputants are appealing to different standards of truth and falsity—namely, the different standards internal to different moral outlooks. Let me now formulate two criticisms of moral relativism.

The first is that the inference from moral pluralism to moral relativism is invalid. From the fact that there are many moral outlooks, it doesn't follow that none of them is true, or that the propositions they generate are true only within the relevant outlooks. If, as Christians believe, ethical propositions are true if and only if God endorses them, then no matter what diversity of human moral outlooks we may find in the world, some ethical statements are true and others are false, regardless of the outlook to which they belong. Very likely, most of the moral outlooks found in the world contain some true claims, and very likely all of them contain some false claims.

The second criticism of moral relativism[3] is that it's inconsistent in ruling out moral criticism of people occupying one moral framework by people occupying a different framework. Thus, Christians may not, according to moral relativism, criticize the Nietzschean practice of dominating one's weaker neighbors for one's own glory; and the Nietzschean is likewise prohibited, by the doctrine of relativism, from criticizing Christians for their generosity to the needy and concern to preserve the dignity of the poor and the less gifted. But if relativism is the view that prohibitions of behavior are correct only from within some moral framework, then we may ask, "To which framework does the prohibition against criticizing actions belonging to other groups' frameworks belong?" It doesn't belong to either the Christian framework or the Nietzschean framework. In fact, it doesn't seem to belong to any naturally existing moral framework. It belongs to the *relativist* moral framework, and from that framework it pronounces a universal prohibition against criticizing other frameworks. So relativism makes the kind of moral judgment that it prohibits, namely a prohibition applying to all moral frameworks. Another way to put the matter is to say that relativism, the view that all moral standards are relativistic, implies a non-relativistic moral standard, and so is self-referentially inconsistent.

A moment ago, I said that probably most moral outlooks contain some moral truths and that probably all of them contain some moral falsehoods. It may seem that Christians must believe that the Christian outlook contains only true moral propositions and no false ones, but this claim seems too strong, unless we identify the Christian outlook with God's outlook. We have good reason not to do that. The Christian outlook of one period of history or one group of Christians may

---

[3] The following is my reformulation of an argument by Bernard Williams in *Morality: An Introduction to Ethics* (San Francisco: Harper and Row, 1972), 20–26.

contradict, on some points, the Christian outlook of another period of history or another group of Christians. For example, some Christians have held that there is no such thing as a just war, and others have held that there is; Christians have not always regarded human slavery as an offense against God and the slave. Of course, we could stipulate that "the Christian outlook" means "God's outlook, whatever that is," but in that case, we couldn't identify the Christian moral outlook with any actual historical instantiation. So we must not, I think, identify the ethical outlook of the Christian church with the final ethical truth. But having said this, Christians must also say that the worldwide and agewide Christian tradition, based as it is in God's revelation of himself in Jesus Christ, is the best place to look for the ethical truth. Christians will be confident that in main and fundamental matters, the outlook of the church, defined in that broad sense, is the moral truth.

If Not Relativism, Then Skepticism?

I have pointed out that moral relativism doesn't follow from moral pluralism and that it's an internally inconsistent view. I have affirmed as well, with what some readers may feel is too much communitarian bravado, that Christians can be confident that they possess the broad outlines of moral truth. But I have done this in the context of admitting that there are people both in our society and in societies across the world who, without being stupid or crazy or pig-headed, disagree fundamentally with Christians on some moral matters. And to say that they disagree "fundamentally" is to say that, as long as they stay within their moral outlook, Christians may not be able to give them reasons acceptable to them to abandon their moral outlook and adopt the Christian one. Relativism doesn't follow, strictly, from pluralism, and it's incoherent; but isn't there, after all, something arbitrary and irrational in our adhering to our outlook in these circumstances? And if so, then doesn't at least a kind of moral skepticism that has been associated with relativism commend itself?

Skepticism, in this sense, is the view that we don't know some important things that we tend commonsensically to think we know. For example, people tend to be very confident about the existence of things like chairs, other people, that the earth has existed for more than fifty years, and that their toes continue to be there even when their shoes are on. Skeptics argue that people don't in fact know such things, and their argument often takes the form of pointing out imaginable scenarios in which we have all the experiences that in fact we have, but actually there aren't any chairs, or our toes disappear when we can't see (or feel) them, and so forth. The question is then asked, "Can you show, once and for all, that these imaginable scenarios don't in fact hold?" And then, since it turns out that we can't show this, the skeptic commends to us the conclusion that we don't know all these commonsense things.

Moral pluralism suggests something like this argument: In the face of living human beings who clearly are intelligent and of good will who think humility isn't a virtue and are unmoved by our best arguments, the conclusion that Christians don't know whether humility is a virtue can seem compelling. Given the undeniable reality of moral disagreement, skepticism about values may seem much more compelling than the corresponding conclusion that we don't know whether there are chairs. Most of us don't actually know anybody who thinks there are no chairs.

If we're reasonable people, then shouldn't moral pluralism disable us morally, shake us in our confidence that, say, Christian morality (or pick your own preferred framework) is the moral truth? If we can't show, to the satisfaction of all intelligent and sane people of goodwill, the superiority of our own morality, aren't we irrational to continue in our confidence that our morality is the moral truth? Must we not admit that what seems to the naïve or sheltered to be moral truths are really just socially conditioned prejudices of preference? Modern philosophers have tended to think so, and much of modern moral philosophy has been an attempt to supply the "foundation" of morality, which is to say the indisputable premise from which morality can be derived and which any rational person can see to be true.

The Failed Modern Search for Moral Foundations

In response to the threat of moral skepticism posed by moral pluralism, philosophers in the modern period have sought compelling non-controversial common grounds on which to base our moral beliefs and by appeal to which to resolve moral disagreements. Thus, by finding *the* fundamental principle of morals, to take the "fundamental" out of the fundamental moral disagreements. Once the foundation has been discovered, disagreeing parties can go back to it to find out which of the competing moral claims, if any, actually derive from the foundation. Such a foundation will remove the arbitrariness that seems to underlie moral commitments, and thus restore confidence in those commitments. Here, I survey just four prominent and representative attempts to find such non-controversial foundations, and I indicate why they fail. In Chapter 3, we'll briefly survey some others.

Sentimentalism: Hume and Smith

David Hume (1711–1776) and Adam Smith (1723–1790) are known as "sentimentalists" because they think the distinction between right and wrong, good and evil, is grounded ultimately in human emotions, which, they plausibly note, is our most fundamental power of perceiving values—in the present connection, the values of actions and character traits. Hume calls actions and character traits "mental qualities" because actions, according to him, are good or bad depending on the mental state of the actor: His motivation, intention, or attitude in performing the action, and character traits are qualities of a person's mind. These are what we evaluate when we experience emotions about them. When we admire someone's bravery, we see him and it as good; when we feel guilty or ashamed of our lie or mendacity, we see it and ourselves as bad; when we feel proud of our generosity, we see it and ourselves as good; when we despise someone for his corruption, we see it and him as bad.

We may think that such emotions are responses to the values that the traits have independently of our emotions and that our emotions are responses (like sense perceptions, sometimes correct, sometimes not) to those values. For example, in the best case, the insult that angers me is objectively bad, and my anger is a response to that badness. At least sometimes, emotions are true *to* what they are about. The insult really was unjust, and my anger was an accurate evaluative take on it because the insult *was* bad. But the sentimentalists think it works the other way around. I projected the badness of the insult onto it: My anger slapped the (negative) value onto it, *making* it vicious. As Hume says,

> moral distinctions depend entirely on certain peculiar sentiments of pain and pleasure, and . . . whatever mental quality [that is, character trait or action] in ourselves or others gives us a satisfaction, by the survey or reflexion, is of course [that is, necessarily] virtuous; as every thing of this nature, that gives uneasiness, is vicious. Now since every quality in ourselves or others, which gives pleasure, always causes pride or love; as every one, that produces uneasiness, excites humility [that is, shame or guilt] or hatred [contempt]: It follows, that these two particulars are to be consider'd as equivalent, with regard to our mental qualities, *virtue* and the power of producing love or pride, *vice* and the power of producing humility or hatred.[4]

The "sentimentalist" strategy must involve the mental state being basic to the value of its object; it is not so much a *response* to the object as a *constituting* of the object's value. The "value" of a good or bad action or character trait is projected upon, or injected into, the object by the mental state. This projecting, rather than perceiving in the usual sense, is what enables the mental state to be the foundation of the value. Hume and Smith are aware that people sometimes rejoice at evil and get angry about what in reality is good. For example, when the chief priests saw that Judas Iscariot was willing to betray Jesus, they rejoiced (Mark 14:11). So the sentimentalists must provide a way of sorting out emotions that can be trusted as projections of moral values from ones that can't be trusted. For this purpose, they introduce the notions of sympathy and an impartial point of view. Sympathy is the ability to take someone else's emotional point of view, and impartiality rules out special interests. To project real values, emotions must take

---

[4] Hume, *Treatise of Human Nature*, Book III, Part III, Section 1, 574–575 in ed. L. A. Selby-Bigge (Oxford: Oxford University Press, 1888), https://davidhume.org/texts/t/3/3/full.

the sympathetic perspective of an "impartial spectator."[5] For example, the impartial spectator won't be able to sympathize with the chief priests' joy that Judas is willing to help them get Jesus killed. And if you slapped a negative value on the official who told the truth about the security of the 2020 election because you wanted everybody to believe falsely that you won it, the impartial spectator won't be able to endorse your anger, and the negative value it slapped on won't stick.

Impartiality isn't indifference, and the impartial spectator isn't indifferent. A person who doesn't care, one way or the other, about the moral qualities of actions and people won't have emotions about them at all, and so won't be capable of sympathy, which is the ability to track other people's emotions with something like corresponding emotions of one's own. In particular, the impartial spectator must care about justice, truthfulness, compassion, and the like: She tracks the emotions of the moral person. She can track them because she can feel them herself, in at least an attenuated way. In viewing the chief priests' joy, for example, she'll feel something like horror at the thought of betraying an innocent man to be killed, and this horror will be about both them and their joy. The chief priests horrify her as beings who are capable of feeling such a horrifying joy.

As modern moral theorists, Hume and Smith offer sentimentalism as a way to address the problems of relativism and skepticism that are rooted in moral pluralism: an emotion with which a perfectly impartial spectator can sympathize is a reliable indicator of moral value. Such a value is one on which all rational persons of good will can agree, and can be, thus, the basis for the resolution of what initially seem to be fundamental moral disagreements.

Is it? Can it be? Who is this impartial spectator? "Impartial" can't mean "emotionally uninvolved" or "emotionally indifferent," since the impartial spectator has to be able to feel sympathetic emotions. So the sentimentalist idea is that this spectator cares about the people with

---

[5] See Smith's *The Theory of Moral Sentiments* (1759), Part 3, chapter 2, https://www.ibiblio.org/ml/libri/s/SmithA_MoralSentiments_p.pdf. See also Hume, *Treatise* 472, where he says that the trait has to be "considered in general, without reference to our particular interest." The impartial spectator isn't absolutely disinterested; to have the moral emotions, she must have a moral interest. But in being "disinterested," she sets aside her private interests.

whom she sympathizes, and thus cares about what they care about, but not in the way that one particularly concerned with them, such as a family member, friend, partner, colleague, or the like would do. The impartial spectator has only the concerns of the generic human being, but presumably she has these concerns in a suitably intense and fine-tuned way.

Thus, for example, if a person is justifiably angry about having been cheated on a road-building contract, the impartial spectator will be able to validate the moral judgment implicit in the individual's anger only if she cares enough about justice to share his anger by way of sympathy *and* knows enough about road-building contracts to know whether the individual has really been cheated. This is an instance of Benedict's point about cultural differences being moral differences: Not every society has road-building contracts.

So it seems that the impartial spectator will have to belong to a culture—in this case, one that contains road-building contracts or at least contracts of some similar kind. But if, to validate moral perceptions, the impartial spectator has to belong to the culture of the persons whose perceptions she is validating, how is she to transcend those features of the culture that distinguish its moral outlook from rival moral outlooks? Why should we think that a Nietzschean impartial spectator and a Christian impartial spectator will agree on whether it's OK for the rich to use their wealth to dominate the poor? Why should we suppose that an Aristotelian impartial spectator, who believes in natural slavery, will agree with a Christian impartial spectator who thinks that all have equal inherent rights to self-determination? Emotions depend on ways of thinking about what the emotions are about, and morally relevant emotions depend on culturally transmitted ways of thinking about right and wrong, good and evil, virtues and vices—exactly the kinds of things an impartial spectator would have to think about to have his or her sympathetic emotions. If enculturation is necessary to the formation of an impartial spectator, it's hard to see how she is going to render any other moral judgments than the canonical ones for the moral outlook to which she belongs. In that case, the impartial spectator doesn't provide a standpoint from which to adjudicate the fundamental disagreements characteristic of a morally pluralistic situation.

Moral Rationalism: Immanuel Kant's Proposal

In his *Groundwork of the Metaphysic of Morals* (1785) and *Critique of Practical Reason* (1788), Kant attempted to find in pure practical reason a universal basis of moral judgments. The idea in speaking of pure practical reason is in part that the most basic principle of morality is something like a rule of logic: If you violate it, you do yourself the violence of becoming unreasonable, irrational, and not making sense. For example, it's a principle of logic that "If [(if p is true then q is true), and p is true], then q is true"; and if I violate this principle by saying "[(If p is true then q is true), and p is true], but q is false," then I contradict myself and thus end up asserting nothing, jabber on though I will. If any principles are universal, it does seem that the rules of mathematics and logic are universal. So if Kant can make this proposal compelling, he will have achieved what modern moral philosophy deems required to avoid moral skepticism: to provide a way by which, in principle, all seemingly fundamental moral disagreements can be resolved.

Kant calls his proposed principle of pure practical reason the Categorical Imperative, and he offers several formulations of this supposedly single principle. In the present brief discussion, I'll consider just two of them: "Act only on that maxim which you can at the same time will that it should become a universal law" and "So act that you use humanity, whether in your own person or in the person of any other, always at the same time as an end, never merely as a means."[6]

The first formula, in some applications, comes closest to looking like a law of logic. Let's say you are deliberating whether to tell the truth in a certain situation. If you decide to lie, then the maxim of your action will be, "Tell falsehoods with the purpose of deceiving." Now, applying the first formula of the Categorical Imperative, you ask yourself whether you can will this maxim to be a universal law. Can I be willing that everybody always follow the rule, "Tell falsehoods with the purpose of deceiving"? It takes little reflection to see that if this rule were

---

[6] *Groundwork*, 4:421, 429. Immanuel Kant, "Groundwork of the Metaphysics of Morals and Critique of Practical Reason," in *The Cambridge Edition of the Works of Immanuel Kant: Practical Philosophy*, ed. Mary J. Gregor (Cambridge: Cambridge University Press, 1996), 73, 80.

universally followed, in a short time, no one would trust anyone else's word. But you can't practically have the purpose of deceiving people in a world where no one trusts anyone else to tell the truth. Consequently, to be willing that this maxim be universally followed is to be willing to live in a world where this maxim can't be followed. So we have a contradiction, and it seems as though the Categorical Imperative is like a rule of logic: Violate it and you contradict yourself. And you violate the categorical imperative every time you perform some action whose maxim you can't will to be a universal law. Acting immorally is just irrational.

The first thing to note is that maxims that are very circumstantially specified don't create contradictions in the way illustrated. For example, let's say the lie you are contemplating is a small but perfectly immoral one on your income tax form, and that you are motivated by a desire to save up money to buy yourself an iPhone, and your name is Jan Pieter Ruiklekker. Now the maxim that is subject to universalization is, "Let people named Jan Pieter Ruiklekker who want to buy an iPhone lie in this particular way on their income tax forms." Can we, without contradiction, want there to be a world in which this maxim is universally acted on? Such a universal practice would make so little difference in the world that there seems to be no logical problem at all in universalizing it. And the maxim of every immoral action that anybody ever contemplated *can* be formulated so particularly that there's no problem in universalizing it.

Secondly, note that even when the immoral maxim does result in a contradiction, it does so only on condition of universalization. This condition isn't needed to violate a law of logic. If you violate Modus Ponens (the logical rule referred to above), you will contradict yourself without having to will that everybody should violate Modus Ponens (this is what we might call the teeth in logic—its authority). But if you violate the rule "Don't lie," you don't contradict yourself unless you will that everybody should do it. And now we may ask, "Are you bound by practical reason to will the universalization of your maxim?" There seems to be nothing illogical in lying and hoping that few or none of your associates will follow suit. It seems, then, that the Categorical Imperative doesn't have the authority of the laws of logic.

What about the other formulation of the Categorical Imperative? It sounds appealing, especially to people who are sympathetic to Christian morality, since it commands us to respect all human beings by never treating them merely as means to our own purposes, but always as beings who have their own aims and purposes. It sounds a little bit like the biblical injunction to love our neighbors as ourselves. Christians will no doubt think that this principle is true and reasonable, because it fits with other beliefs about ourselves, other human beings, and God. Furthermore, we will take it to be binding on all human beings. But in claiming that the rule is a formulation of *pure practical reason*, Kant is not just claiming that it's true and reasonable within the Christian framework, and binding on all people. He is claiming that it is somehow *compelling and unavoidable* to all human beings and other rational creatures (once it has been pointed out to them, at any rate), in something like the way the rules of logic are. If the rule lacks *this* kind of status, it will not fulfill the function of ruling out fundamental moral pluralism—it can't be the basis for resolving what seem to be basic moral disagreements.

Do we have reason to think that it formulates a universal law of practical reason in this sense? Must a Donald Trump, on pain of irrationality, admit that everyone (including him) is under an obligation to respect every other human being as an end in himself or herself? Must the Nietzscheans, upon getting it through their heads what is meant and implied by this formulation of the Categorical Imperative, abandon their practice of domineering over weaker neighbors—or alternatively admit that they are violating one of the fundamental canons of universal reason? Or might Trump, in full knowledge of the meaning of the principle, say that in his view another, more fundamental, principle trumps this one—namely that as a "winner" he has a home-made right to do whatever he can and wishes to do to his enemies and other losers?

Kant's proposal of finding in pure practical reason the basis for avoiding moral pluralism and the skepticism that is supposed to follow if it isn't avoided is no more successful than the sentimentalists' proposal of finding it in human emotions sorted by the sympathetic and unsympathetic responses of the impartial spectator.

Social Contract: Thomas Hobbes's Proposal

Another modern proposal is that we think of the foundation of ethics as a contract (agreement, bargain, deal) among people to limit our own actions in exchange for others limiting theirs.[7] The theory initially assumes that we are all basically Trumpians, bargaining selfishly with the aim of getting the "best deal," namely maximal benefits for minimum "costs." We would like to be free to do anything that we would like to do. But if everybody exercised such freedom, we'd all be miserable. We'd take possession of things that "belong" to others; we'd stiff those to whom we owe money; we'd have sex with anybody who attracted us whenever we felt we could get away with it; we'd do away with people who got in our way; we would jeopardize the lives of our "enemies"; and so forth. But a society in which everybody exercised such lawless freedom would be chaotic, dangerous, and economically unworkable. No business would last long enough to become profitable, because people would regularly steal the merchandise or falsely promise to pay for it, or competitors would burn the business down to reduce the competition. Our lifespan would be short, our days full of anxiety and pain, and we'd be unable to pursue the goals that make life meaningful.

So we make a deal: We agree on moral rules. Some of the rules protect property ("don't steal"), others protect relationships ("don't commit adultery," "don't lie to one another"), others protect life ("don't kill"), and so forth. These rules may look like commands from on high, but in fact, according to the social contract theory, they result from implicit bargaining: I won't take your property arbitrarily if you don't take mine; I won't violate your marriage bond if you don't violate mine; I won't lie to you if you don't lie to me; I agree not to kill you if you agree not to kill me; and so forth. The assumption is that morality, though not the best deal I can imagine, is a pretty good deal for

---

[7] An early example of this theory is found in Book II of Plato's *Republic* (358a–359d), where Plato puts it in the mouth of Glaucon and Socrates refutes it. Thomas Hobbes is the early modern philosopher most associated with the view (see his *Leviathan* https://www.gutenberg.org/ebooks/3207). A contemporary example is David Gauthier, *Morals by Agreement* (Oxford: Clarendon Press, 1986). C. Stephen Evans offers an able critique in *Kierkegaard's Ethic of Love* (Oxford: Oxford University Press, 2004), 250–279.

everybody. In return for giving up quite a bit of our freedom, we get quite a bit more freedom: the freedom to possess our property, pursue our marriage, conduct our business in peace, and go about the activity of living in relative tranquility. As long as everybody (or at least most people most of the time) honors it, morality creates order, and order is to almost everybody's advantage.

A basic problem with this theory is that if you adopt the selfish point of view that the theory ascribes to you, it isn't true that acting morally is always to your advantage. Instead, *appearing* to act morally is *often* or *mostly* to your advantage. The person who is really honest is not just seeking the advantages of honesty; instead, she values honesty, she respects the people she informs and is uncomfortable with the prospect of misleading them; and so will tell the truth and play fair even when she could "get away with" being dishonest. Some of her interests are moral. If we stay within the bounds of the theory, it wouldn't make sense to be honest in the way that genuinely honest people are honest. But the theory is supposed to explain such things as honesty and justice. So the theory fails to explain what it sets out to explain.

As an attempt to answer moral pluralism, contract theory needs to assume a very high degree of agreement among people about what they take to be in their interest. But the different moral perspectives that make for a morally pluralistic situation in the first place include diverse concerns and aims. The good Samaritan of Jesus's parable suffers (feels compassion) upon seeing the injured man in the ditch; he is "interested" in the well-being of the man, and so goes and helps him, and pays for an innkeeper to care for him, and then returns later to see that the injured man is recovering well.[8] The interest that he will be seeking to maximize is very different from the interest of the Trumpian, who wants to acquire as much money and power as possible at the least cost to himself. It's hard to see how any "deal" between the Samaritan

---

[8] It may seem odd to call the Samaritan's interest in the well-being of his neighbor *self*-interest. But self-interest is relative to the self. The banker's self is formed in love of money, so that acquiring money is his self-interest. And the Samaritan's self is formed in love for his neighbor, so that his interest—the interest of his self—is in the neighbor's well-being. The Samaritan finds satisfaction of his "preferences" in improving the injured man's well-being.

and the Trumpian can result in an agreement about their fundamental commitments. So the social contract theory of the foundation of ethics doesn't supply a plausible answer to the problem of moral skepticism.

Utilitarianism: John Stuart Mill's Proposal

A fourth way around moral pluralism is presented by the utilitarian tradition of ethical theory. In his *Utilitarianism* (1863), Mill tells us that the highest good is the greatest happiness distributed as widely as possible among creatures who are capable of it. Happiness is pleasure and the absence of pain. Initially, pleasure/pain seems to be a plausible candidate for a non-controversial basis of ethical distinctions. After all, everybody knows what pleasure and pain are, and everybody agrees that pleasure is good and pain is bad, right?

However, unlike some utilitarians, Mill distinguishes different kinds of pleasure. Some are more ethically important than others: the pleasures of sensory stimulation count for less than the pleasures of intellectual accomplishment and understanding, the pleasures of experiencing fine art, or the pleasures of virtue. In Mill's analogy, a hog's delight in eating garbage is less valuable than Socrates's delight in thinking about the form of the Good and the Beautiful. "It is better to be a human being dissatisfied than a pig satisfied; better to be Socrates dissatisfied than a fool satisfied. And if the fool, or the pig, is of a different opinion, it is because they only know their own side of the question. The other party to the comparison knows both sides" (*Utilitarianism*,[9] chapter II).

It's not that pig-pleasure has no weight at all: But if we weigh the same "amount" of pig's pleasure and Socrates's pleasure, Socrates's pleasure will weigh more in the calculation of whether some action should be done. If you're deciding about the utility of a $500,000 municipal investment, and the options are to spend the money serving barbecue to everybody in town or to found a city symphony orchestra, then to justify choosing the barbecue option, the amount of

---

[9] https://www.gutenberg.org/cache/epub/11224/pg11224-images.html, chapter 2.

pig-pleasure to be reaped from it will have to be, let us say, 25 times as great as the amount of Socrates's pleasure to be gained from founding the orchestra. The reason is that a given amount of pig-pleasure "weighs" so much less, morally, than the same amount of Socrates's pleasure. It's like putting lead weights in one side of a balance scale and feathers in the other. Feathers do have some weight, but for the feathers to out-balance the lead, you have to have a *really* big pile of feathers.

So in the phrase "the greatest happiness distributed as widely as possible . . . ," 'greatest' includes this distinction between higher and lower pleasures. If we take an amount of the pleasure of reading Dostoevsky to count for a lot more than the same amount of pleasure of reading Agatha Christie, then the action of promoting the reading of Agatha Christie will be as ethically good as promoting the reading of Dostoevsky only if the first action induces a lot more readers to get busy or induces a lot more reading in the same number of readers. Without the distinction between higher and lower pleasures, Mill's theory would be implausible as an ethical theory. But we can see that with the distinction, we have introduced a new potential for ethical disagreement. Pluralism is back, along with the threat of its degenerating into skepticism.

If utilitarianism is to provide the basis for resolving ethical disagreements, it must be pretty obvious to all sane, well-informed, and open-hearted parties which pleasures are indeed the higher and which are the lower and by how much. But it seems clear that these judgments, in which pleasures are ranked, depend on prior ethical commitments. The confirmed aesthete, for example, ranks the pleasures of art higher than the pleasures of virtue, whereas the moralist reverses this ranking (see Kierkegaard, *Either/Or*). The Stoic ranks the pleasure of contemplating his apatheia higher than the Christian's pleasure in the recovery from illness of her neighbor's child (Rom 12:15). This pluralism can't be resolved by a utilitarian theory that allows or requires the ranking of pleasures into higher and lower. These are disagreements about the ranking of pleasures. And a utilitarianism without ranking will be acceptable only to pig-pleasure devotees. Not to speak of the pleasure that crooks and murderers take in the good prospects of their schemes. So utilitarianism fails to avoid the moral skepticism which, according to modern moral theory, threatens if we don't find a universally acceptable basis for resolving fundamental ethical disagreements.

A Note on the Notion of a Foundation

Certain Christian philosophers have proposed a kind of "foundationalism" that is not the same as the kind I have been criticizing in this chapter. When Alvin Plantinga (*Noûs 15* [1981]: 41–51) and others say that belief in God is "properly basic," they are not proposing a foundation like what Mill and Kant are proposing for ethics. For the Reformed theologians, 'properly' means "legitimately," not "necessarily." They are not hereby denying the rationality of atheism or agnosticism. For those who believe in God, that belief can be foundational in the sense that other beliefs can be based on it (say, that we are creatures who can and should trust God). Similarly, a pluralist in ethics can and should acknowledge that his or her moral beliefs form a web of dependency relations in which one belief (say, that an order of peace is normative for human beings) implies other beliefs (say, that the variants of agapē are human virtues). So the one belief can be thought of as a "foundation" for the other. But this is different from the reductionist project of modern ethical theories in which *everything* ethical other than the foundation is "derived" from some selected undeniable moral concept as the foundation.

Conclusion

We have considered the indisputable fact of moral pluralism and its supposed implications: moral relativism and moral skepticism. And we have seen that a fundamental project of modern moral philosophy has been to avoid moral skepticism by discovering some basis of morality on which all can agree and from which to derive moral conclusions that all can agree on. We have sketched the four main proposals in modern moral theory prior to the modern renewal of virtue ethics and have briefly argued that all four fail to accomplish what they set out to achieve. In the next chapter, we'll begin to consider modern virtue ethics as an attempt to achieve what the other modern ethical theories did not.

2

The Instigators of the Later Movement

Anscombe and MacIntyre

Introduction

It isn't surprising that the two philosophers who kick-started the "return" to virtue ethics in the last half of the twentieth century were both Catholic Christians. From the earliest days of the church, Christian leaders have been preoccupied with the formation of souls. Christian teaching is not just interesting theories about God and the universe but is meant to form the broadly ethical character of the people who accept the teaching: to "inform" their minds and hearts with such qualities as justice, compassion, forgivingness, humility, patience, and gentleness.[1] Elizabeth Anscombe and Alasdair MacIntyre were nevertheless "pure" philosophers, who showed little interest in introducing theological or biblical detail into their ethics. MacIntyre especially insists on strictly dividing the labor of philosophers from that of theologians. In this book, by contrast, I will in later chapters unabashedly appeal to the Bible in expounding Christian virtue ethics. Those chapters will blend philosophy—especially the kind of philosophical psychology that Anscombe calls for—with theology of the virtues as it is found in the Bible.[2] Both Anscombe and MacIntyre saw a return to virtue as a more promising way to address the troubles of contemporary ethics

---

[1] See Ellen Charry, *The Renewing of Your Minds* (New York: Oxford University Press, 1997) and *God and the Art of Happiness* (Grand Rapids: Eerdmans, 2010).

[2] For people who don't accept the truths of Christian faith, it makes sense to exclude theology from philosophy. But for Christian philosophers and any theologians, it's eccentric to exclude Christian beliefs from philosophical work, except for strategic purposes. Every philosopher appeals to truths that are not products of philosophical thinking, and for Christians, the main doctrines of Christianity are truths. See Alvin Plantinga, "Advice to Christian Philosophers" (https://place.asburyseminary.edu/cgi/viewcontent.cgi?article=1019&context=faithandphilosophy).

Virtue Ethics. Robert Campbell Roberts, Oxford University Press.
© Robert Campbell Roberts 2026. DOI: 10.1093/9780197848005.003.0004

than the ones proposed by the sentimentalists, the Kantians, the contractarians, and the utilitarians whose proposed solutions I briefly sketched in Chapter 1.

Elizabeth Anscombe's "Modern Moral Philosophy"

In 1958 Anscombe published "Modern Moral Philosophy,"[3] one of the most influential papers in twentieth-century philosophy. She says that for philosophers of her generation, the central concept in ethics is the concept of obligation, and that in their thought, the moral sense of this word is that of absolute (unconditional) requirement. For example, to say that you *morally* ought to tell the truth is to say that there are no conditions under which you may lie. Immanuel Kant thought that the rule against lying was a "categorical," that is, unconditional, imperative. But, says Anscombe, a rule can have that kind of force only if it's laid down by God. The philosophers of her generation don't believe in God, so they're in a fix. The idea of moral obligation, in the sense that they want to promote, makes no sense, though they have to pretend that it does, because of their strong commitment to the idea of morality. So they surround the word with a certain mood, a certain look in their eyes and tone of voice, and a feeling of referring to something profound. She says that the feeling of need for such hocus-pocus is a misunderstood inheritance from Christianity, which has a "law conception of ethics" (5). The idea of an absolute obligation, says Anscombe, made sense when philosophers believed that God had required certain things of us and prohibited other things by command. But in the absence of such a Commander, there is no law of the sort that unconditional obligation requires.[4]

This is where virtue ethics begins to come in. Anscombe proposes that philosophers can get out of their bind by giving up the idea of moral obligation and substituting the kind of motivational consideration that

---

[3] Elizabeth Anscombe, "Modern Moral Philosophy," *Philosophy* 33 (1958): 1–19.

[4] In a later chapter, I'll argue that the point of the law, in its biblical presentation, like the laws of the city-state in Aristotle's presentation, is to form the character of the people who are governed by the law. To use the language of the Bible, the law is to be "written on their hearts." (See Jer 31:33, Heb 8:10.)

virtue concepts exert. If it makes no sense for an atheist to feel under absolute obligation to deal fairly with others, perhaps she can feel that you really should deal fairly with them anyway, since justice is a virtue (a human excellence), and so a necessary component in flourishing as a human being. We all want to flourish, to be healthy and mature human specimens, don't we? In the place of theological thinking, we put a kind of psychological thinking, a philosophical psychology that centers on concepts that bear on ethical attitudes and actions.

But to jump directly to thinking about virtues is to get ahead of ourselves, according to Anscombe. "In present-day philosophy an explanation is required how an unjust man is a bad man, or an unjust action a bad one; to give such an explanation belongs to ethics; but it cannot even be begun until we are equipped with a sound philosophy of psychology" (4).

The idea, I think, is that we need to know, about ourselves, why we, as creatures with certain generic defining features, do well only if we're just, humble, courageous, and so forth. Once we know who we are, then we'll be able to see what's "compelling" about virtues—compelling even, in principle at least—to people who don't have them but do understand the psychology. This knowledge would be ethically compelling by way of insight into the normative demands that our nature, as characterized by this psychology, places on us. It would have the form,

> *If you want to be human (a person)* [as you, being the kind of being you are, inevitably want to be], *then here's what you have to be* [just, courageous, humble, and so forth].

Assuming that human beings *have to* desire to be human beings, then the knowledge of what it takes to be that would have an ethically motivating force which, though conditional in form, would be categorical in force. People who confronted a psychology of this sort but didn't feel the pull (the attraction, the need) of virtues would be people whose imagination was wanting. Which is to say, they wouldn't know, in the sense of appreciative personal understanding, what kind of being they are. And, for each of the particular virtues, they would fail to understand its crucial role in making them the kind of being that they desperately want to be. (That they don't feel "desperate" about their need to be virtuous would be a symptom of their failure to understand basic human moral psychology.)

Anscombe proposes that philosophers begin with applying philosophical psychology to the concepts *action*, *intention*, *pleasure*, and *wanting*, and "eventually it might be possible to advance to considering the concept *virtue*; with which, I suppose, we should be beginning some sort of a study of ethics" (15). Anscombe herself wrote a dense little book on intention, and other philosophers in her wake have written about such virtue-related concepts as *will*, *emotion* (passion), (moral) *perception*, and *practical reason*. All of these concepts, and others, are important if we are to understand the concept of a virtue.

According to Anscombe, the philosophers of her generation rejected the earlier "Christian" foundation of ethics in the commands of God. They followed this rejection with what seem to be two incompatible positions: They retained the moral "ought" with its aura of absoluteness, but since it lacked theological teeth, they went on to suppose that there is no kind of action that is prohibited in every circumstance. Anscombe's example of a test case is the action of knowingly condemning an innocent person for a crime. Imagine a situation in which you can prevent a maniac from nuking the country next door only by condemning a person to death for a crime you know he didn't commit. Anscombe wants to retain the idea of actions that are absolutely prohibited: If somebody really thinks that in some circumstances it's not beyond the pale to condemn an innocent to death, "I do not want to argue with him; he shows a corrupt mind" (17).

But she's trying to find a way for atheists to do ethics, and she proposes that they do virtue ethics (she doesn't use this term) instead of the ethics of obligation, which she thinks they can't coherently do. She hopes that if we can clarify the idea of justice as a personal virtue, we will see something like an absolute prohibition of injustice. Unjust actions will be seen and felt to be so odious, and actions that correct injustices so fetchingly attractive, that we'll spontaneously shrink from the former and crave the latter. Anscombe's paper has a strongly aspirational quality. It's proposing to do moral philosophy in a way that it isn't yet done. Apparently, it would work this way: You will realize that, because justice is a virtue, to perform an unjust action is to corrupt your humanity, and when you fully understand that prospect (we will understand this once we have the philosophical psychology that she envisions), it will appear absolutely intolerable to you. In this way, the concept of justice as a virtue (and similarly for the concepts of the other virtues) will become a basis of "obligation" that is an alternative to the commands of God. Virtue ethics (philosophical moral psychology) will be a way of ruling out relativism and skepticism.

Alasdair MacIntyre's *After Virtue*

In *After Virtue: A Study in Moral Theory* (1981), Alasdair MacIntyre established himself as the most distinguished exponent of the virtues in twentieth-century philosophy. Along with Anscombe he is considered a groundbreaker in the virtue ethics movement, though the phrase "virtue ethics" doesn't occur in his book; nor, as far as I know, does he describe himself in this phrase in any of his writings.[5] Later, when we come to those writers who forthrightly defend "virtue ethics," we'll see why he doesn't.

MacIntyre looks at what I have called moral pluralism—the situation in which various parties dispute endlessly with one another about practical moral questions like abortion and the justice of taxation, and where philosophers and other thinkers wrangle endlessly about the ultimate basis of moral concepts—and postulates that this situation can be explained historically as a loss of the tradition of the virtues, especially in the strand that centers in Aristotle's *Nicomachean Ethics* in the ancient world and was developed in greater depth and detail in the writings of Saint Thomas Aquinas. According to MacIntyre, this Aristotelian *tradition* is the right one, and it is the one that modernity has "forgotten."

MacIntyre says the repudiation of the Aristotelian tradition that we have inherited took place in Europe during the fifteenth to the

---

[5] He refers to "virtue ethicists" as a group of philosophers who are doing something different from his own project. See Alasdair MacIntyre, *Ethics in the Conflicts of Modernity: An Essay on Desire, Practical Reasoning, and Narrative* (Cambridge: Cambridge University Press, 2016), 66.

seventeenth centuries (*After Virtue*, 117). Especially Martin Luther, among the Protestant reformers, was wary of the influence of the Aristotelian virtue tradition, on the grounds that thinking about ethics in terms of personal virtues put human agency in competition with God's sovereign will in matters of salvation.[6] We are saved by God's grace alone, and any hint that we contribute to our salvation by forming good traits like justice, compassion, and courage, or that salvation depends on such personal formation, or that we sinners would have a residue of virtue sufficient to make virtue appealing to us, was to be discouraged.

But MacIntyre doesn't think of the Aristotelian tradition as a collection of uniformly true beliefs. For example, he thinks Aristotle erred in supposing that some people have a natural slave nature, that women don't have all the faculties of mind, and that to have optimal moral formation people have to live in a city-state. A tradition is an ongoing conversation among people who share some broad starting points for their thinking, for example, the idea that we have to have virtues if we are to achieve and enjoy a distinctively human way of life.

MacIntyre thinks that moral pluralism results from taking fragments of thought inherited from this Aristotelian tradition out of their original context and defending or using them outside that proper context, either as practical guidance or as the basis of theories. In the moral theories that we examined in Chapter 1, we can see a process of picking fragments from an outlook in which they made sense as aspects of the whole and trying to use them outside that context. Thus, modern sentimentalism abstracts the important and legitimate role of *emotions* in Aristotle's ethics and makes it the basis of morality, something it isn't properly fit to do. Kant takes the important and legitimate role of *reason* in ethics and makes "pure" practical reason the ultimate basis of morality, again, a task that "pure" reason is not up to. Contract theory takes the important and legitimate ideas of *agreement* and *community* in the earlier ethics and tries to make them function as the ultimate basis of morality. And the utilitarians and other consequentialists take the perfectly legitimate concern with *pleasure, happiness,* and the

---

[6] See Jennifer Herdt, *Putting on Virtue: The Legacy of the Splendid Vices* (Chicago: University of Chicago Press, 2008).

consequences of human actions out of their proper context and try to develop an entire moral theory on their basis. All of these theoretical efforts fail because they abstract a legitimate moral concept from its proper and original setting and put it, abstracted, to a use for which it's unsuited. At the same time, rather than unifying ethics on a single foundation, ethical theory confirms the fragmentation of ethics by its selectivity, reductive artificiality, and contentiousness. Endless disagreement about moral practice such as how to treat pregnancy and the beginning of life, or about justice in relation to the practice of taxation, also stems from the "forgetfulness" and thus abandonment of the Aristotelian/Thomist tradition of the virtues. In *After Virtue*, MacIntyre begins a recovery of the Aristotelian tradition of the virtues and thus points the way to resolve the modern problem of moral pluralism and its consequences.

Twenty-six years after the first edition of *After Virtue*, in the Prologue to the third edition (2007), MacIntyre tells us that though he was an Aristotelian in 1980 when he wrote the first edition, he was not yet a Thomist and so didn't appreciate the Aristotelian "moral biology." Aristotelian biology is the idea that human beings, like all other living things, have a species nature that "demands" a specific formational outcome if the individual animal or plant is to reach maturity or full potential and thus be a *good* and properly functioning specimen of its kind. Each species has a characteristic way of functioning within its environment, and this way of living is its distinctive "end" or "telos." This is biology because it belongs to the science of living things. Applied to ethics and the human species, Aristotle's moral biology (fundamental anthropology) is the idea that we reach our telos or maturity as human beings only if we acquire the virtues of justice, wisdom, temperance, courage, liberality, and so forth. If I lack the virtues, I am a stunted human specimen, like a pin oak tree that attained only three feet of height because it grew up among the rocks on the edge of a desert where it received only enough water and soil nutrients to survive, but not to flourish. We need the virtues because they fit us to live the characteristically human life. If Aristotle's human biology is correct, it rules out the endless debates over ethical issues by fixing moral standards in a compelling way: It roots them in our human nature. That, at any rate, is the theoretical hope.

MacIntyre expounded and defended a version of Aristotelian moral biology in *Dependent Rational Animals* (1999). But as I say, when he wrote *After Virtue* (1981), he had not yet accepted that crucial part of the Aristotelian moral tradition. Yet in the 2007 Prologue, he stands staunchly by what he wrote in *After Virtue* and insists that it is Aristotelian. How did he propose in the earlier work that the concept of human virtue resolves or heads off the problem of moral disagreement and thus of moral skepticism? And how is his answer there related to the Aristotelian biology that he early shuns and later embraces?

The crucial elements in MacIntyre's earlier argument are (1) the idea of *a practice with its internal goods*; (2) the idea of *a self with a narrative structure*; and (3) the idea of *a moral tradition*. The basic argument seems to be that all three of these central and peculiarly human ways of "functioning" presuppose Aristotelian-type virtues. 'Presuppose' is my word; MacIntyre often talks of the virtues' "sustaining" the human functions.[7] Without the virtues, along with the moral standards that they embody, human life, with its essential functions, degenerates in various ways.

Human Practices

What is a practice? What is an internal good? A "practice," in MacIntyre's special sense, is a type of activity that has standards of excellence and is pursued in coordination with other people. In trying to achieve excellence in a practice, you improve your abilities and bring about good things that are special to the activity. To qualify as a practice, the activity has to be complex to a certain degree: "Tic-tac-toe is not an example of a practice in this sense, nor is throwing a football with skill; but the game of football is, and so is chess. Bricklaying is not a practice; architecture is. Planting turnips is not a practice; farming is. So are the enquiries of physics, chemistry and biology, and so is the work of the historian, and so are painting and music."[8]

---

[7] See his summary in Alasdair MacIntyre, *After Virtue: A Study in Moral Theory* (Notre Dame, IN: University of Notre Dame Press), 222–223.

[8] MacIntyre, *After Virtue*, 187.

To be a good "internal" to a practice, the good must belong strictly to the practice. Some people make lots of money playing football or practicing architecture and become famous. Money and fame are goods, and participants get them from the practices, but money and fame aren't "internal" to football or architecture: You can get them in many ways, and you could engage excellently in these practices without acquiring (or even seeking) money and fame; these goods don't belong strictly to these practices. But to achieve excellent strategies in football or beautiful, commodious buildings by architecture, or the pleasure that is specific to expertise in them, you have to pursue *these* practices. So brilliant plays and excellent buildings are goods internal to football and architecture. To get them, you have to practice football and architecture well.

Practices have traditions—the know-how, the methods, the standards—that are passed from one generation of practitioners to another. These traditions can flourish only if enough people who practice them have certain virtues. If practitioners of pottery-making stingily guard their discoveries in the mixing of clay or glazes, the community of potters is held back a bit, and the practice suffers. Here, a generous spirit of sharing secrets among potters fosters the community of potters and their practice. In science, dishonest or self-seeking researchers hold back their community and its practices. In football, coaches and players who are too "proud" to learn from others, or players who spread a spirit of unhealthy competition among players on the same team, damage the practice and hold back other participants who depend on them. So we can see that virtues like fairness, generosity, truthfulness, and humility have to be fairly widespread among practitioners if a practice is to flourish and develop and yield the goods internal to it.

MacIntyre notes that he isn't claiming that no practitioner has vices or lacks virtues. Dishonest scientists and selfish violinists exist. But he insists that the traditions of science and violin playing couldn't exist without there being such virtues in many of their practitioners. And it seems that no practitioner who completely lacked respect for truth would get very far as a scientist, and further, that practitioners who are defective in the virtues will also miss enjoying some of the internal goods that are fruits of their activities. The practice of science includes devices, such as peer review, that aim to keep dishonest practitioners "honest," thus showing the importance of honesty to science. Goods internal to practices have a way of taking captive the mind and heart of their practitioners, so that the latter find themselves motivated to be truthful, humble, generous, and just where those goods are concerned. Richard Feynman, the great twentieth-century physicist, was happy enough to cheat on his wife, but he observed a strict scientific integrity because he loved so much the goods internal to science.[9] (Apparently, he cared less about the goods internal to marriage.)

MacIntyre isn't a Marxist, but he agrees with Karl Marx's idea about the evil of the "alienation" of the worker from his or her work. A person is alienated from her work to the extent that she pursues it only for goods external to it. Many people who work at MacDonald's do so for the money, and thus for food, clothing, and shelter. Were it not for the money, they wouldn't do it. Indeed, the "practices" inside a MacDonald's are so routinized and simple that they don't qualify as practices at all. Creativity and progress in execution are nearly excluded. The worker functions as an impersonal means to the end of cranking out hamburgers and shakes. What about the executives with large salaries who oversee the network of MacDonald's franchises across the world? Are *they* engaged in practices with internal goods? It is plausible that some of them do what they do simply for the money they make, and thus for the large houses, the yachts, and so forth that money can buy. They would switch to an entirely different industry if offered a job that paid significantly more. If so, then some of them, too, are alienated from their work.

What about college students? Some students take courses in mathematics, English literature, history, the sciences, philosophy, and so forth because they love mathematics, or reading great literature, or want to understand human history or the sciences. Such understanding and skills are goods internal to the practice of these disciplines, so such students are not alienated from their studies. But seemingly more and more, students are encouraged to go to college "to get a well-paying job." If this continues to be their main goal throughout the college

---

[9] See Richard Feynman, *You Must Be Joking, Mr. Feynman*, as told to Ralph Leighton, ed. Edward Hutchings (New York: W. W. Norton, 1985), 341.

experience, they are alienated from their studies. They study for the sake of grades, and they want grades to get a good paying job. But those are not the goods internal to philosophy, literature, history, and mathematics. Such students are alienated from their work.

The Human Self

So, to the extent that practices with goods internal to them are important to human social life being *good*, that life will need to be populated with people who have qualities like justice, courage, generosity, truthfulness, and humility. But this raises the question, "What is it to have such qualities?" In particular, what kind of being do you have to be, to be just, generous, courageous, and so forth? This is the psychological question that Anscombe seems to be referring to, as the key to finding why the virtue concepts are compelling. MacIntyre's Aristotelian answer is that you have to be a self with a certain kind of psychological continuity, and he calls this continuity "narrative unity."

The characters in stories aren't just bursts of action, emotion, and thought flashing randomly here and there on a narrative landscape, but are *persons* that have a continuing single personal identity throughout the changing circumstances of their lives as well as through their actions and the psychological changes they undergo. At different times in the narrative, the character has different experiences, responds differently to them, performs different actions, and is related in various changing ways to other characters in the story. Yet throughout these actions, events, and developments, if the character is *a character* in the story, he or she also remains the *same one*. Furthermore, the narrative that shapes the identity of a character may extend to well before the birth of the character and beyond his death, and be also the narrative of his culture, his nationality, and his more local community.

This is the kind of self it takes to be the seat of virtues (and vices), which are traits (qualities) of character in this sense. If we think that a particular person is generous—that she is a generous *person*—we don't just think that, randomly and impulsively she now and then inexplicably behaves generously. We think, rather, that her action arises "from a firm and unchanging state of character" (NE 2.4, 1105a30). A self can have virtues, says MacIntyre, only if it's the sort of being that can be a character in a narrative.

Thus, we can identify two kinds of narrative unity or consistency: On the one hand, if a person is a character in a story, that person will be the same person throughout the story, regardless of whether he or she is virtuous or vicious or wavering between the two. On the other hand, if the person has the virtues, we can see a more particularized kind of consistency: He is (let us say) consistently kind, self-controlled, fair in his dealings with others, truthful, and compassionate. The first kind of consistency comes "automatically" with being a person at all; the second kind comes with being a good (or bad) person. Because the life of each of us has narrative unity in the first sense, each of us is faced with the question what kind of narrative unity our life will have in the second sense.

At a fairly young age, people become aware that we human beings come in generations: I am the son of these parents, and they are the children of my grandparents; and my grandparents were children of my great-grandparents, and so on. And I will someday probably be a parent, and then later a grandparent. And like my grandparents, I will then be near the end of my life. And the reflective young person may think: Will I have lived a life that is as good, or as bad, as my parents and grandparents? How will I manage my life? And if that child has received a decently good upbringing, he will hope to live a good life and will think of doing so as being at least partially his to choose. And he will evaluate his life by moral standards: Did I do something worthwhile? Was mine a life of integrity? Did I respect my fellow human beings and treat them well? If his upbringing has been less good and less human, he may evaluate his life in other terms: Will I have been more famous than my parents? Will I have been wealthier than my parents? Will I have had more power over others than my parents had? But in either kind of case, he will think of and evaluate his life as having the form of a story with a beginning and an end, and he will think of it as having been good or bad (or a mixture of these) in whatever terms he thinks of good and bad.

All this may seem obvious. You may ask, "How could anybody think otherwise about the human self?" MacIntyre's answer is, "Lots of modern people." Throughout *After Virtue*, MacIntyre stalks a degenerate modern concept of the human self that he calls "emotivist." Emotivism is the modern name that some twentieth-century philosophers gave to a theory that goes back to the sentimentalists of the eighteenth century. The theory is that when we attribute qualities like good and evil to some event—say, an earthquake or a human act of kindness—we are not quite ascribing a quality to *the event* (though we do *seem* to be doing that). Instead, we are really saying *how we feel* about it. So if I say to you, "I admire your compassion and generosity in helping that poor man you found wounded in the ditch," I'm not really talking about the value of your qualities as a person or of your action. Instead, I'm saying "I feel good about you and what you did." So according to emotivism, when we ascribe a value (negative or positive) to something, we're not talking about a quality in the thing; we are talking about ourselves and how we feel about the thing. Qualities of good and evil are "projections" of our feelings. And if this is true, says MacIntyre, the self "can have no rational history in its transitions from one state of moral commitment to another" (*After Virtue*, 38).

Feelings always occur at one moment or another: They often change from one moment to another, and different people have different feelings about the same thing. So the emotivist *self* is a self that has its existence only in the moment. A human life (which is, after all, the life of a self) therefore doesn't have a narrative structure in which it is a continuing being that changes by deciding to do this or that, performing actions, thinking thoughts, and undergoing various experiences, and so has a past, present, and future, and *develops* as a self. According to the emotivist theory, the whole "story" of the self is just in the moment (and that's not a *story*).

A paradigm and celebration of this kind of self is the character Meursault in Albert Camus's novel *The Stranger*. Meursault just drifts with the currents of his environment, responding to the "stimuli" that they present. He has no ambitions, no projects, no aspirations other than his current comfort. He is a character in Camus's story, but he has no character; he is neither good nor evil. Camus, in this period, is regarded as an existentialist thinker, and the avowed existentialist Jean-Paul Sartre interprets him as such.[10] So another term for the emotivist

---

[10] Jean-Paul Sartre, "*The Stranger* Explained," in *We Have Only This Life to Live*, ed. Ronald Aronson and Adrian van den Hoven (New York: New York Review Books),

self is the existentialist self. But if the emotivists and existentialists are wrong about the nature of the self, as they most certainly are, then, thinks MacIntyre, we need the virtues. The virtues are qualities that a self with a narrative structure needs if that self is to be both good and true to its own nature as a self.

We each seek our own good, but we may do so foolishly and ineptly; or wisely, circumspectly, and effectively. This clause in MacIntyre's summary claims that the latter course requires that we have the virtues. We may need to be courageous to choose the virtuous and truly "happy" course; we will need to be truthful and just and forgiving and generous in dealing with our associates who are also seeking their good, and by our wisdom we will realize that their good *is* our good; and so forth. One of the contrasts suggested by insisting on the "whole life" is that often what appear to be short-term gains in achieving our good are illusory and so need to be "seen through" in a way that requires the virtues. And even when in some sense we see that our true good is not what seems immediately most advantageous, we may need to rule virtuously against our insistent inclinations. All this requires the virtues.

Moral Traditions

We have already noted the importance of virtues to sustaining the traditions from which we have inherited many practices with internal goods such as architecture, the sciences, and violin playing. The

16–43. Sartre speaks of the novel as presenting a "succession of inert present moments" (43). https://books.google.com/books?id=2QuTTX0WekgC&printsec=frontcover&source=gbs_ViewAPI#v=onepage&q&f=false.

Electronic devices can induce a first-personal experience of what it's like to be an emotivist or existentialist: We happen on a page that's interesting for a moment, then click on a link that brings us to another page that's a little bit interesting, which has a link to another page, and so forth, and before we know it an hour has passed of going passively with the algorithmic flow, being momentarily stimulated by this and that but without setting any course of our own, any course set by our own life purposes and considered choices. If all (more or less) is well with our soul, something in our character (probably with help from our environment) calls us from this emotivist lapse, we wake up and kick ourselves for having wasted an hour of precious time. Dusting ourselves off, we resume the narrative of our actual life. Thanks to a reader for OUP for suggesting this illustration.

notion of a good *internal* to a practice is that if you want *that* good, you have to engage in the practice, and you have to do so well. But to engage well in the practice, you have to accept, from the tradition of the practice, the *ways* of doing things that the tradition has come to understand as needed for reaping those internal goods. For example, the tradition of violin playing offers standards of excellence of performance and ways of fingering and bowing, as well as criteria of interpretation of the violin repertoire, that you must master if you are to reap the goods internal to the practice. If you are very creative, you might deviate from the tradition in certain limited ways, adjusting the tradition and adding something of your own to it; but if you do, you will do so *as* a practitioner of the tradition that you are adjusting and advancing.

We can think of living a life as comparable to a practice. Just as violin playing can be done well or not so well, a person can live his or her life well or not so well. Just as violin players have developed, over the years, a tradition of how violin playing is done well (and there might be different "schools" with somewhat different proposals about what makes for good violin playing, but all the schools would have something to say about fingering, bowing, and posture, and all would aim at precise intonation), so traditions have developed about what it is to live a whole life well, and these are the "moral" traditions. Possible examples are the heroic tradition (depicted in Homer's epics), the Hebrew tradition (depicted in the Hebrew Bible), the Confucian tradition (embodied in the *Analects*), the Stoic tradition (promoted in various Stoic documents), and the Aristotelian-Thomistic tradition (expounded in the ethical writings of Aristotle and Aquinas). All these are traditions about how to live a human life well—how to pursue that all-encompassing "practice." MacIntyre's point would be that to practice well the living of a human life according to any of these traditions necessarily involves the formation of a human self that takes into consideration its narrative structure, and traits that by their "constancy" reflect and conform to this narrative structure.

According to the Aristotelian moral tradition, the virtues are the way to live the good life, and thus reap the goods internal to doing so. The state of a person's life who practices the virtues is what Aristotle calls *eudaimonia*. Sometimes, this Greek word has been translated "happiness," but this can be misleading, since it is natural to say, "I made the children happy by giving them candy" and "the drunk has been happy since he got his hands on a bottle of wine a few minutes ago." It's better to translate eudaimonia as "the good life." *Eudaimonia* is the good internal to the "practice" of living a life of virtues. According to Aristotle, *eudaimonia* is the highest good for a human being, and to achieve that good you need to be just, temperate, courageous, and practically wise, as well as to have some lesser virtues. Aristotelian eudaimonia is a variant of what the Jewish scriptures call shalom: an order of peace and well-being. It's a social-relational package consisting of virtuous persons interacting in a social environment that befits human nature. I say "variant" because Jewish shalom crucially requires a positive, loving, ongoing, personal relation with God as the Lord, and eudaimonia does not. Central to Aristotelian eudaimonia is the social context of the city-state, whereas the context of shalom is the reign of God.

So if the virtues are means to *eudaimonia*, they aren't means *external* to that good, in the way that money is a means to getting a yacht or a hamburger. Simple Christians have sometimes thought of the virtues that way: If I'm compassionate and generous, I'll be rewarded in Heaven. But that's not the right way to think of the virtues, either as a Christian or as an Aristotelian. Rather, the virtues are the *very way*, or a crucial part of the very way, that the good life is lived. So they are means that are also a large part of the end. The *goal*, which is eudaimonia or blessedness, is the *practice* of the good life (the excellent practice of a human life). It is not something *beyond* and somehow *caused by* the good life. Eudaimonia (blessedness) is the dominant and comprehensive *characteristic* of the good life.

A Metaphysical Grounding: *Dependent Rational Animals* (1999)

I noted earlier that though MacIntyre has continued to affirm the main arguments of *After Virtue*, he has acknowledged that they're incomplete. They need to be supplemented with an account of the kind that he calls "metaphysical biology." Earlier I called this a fundamental anthropology. Thus, he writes in the Prologue to the third edition (2007), "But I had now learned from Aquinas that my attempt to provide an account of the human good purely in social terms, in terms of practices, traditions, and the narrative unity of human lives, was bound to be inadequate until I had provided it with a metaphysical grounding."[11] A metaphysical grounding is an answer to the question, What kind of nature do beings have to have to be beings who have practices with internal goods, selves that seek the good of their whole life, and moral traditions? MacIntyre answers this question in *Dependent Rational Animals* (1999). The answer is in the title: We humans are dependent rational animals. Aristotle had already stressed that we are rational animals, so Aquinas's addition is the idea that we are fundamentally dependent. We are fragile creatures, creatures with a long dependent infancy and childhood who, if we live long enough, will become again dependent on others for our continued existence and quality of life, creatures among whom some of us are disabled and permanently dependent on others. Even in our prime, we depend on others for services, help, and collaboration. Our fundamental dependency has implications for the nature of our rationality, as we will see.

MacIntyre's fundamental anthropology in *Dependent Rational Animals* consists largely of extended comparisons of being human with being an intelligent animal like dolphins and gorillas. The point of the comparison will be to mark its limit: the line between being intelligent and being rational. Dolphins are among the most intelligent animals. They engage in socially coordinated, improvisatory goal-directed behavior. For example, in fishing they employ scouts that signal to the rest of the herd when fish have been sighted, and the rest of the herd respond by changing swimming direction. They sometimes herd fish into a narrow inlet to entrap them, but if this strategy doesn't work, they may drive them out to sea where other dolphins are waiting. In the course of such goal-directed behavior, dolphins make use of perceptual recognition and perceptual attention, and respond to what is perceived with appropriate action and emotion. Thus they exhibit the ability to act for reasons, changing them as circumstances change. They display developmentally essential patterns of receiving and giving. Adult dolphins have received from their elders an

---

[11] MacIntyre, *After Virtue*, third edition, Prologue, unpaginated.

understanding of fishing, and they pass it on to the next generation; and they care for their young in other ways. So dolphins are intelligent animals, and their intelligence is devoted partly to receiving nurture from others and, in turn, nurturing others in the ways of dolphin intelligence.

Human beings, too, are intelligent animals. But we differ from other ones in being also rational animals, and ideal human development is toward a goal that no other intelligent animal has: that of becoming "independent practical reasoners." Mature human beings are *agents*—sources of actions—in a way that no other intelligent animal is. To be the kind of being that can achieve this, we need to be able not only to have reasons for our actions and emotions but to evaluate our reasons and to choose the best ones and the ones that we ought to act on. This goal makes us vulnerable and dependent in a way that other intelligent animals are not. Our parents need to have given us a kind of moral upbringing that allows us both to evaluate well our reasons for action and to be motivated to act on the reasons that result from such evaluating.

This requires that our parents or other guardians exercise toward us the virtue of "just generosity." Generosity is the virtue by which we are moved by the prospect of another person's good for his or her sake, and just generosity is generosity that recognizes the other's good as owed to him or her by us. For example, justly generous parents recognize that what they generously give to their children is something that, as parents, they owe to their children. Gratitude is the virtue by which we recognize that the giver has generously given us what we needed to become what we are—independent practical reasoners, mature human beings. So, where human life is being carried on as befits it, all are grateful to our parents for what we have received from them and justly generous toward our children. Thus, persons living within this moral tradition will have a vivid appreciation of being dependent rational animals. Our being dependent animals affects the shape of our being rational animals, and our being rational affects the shape (or content) of our dependency.

What does our rationality have to be like for us to have the virtues of just generosity and the corresponding gratitude? It is a kind of rationality that allows us explicitly to understand and appreciate our own social nature, and thus to contemplate our needs as a certain kind of intelligent being and our good of having those needs fulfilled. This rather "philosophical" kind of understanding seems to distinguish human rationality from the kind of intelligence that merely intelligent animals have. Notice, however, that this kind of "philosophy" isn't the special preserve of professional philosophers such as philosophy professors: Any reflective person who has received a good upbringing in the moral tradition can have it. Other virtues that are characteristic of fully formed dependent rational animals are compassion (MacIntyre follows Aquinas in calling this *misericordia*) and forgivingness (which MacIntyre does not mention). All four of these virtues are from the Christian moral tradition and are absent from Aristotle's list.[12] All four, or near equivalents of them, have been taken up, theologically sanitized, by some parts of secular ethics.

Conclusion

For Elizabeth Anscombe, the turn to moral psychology, and ultimately to a study of the virtues, was a way of rescuing atheist philosophers from an unworkable concept of moral obligation. Whether or not she rescued any atheists, she set a-humming a philosophical factory that for the last several decades has cranked out many works of moral psychology, including MacIntyre's. For Alasdair MacIntyre, an exploration of the virtues as required by the fulfilling human pursuit of goods internal to practices, the good of having a self with a narrative structure, and immersion in a moral tradition that aspires to both the Aristotelian virtues and the virtues of us dependent rational animals is the way to transcend and resolve the moral fragmentation and interminable moral disagreements of modern life. Neither of these "founders" of the modern study of the virtues calls their activities "virtue ethics," though both fall under the broad category of the virtue ethics that this book is about. We turn in the next chapter to a group of philosophers

---

[12] See Chapter 4 for how the virtue of generosity differs from Aristotle's virtue of liberality and for what Aristotle has to say about compassion.

who do accept the title of "virtue ethics" for what they pursue. In general, I will argue that they are trying, in a less profound and complex way than Anscombe and MacIntyre, to avoid the evils of moral skepticism that motivated the modern ethical theories briefly examined in Chapter 1.

3

Virtue Ethics Today

"Pure" Virtue Ethics

Introduction

What is this thing we call "ethics"? Let's distinguish ethics as the study of ethics from ethics as what the study of ethics studies. This book, like courses in ethics that you might take in college, is an example of the study of ethics. In this chapter, we will be looking at two things. First, we'll be figuring out what the study of ethics (and this book) is properly *about*: What are some of the main things that need to be considered in a study of ethics? But in addition to that, we'll be interested in considering different *ways* of studying ethics, and we'll ask, "What is the best way to study ethics?" We won't only be studying ethics, but studying the study of ethics. Two different ways of studying ethics that will loom large will be *ethical theory* and what we might call *exploration of ethical concepts*. The expression "virtue ethics" is ambiguous, inasmuch as it can mean either (1) an ethical theory in which the concept of virtue is foundational or (2) an exploration of ethical concepts centered on the concept of a virtue. I'll be proposing that the latter is the better kind of study of ethics and that it's better for two reasons: It's better because it's more respectful of the way the ethical concepts actually work; and it's better because it has more potential to promote ethics: ethical living by the study's practitioners (you and me). The latter seems to me to be the most important purpose in studying ethics. In the next section, we'll survey some possible ethical theories, both the ones we surveyed in Chapter 1 and several others. We'll use our consideration of them as a way of starting to collect a list of ethical concepts: the things that a study of ethics might be about.

Virtue Ethics. Robert Campbell Roberts, Oxford University Press.
© Robert Campbell Roberts 2026. DOI: 10.1093/9780197848005.003.0005

Ethical Theories and the Many Proposed
"Foundations" of Ethics

In Chapter 1, we briefly explored four rival theories from the modern history of ethics which, we said, are efforts to find and establish the foundation of ethics. Each of the four theories identifies some aspect of ethics that it supposes to be the (one and only) foundation: Kantian ethics (deontology) proposes pure practical reason (something indisputably *right*); utilitarianism proposes pleasure, happiness, or well-being (something indisputably *good*); social contract theory proposes *agreement* or *contract* (what is agreed on may be various ethical rules, what to count as right or good, but basic to establishing either of these would be the agreement or "deal" that establishes what is right or good); and sentimentalism proposes that the foundation is *mental states of approval*—feelings, judgments, intuitions, perceptions, and so forth (the right, the good, or the virtues get their status as such from our mental approval of them). The basic idea behind the theories is that all of the aspects of ethics that are *not* chosen to be the foundation derive their ethical status, in one way or another, from the chosen foundation. They depend on the foundation for their ethical status.

So the answer to the question, "What is ethics (as what the discipline of ethics studies)?" in each of these four theories, is that ethics consists of at least these four items:

— The right
— The good
— Agreement, contract, promise, covenant, "deal"
— Emotions, judgments, or intuitions about what is right and/or good and perhaps more basically still, the innate human disposition to form such mental states

All four of these items are indisputably concepts that we use in the course of daily ethical life. We say, "yes, he did the right thing, even though he had misgivings." We say, "he made the right decision, because it's ultimately for the good of the community." We say, "it was only right for him to do that, because that's what he agreed to do."

We say, "it's wrong to go against your conscience (that is, what you judge and feel to be right) even when your conscience misleads you." When we speak and think in these terms, we're practicing ethics (not studying ethics). These, then, are items belonging to ethics, not as a theory or academic discipline, but as a standard for living, as what the philosophical discipline of ethics is about. If we live ethically, we try to do what is right, to bring about good and eliminate evil, to keep our agreements with one another, and to make proper ethical judgments and feel proper ethical emotions about what we and others do, the good or bad traits of people, and about states of affairs in the world.

If all ethical people use all the concepts that are the basis of the ethical theories that we surveyed in Chapter 1, what is there for the theories to disagree about? We said that the theories differ from one another—and become rivals—because each chooses one of these concepts and makes it the foundation for all the rest. The theories are incompatible with one another, not because of the concepts they acknowledge to be legitimate, but because of the *orders* or *arrangements* of the concepts that they propose. To follow the metaphor of the building, what one theory proposes as a window or a wall, another theory proposes as the foundation. Given the rule that an ethical theory can have only one foundation, the theories have to be rivals of one another. Since these four concepts don't seem to be rivals in everyday ethical life, we may begin to think there's something wrong with the enterprise of ethical theory. If we decide that ethical theories have lost their purpose and are only a hindrance to ethical understanding, is there any other way to study ethics? But we are getting a little ahead of ourselves. Where does virtue ethics fit in this picture?

In his paper, "The Primacy of Character,"[1] Gary Watson points out that John Rawls, who was perhaps the greatest ethical theorist of the twentieth century, thought that ethics had three aspects: the right, the good, and moral worth. Moral worth is an aspect of ethics not yet mentioned in this chapter, and not considered as a foundation of

---

[1] In *Identity, Character, and Morality: Essays in Moral Psychology*, ed. Owen Flanagan and Amélie Oksenberg Rorty (Cambridge, MA: MIT Press, 1993), 449–469, 449. See also Jason Kawall, "In Defense of the Primacy of the Virtues," *Journal of Ethics and Social Philosophy* 3 (2009): DOI: 10.26556/jesp.v3i2.32.

ethics in any of the four theories sketched in Chapter 1. Moral worth is the excellent moral formation of human persons, in other words, good character or the virtues. Watson notes that Rawls acknowledged only two kinds of moral theory, one based on the right (Kantian-style ethical theory, what you ought to do: "deontology") and one based on the good (utilitarianism and other consequentialisms: what ought to be brought about). Rawls thought it obvious that moral worth would have to be derived either from the right or from the good. That is, traits of persons would qualify as ethical virtues only if they got their worth by being proper orientations to the right (for example, the sense of duty or the virtue of justice) or by being dispositions to bring good into the world (kindness, generosity, compassion). In a deontological theory, what is good gets to be good by being what we should do, and in a consequentialist theory, what is right gets to be right because it brings more good into the world.

Watson spends his paper considering the possibility that Rawls was wrong about this. There's a third option for moral theory. Moral worth (character) is a possible foundation: Derive the right and the good from the virtues.[2] Thus, "the primacy of character" as in what Michael Slote calls "pure virtue ethics"[3]—an ethical theory different from the four that we discussed in Chapter 1: a theory that makes the concept of virtue foundational for ethics and derives everything else from that single foundation. I will adopt Slote's terminology, thus distinguishing between virtue ethics simply as ethical reflection that centers on the concept of virtue (as in this book and as in the ethics of Aristotle, Aquinas, and many others), and "pure virtue ethics," which is a theory that makes virtue the fundamental ethical concept, the foundation and basis of all the other ethical concepts. In either case, the introduction of virtue ethics obviously adds a fifth item to the above list of the elements of ethics: the concept of virtues (and vices): psychological norms of ethical excellence. But our collection of aspects of ethics isn't yet complete.

---

[2] As to the sentimentalist option, it seems plausible that to have dependable ethical judgments, emotions, and intuitions, one needs to be a virtuous person, so virtue would be foundational for these as well.

[3] Michael Slote, *Morals from Motives* (New York: Oxford University Press, 2001), 3–10.

Linda Zagzebski has proposed a theory in which exemplars—persons of outstanding and impressive moral character—form the foundation.[4] Exemplarist moral theory is the proposal that individual virtuous people, in their capacity as exemplars of the virtues, are foundational to everything else in ethics. According to her theory, we pick out certain individuals from the crowd of human beings we know of and notice that they are unusually excellent *as people*. We do this by finding ourselves admiring them. If we are reflective enough in our admiration for them, our admiration is a reliable way of identifying them as moral exemplars. As we become reflective about these people and the fact that we admire them, we ask, *Why* do we admire these people? What sets them apart from others? And we might conclude that they are unusually compassionate, or generous, or humble, or fair, or truthful—and our admiration would become more articulate by identifying their specific virtues.

Thus, Zagzebski thinks, individual moral exemplars are basic to the other aspects of ethics, including the virtues. She proposes this as a new theory, different from any of the other five that we've mentioned in this chapter. We might worry that in making the emotion of admiration so crucial in her theory, she is actually proposing either a version of sentimentalism or, if we stress the reflectiveness of an individual's admiration of the exemplar, perhaps a version of ("pure") virtue ethics. After all, it takes some virtue to admire and understand virtue. Here we see a problem that bedevils efforts to satisfy the "purity" condition on ethical theories: that their purity is threatened by the preferred foundation's need to be supplemented or combined with some other aspect of ethics to be plausible, thus undermining the theory's "purity." Zagzebski's theory is interesting less because it is plausible than because it is an effort to take yet a different item from among the aspects of ordinary ethics and make it the foundation, thus creating one more

[4] See her *Exemplarist Moral Theory* (Cambridge: Cambridge University Press, 2018) and my review of the book in the *Australasian Journal of Philosophy* 2019. Attention to moral exemplars is important in our moral thinking, both because we inevitably play the role of exemplar to our children, spouse, friends, and colleagues (and maybe to others as well) and because the role of exemplar is so important in moral education. When we pay real attention to the fact that others are influenced by our conduct and attitudes, it has a tendency to sober us up and make us more serious about how we come across.

kind of ethical theory. So we have added the concept of a moral exemplar to our list of the conceptual aspects of ethics.

Modern "neo-Aristotelian" ethical theorists like Rosalind Hursthouse[5] tend to think of Aristotle's ethics as a variant of what they themselves do when they are "doing ethics," namely ethical theory. Here, the foundation is yet a different item in the array of aspects of ethics: a conception of human nature, and thus a notion of what it is for a human being or community of such beings to "flourish," to live well the life that is characteristic of our species. As we saw in Chapter 2, Aristotle thinks that we human beings are "rational animals." This summary phrase doesn't tell you in much detail what Aristotle thought we are, but we learned from MacIntyre that Aristotle does *not* emphasize that we are *dependent* rational animals, as Aquinas and other Christians think we are. In any case, Aristotle thinks of the virtues as ways of being "complete" or mature or excellent specimens for beings who are "rational animals" as he conceives us to be. If Aristotle's ethics is a variant of foundationalist ethical theory on the modern model (I will argue in Chapter 4 that it isn't), then the foundation would be human nature conceived as Aristotle conceives it, and neo-Aristotelians, if they are pushing a modern ethical theory, would be proposing that human nature as *they* conceive it is the foundation of ethics. This would be a sixth possible ethical theory.

Jorge Garcia has proposed an ethical theory according to which ethical roles such as parent, information-giver, friend, shopkeeper, and so forth, are fundamental, and virtues enable us to fill these roles properly.[6] Ethically speaking, we human beings seldom if ever function simply as human beings. We are nearly always (arguably always, says Garcia) filling one or more social roles such as friend, parent, child, teacher, student, fellow citizen, partner, spouse, neighbor, employee, employer, helper, researcher, and so forth. Similarly, we have our obligations, not just as human beings, but as husband, son, letter carrier, physician, patient, promise-giver, and so on. The virtues help us fill these roles well. So social roles are at least as fundamental to the

---

[5] Rosalind Hursthouse, *On Virtue Ethics* (Oxford: Oxford University Press, 1999).

[6] See his "Roles and Virtues," in *Routledge Companion to Virtue Ethics,* ed. Lorraine Besser-Jones and Michael Slote (New York: Routledge, 2015), 415–423.

moral life as virtues and obligations: "we regard the moral virtues as themselves derived from and relative to the agent's roles" (420).

Garcia's commitment to the fundamental status of a social role vis-à-vis virtues comes out when he briefly considers virtues that don't seem to be necessarily social in nature. "We don't talk of being courageous, temperate, or prudent *to* someone, but it may still be that these are only virtues in that they make us good in relation to ourselves; in being temperate I am good to myself."[7] Though he doesn't say so explicitly, Garcia seems to flirt with the idea that another role we fill might be being ourselves, as when a famous actor plays himself in a play in which he himself is one of the characters. But this move would undercut Garcia's point about the fundamentality of social roles: No matter which role we may be playing at a given moment—mother, daughter, social worker, amateur musician—we are almost always "playing" ourselves. The only time we're not playing ourselves is when we are literally stage-acting a role or pretending to be someone we aren't. In that case, though in the ordinary sense we may be playing the role of Abigail Adams or Odysseus, in Garcia's sense of "play a role," we are playing the role of an actor, and the person who's playing that role is us. But being oneself isn't a role in the way that the social roles are roles. The concept of a self is another basic ethical concept; after all, it is a self—an individual human being—who plays the various social roles, and the self is the location, so to speak, of the virtues (and vices).[8] So the notion of a social role seems to presuppose the notion of a self, threatening the "purity" of a role theory of ethics. Though being oneself seems bogus if presented as one more social role, nevertheless, real social roles are pervasive in the moral life, and it takes virtues to fill these roles well. We owe Garcia a debt for pointing this out.[9]

Another kind of theory that is sometimes proposed is a divine command theory: The foundation of ethics is the commands (or will) of

---

[7] Garcia, "Roles and Virtues," 415–423, 416.

[8] For an ethical exploration that focuses on the concept of a self, see Søren Kierkegaard's *The Sickness unto Death* (Princeton: Princeton University Press, 1980) and many other works; and my exposition of Kierkegaard's ethics in *Recovering Christian Character* (Grand Rapids: Wm. B. Eerdmans, 2022).

[9] We might connect roles with MacIntyre's notion of a practice. Practices seem to be pursued by people in various roles—roles like musician, chess player, governor, architect.

God. Recent divine command theorists have limited their foundational claims: Divine commands are the foundation of *obligation*, but not necessarily of the distinction between *good* and *bad*; the latter derives from God's goodness, which cannot be a result of God's commands. The commands of God are the fundamental basis of "the right."[10]

Certainly, the commands of God seem very fundamental to the moral life of believers. But non-believers too can have a strong sense of obligation. And again, as in so many other cases of proposed foundational concepts, God's commands seem to need help from other aspects of morality to create obligations. In particular, human nature needs to have some features that enable beings of this kind to respond to God's commands by becoming obligated. For example, you can't become obligated in response to a command that you don't understand. God doesn't direct his commands to snakes and squirrels and salamanders, because they wouldn't understand the commands even if they "heard" them. Thus, something like Aristotle's claim that we are rational animals needs to be true if we are to be able to be obligated by God's commands. This aspect of morality is just as fundamental and necessary to our being obligated as God's commands are. And we need not only to understand what is commanded in some basic sense but also to be able to adapt our will to conform our heart to what we understand. Thus, our nature needs to be not only rational in some bare sense but also to be rational in a way that is also "passional." We need to have what the New Testament calls a "heart" that can be affected by thoughts.

Thus, in addition to the right, the good, agreement, and moral "intuitions," aspects of ethics as a practice and way of thinking include

Virtue concepts
Moral exemplars
Social roles (parent, child, information-giver)
The (human) self
Commands (or will) of God
A conception of human nature

---

[10] See Robert Adams, *Finite and Infinite Goods: A Framework for Ethics* (Oxford: Oxford University Press, 1999). See also Evans, *Kierkegaard's Ethic of Love*.

Before virtue ethics came on the scene, by far the most popular materials for use as moral foundations were the right and the good. But all ten items from the array have been the focus of ethical reflections by one philosopher or another, and many of these have been proposed as foundational for ethics.

"Pure" Virtue Ethics

The major ethical theories of the nineteenth and twentieth centuries had places for the concept of virtue. For Immanuel Kant, virtue is a strength of will by which a person resists natural inclinations that are inconsistent with duty or respect for the moral law. It's a power by which the virtuous person resists temptations to forsake his duty.[11] Thus, for Kant, virtue is entirely subordinate to the concept of the moral law prescribing duty. For John Stuart Mill, a major defender of utilitarianism, virtue is a disposition to maximize pleasure or happiness for oneself and others. Think of how the virtue of fairness among a society's leaders and citizens makes for an overall happier society. Mill notes that virtue can itself become an object of pleasure for virtuous people, so it can be not only a means to happiness but a part of it.[12] The ability to take pleasure in virtue is not automatic and universal among humans, the way some dispositions to pleasure are, but has to be learned. Here we see that Mill too has a place for virtue in his moral theory, but that the place he gives it is subordinate to "utility"[13] (pleasure or happiness), which is the only thing that is originally and in itself good according to his theory. We've seen that the sentimentalists,

[11] See *The Metaphysics of Morals*, Part II: Metaphysical First Principles of the Doctrine of Virtue, in *The Cambridge Edition of the Works of Immanuel Kant: Practical Philosophy*, ed. Mary Gregor (Cambridge: Cambridge University Press, 1996), 507–540; See especially 524–527.

[12] See John Stuart Mill's *Utilitarianism* (1863), 65–66. The page numbers are to a pdf reproduction of Mill's text of *Utilitarianism* available at https://www.utilitarianism.com/jsmill-utilitarianism.pdf.

[13] In Mill's *Autobiography*, he claims that he invented this special usage of the word 'utility,' and a strange one it is. In the context of utilitarianism, utility is a synonym for pleasure, happiness, or well-being. Philosophers have become accustomed to this usage, but it continues to confuse many other English speakers.

too, talk about virtues and claim that the concept of a virtue derives, as a projection, from our sentiments of moral approval.

So you could say that Kant, Mill, and Hume, and indeed any deontologist, consequentialist, or sentimentalist, can have a "virtue ethics" as part of their theories. After all, the concept of virtue or virtues is a natural one for anybody's array of ethical concepts. Virtues aren't the foundation, but within each of the theoretical constructions, they are an important wing of the structure.

By contrast, Michael Slote wants a virtue ethics that is "pure"—one in which virtue, and neither duty nor utility nor sentiments, nor any other ethical concept, has the primary place, the place of the foundation. "Purity" in a moral theory can be defined as the theory's ability to make do with a single solitary foundation, unsupported by any other of the elements of an ethics. This kind of purity is an ideal in the construction of ethical theories in the modern style: To the extent that a theorist has to call in other items from ethics to build his favorite kind of foundation, his theory falls short of the ideal. Kant's theory is a "pure" deontology, because everything that isn't deontological is subordinate to duty (as dictated by practical reason). And Mill's theory is a "pure" utilitarianism. In a way, purity is the essential mark of an ethical theory, since theories differ from one another by which item from the conceptual array is taken to be the foundation. A foundation that has to rely on something else to hold it in place is not quite the (one and only) foundation. We have seen that purity is hard to come by in an ethical theory. Proposed foundations have a way of sneaking a little help from some of the things they are supposed to be holding up.

Slote proposes a "pure virtue ethics" in which the moral quality of an action is "*entirely* derivative from *independent* and *fundamental* aretaic (as opposed to deontic) ethical characterizations of motives, character traits, or individuals . . . ."[14] Though he mentions character traits and individuals, for Slote the state of the agent that determines the moral quality of the agent's actions is the agent's motive. He supposes that

---

[14] "Aretaic" is a fancy word for "having to do with virtue." In Greek, the word for virtue is *aretē*. Slote's paper is "Agent-Based Virtue Ethics," in *Virtue Ethics*, ed. Roger Crisp and Michael Slote (Oxford: Oxford University Press, 1997), 239–262. The quotation is from p. 239, italics added.

motive is the essence of virtue.[15] Thus, if we wish to know whether a particular action is a good one, we will try to determine the agent's motive in performing it. If the motive is virtuous, then the action is good, and if the motive is vicious, the action is bad.

Let's take him at his word and see where it leads. So, if I give 20 $1 bills to a beggar out of a morally indifferent motive such as a desire to relieve the discomfort of sitting on a fat wallet, my action is morally indifferent; and if I do so out of a morally good motive, such as compassion for the beggar, my action is good; and if I perform it out of an evil motive such as a desire to humiliate my walking companions, my action is bad. Let's agree on the point about the moral quality of these motives and that, in *one* sense, what I "did" is to be evaluated by reference to my motive. But is this the *whole* story about the moral goodness or badness of the action?

The motive is the "independent and fundamental" moral element. This means that if you want to know what makes the motive of compassion good, you can't appeal to its *rationality* by saying that we all want to be treated compassionately when we are in trouble, so we should treat others that way when they are in trouble; or to its *consequences* by saying that the world is a sweeter place to live if people have compassion for one another; or to a *commandment of God* that we should love one another; or to *human nature* by saying that being compassionate is part of natural human functioning and fulfillment. No, if the motive of compassion is "independent and fundamental," then its moral status doesn't derive from any other consideration. You can't explain in any other terms what makes the motive good. It just *is* good. There, explanations come to an end.

Thus, the "purity" of this virtue ethics is a straitjacket on explanations. It seems to me to be just common sense that we can explain the goodness of the motive of compassion in all four of the

---

[15] I think this supposition is false. The virtues that I call substantive are indeed "defined" by their motives, because they are essentially concerns for parts of the good. Think of generosity, justice, truthfulness. But other virtues, such as courage and perseverance, are not defined by their motives; courageous and perseverant actions, for example, can be motivated by other considerations, perhaps even by evil motives. To the extent that such actions are morally good, they borrow their motives from the virtues that *are* defined by the motives. (See Chapter 7 for details.) Motive is not the essence of virtue in general.

ways that Slote's "pure" virtue ethics rules out. To be moved by compassion is rational (makes sense), makes the world a better place (has good consequences), is commanded by God, and fulfills our human nature. Note that each of these four explanations appeals to one of the "foundations" of another theory. One is tempted to think: All the theories are right in appealing to a genuine explanation, and all are wrong in regarding their favored explanation as a unique foundation. Moral theories are awkward simplifications.

Can you do the right thing for the wrong reason? If so, Slote must be wrong to claim that motive defines the rightness of all right actions. He addresses this objection by bringing up Henry Sidgwick's example of a prosecutor who does his duty in prosecuting a defendant but does it from malice. Thus, the prosecutor does what is right from a wrong motive. Slote's attempted answer is that if the prosecutor prosecutes at all, he does it from *some* sense of duty and thus a good motive—because if, horrified by his malice, he decided not to prosecute, his inaction would result from "insufficient concern for the public good" (242).

But to insist that the prosecutor acts from a sense of duty is simply to reject the plausible example. Perhaps Slote is confusing doing your duty with doing your duty from a sense of duty. But we often do our duty without doing it from a sense of duty. I do my duty to my children when I do it out of love; if I actually had to call on duty to make me do my duty, the action would have less moral value, or the wrong kind. One genuine possibility is that the prosecutor does his duty from malice, without any compunction. He happens to hate the defendant, and his hatred doesn't horrify him. The defendant is guilty and indeed needs to be prosecuted, and the prosecutor, in his role as prosecutor, has a duty to prosecute him. But the prosecutor's hatred of the defendant swamps his sense of duty. Doing his duty—prosecuting the criminal—is a joy to him, not because the man deserves it or because it is his duty to prosecute criminals, but because of his personal hatred (say, a racist hatred) for this individual. His hatred is so intense that he would seek to convict the defendant even if he knew him not to be guilty. But he prosecutes the defendant skillfully, using true premises and excellent reasoning. So he does the right thing for the wrong reason.

Another objection to Slote's pure virtue ethics: If to do the right thing just *is* to act with virtuous motivation, then a person of virtue can perform any action whatsoever and it will automatically be a good action: "it cannot morally matter what [the virtuous person] actually *does*" (243, italics original). Slote says his theory isn't vulnerable to this objection, since even the virtuous person isn't always ideally motivated, and so can fail to act virtuously: Not every action that the virtuous person performs is virtuously motivated.

Slote's comment is true but irrelevant to his theory. Slote's foundation isn't virtue itself, but episodic virtuous motivation. Virtues aren't episodes, like actions and emotions. They are dispositions, *readinesses* to act and feel in certain ways. As MacIntyre notes, a virtue is an attribute of a person over time, not just a snapshot of his motivation at a particular moment, as an "emotivist" might suppose. An action is good or right, according to Slote's theory, not because the agent is a dutiful or compassionate *person*, but because this action is motivated by an episode of dutiful impulse or feeling of compassion. A person who wasn't characteristically moved by the sense of duty or concern for others might, on a particular occasion, be motivated in one of these ways. Maybe he's with a dutiful or compassionate person, and that person's virtue "inspires" him for the moment. Or maybe he's in the middle of a novel, or has just heard a sermon, that has a momentary effect. For Slote, such an action would be perfectly right or good, because the motive was "virtuous." Or consider the reverse case of a virtuous person who wasn't moved by duty or compassion because he was in a bad mood or didn't get enough sleep last night. He could fail to act well according to Slote's theory, even if he performed his duty or did the compassionate thing. In neither case is it the person's virtue or lack of virtue that determines the rightness or goodness of the action.

But focusing on actions instead of persons doesn't get him out of the woods either, because actions can be impeccably motivated, and still be bad. Let's say that my motive in giving the beggar $20 is pure compassion. I really want him to be OK, I care about relieving his suffering, and I care for his sake. But unbeknownst to me, he's been having suicidal thoughts. If I had given him a couple of dollars, he would have bought a cheap beer with it, but with $20 he can go into a pharmacy and buy a bottle of something that will put him out forever if he consumes the whole bottle. Let's say he does this, so my act of compassion turns out to be inadvertent assisted suicide. I think anybody who isn't being driven by a reductive theory will want to say that I have acted badly or performed a bad (unfortunate) action, insofar as, in these circumstances, it was inadvertent assisted suicide, even though I was moved by a good motive. I did the wrong thing. We acknowledge the possibility of such misfired action when we deliberate carefully about the consequences of our actions. We don't only want our motives to be good; we want our outcomes to be good too. The possibility of an action that's good in one respect and bad in another is a natural one that Slote's theory rules out.

So this isn't just virtue ethics, but virtuous motive ethics, and it's motive ethics ideally to the exclusion of any element that is not a motive. In the virtue's role as basis or foundation for other items in the array of moral concepts/phenomena, it's the motive aspect of the virtue that represents the virtue, rather than, say, the power of judgment aspect, or the agent-efficacy aspect, or the consistency-over-time aspect. Slote writes as though an action's motive can be fenced off from such ethical items as rules, principles, thoughts, identified goals, reasoning, powers of execution (for example, the difference between mere wishes and entrenched concerns), and the reliable consistency of character. But arguably, a motive is not definite unless it contains the cognitive element (ethical understanding), and not effective unless it's backed up with executive powers. A motive that really moves a person to excellent action will need to be backed by executive power, by normative practical reason, and the regularity over time that Aristotle and MacIntyre point out. To be fully virtuous, ethical motives must be rational, effective, and reliably consistent. In the way that it moves the agent, the motive needs to partake of practical reason, which Kant makes the basis of ethics; effectiveness of agency, which any utilitarian theory must stress; and the reliable consistency over time that characterizes the keeping of contracts. All these features need to be built into the idea of moral motivation if that motivation is to be ideally virtuous.

The Ideal of Purity as a Source of Confusion

In her book *On Virtue Ethics*,[16] Rosalind Hursthouse makes many good points about the concept of a virtue and offers many insights about the nature of particular virtues. As an example of the latter, I commend the four paragraphs that start on p. 11, where she offers a brief but rich discussion of the virtue of honesty. She says that her brand of virtue ethics doesn't play the "primacy" game, with its program of deriving from the concept of a virtue all the other main ethical concepts, and those four paragraphs are a poster child for that brand. In her Introduction, her stance is that of a peace-maker: Virtue ethics should live side-by-side with deontologies and consequentialisms, supplementing them and being supplemented by them. She hopes that at some time in the future, ethicists may drop such labels and erase division lines among ethical theories. Later in the book, she says, "So where do I stand on the 'primacy of character'? For a start, I need a phrase that explicitly disavows any foundational or reductivist role for it, so I shall say I subscribe to the thesis that the concept of the virtuous agent is the focal concept of ethics" (82–83). This sounds like the view of virtue ethics that I'm promoting in this book, except that I wouldn't say that the virtuous agent is *the* focal concept of *ethics*. It is *a* focal concept of ethics and *the* focal concept of *virtue* ethics. Hursthouse is well aware that at the present moment in the history of philosophy, it's implausible to think that anyone will be able to establish a foundation of ethics secure enough to rule out relativism and skepticism. Yet, as we've seen, the form of the foundationalist project abides with us alive and well. It is telling that a philosopher as keenly aware of the futility of the foundationalist project as Hursthouse, when explaining what virtue ethics is, so frequently compares this approach, as she understands it, with the standard ethical theories. Also, three times she describes virtue ethics as a "rival" of the other ethical theories (see 2, 26, 29). But if virtue ethics is just ethical reflection that focuses on the virtues, it's not a rival of the other theories, but a different kind of enterprise altogether. Hursthouse seems confused as to whether virtue ethics, as she

---

[16] Hursthouse, *On Virtue Ethics*, 1999.

understands it, is or isn't an alternative to ethical theory in the modern sense. One indication is that she repeatedly seeks to "derive" norms for actions and policies from the notion of a virtue, and often the results are awkward and implausible.

Consider lying. Why not lie? What's wrong with it? The Kantian will say that to lie is to act on an irrational (ununiversalizable) maxim: Lying violates practical reason and thus the dignity of the person to whom the lie is told. The utilitarian will say that lies are out (when they are out) because they have bad consequences. They lead to confusion, disillusionment, injustice, reduced practical effectiveness, social antagonism, and other evils. They reduce "utility." The social contract theorist will say that we shouldn't lie because we have made an implicit pact with others to tell the truth, and that if we didn't have and follow such a rule, social life would be much more difficult than it is. The contract will work only if enough people keep it. The sentimentalist will say that, among people whose humanity hasn't been corrupted, lies and liars are disgusting. Hursthouse declares:

> According to virtue ethics—and in this book—what is wrong with lying, when it is wrong, is not that it is unjust (because it violates someone's 'right to the truth' or their 'right to be treated with respect') but that it is *dishonest*, and dishonesty is a vice. What is wrong with killing, when it is wrong, may be not so much that it is unjust, violating the right to life, but, frequently, that it is callous and contrary to the virtue of charity. (6)

Hursthouse's 'not x, but y' way of thinking seems at odds with her peace-making project and suggests that she sees virtue ethics as an alternative to rights-based theories. If we think outside the theory model that drives so much of current philosophical ethics, we will have freedom to allow a number of different explanations of what's wrong with lying. Lying seems bad for *all* the following reasons:

a) it makes for bad relationships with people
b) it often leads to confusion and disruption
c) it is disrespectful of people
d) it violates the hearer's right to the truth

e)   it is dishonest, and dishonesty is dysfunction in the liar
f)   truthfulness is a virtue, and lying tends to ruin it
g)   it is (often) a betrayal of trust
h)   it disgusts and horrifies the pure of heart

Thinking non-theoretically about lying allows us to draw connections to any part of the ethical conceptual array that will enrich our understanding (ethical wisdom). If our philosophical activity is exploration of ethical concepts rather than ethical theory, we may still find a place for something called "deontology" or "virtue ethics." But in that case, these will be themes of conceptual exploration rather than rival theoretical standpoints. Deontology will be the study of the concept of obligation in its connection with other ethical concepts—without supposing that obligation is a privileged ethical idea, more basic or foundational than others, to which the others must be subordinated. And virtue ethics will be the study of the virtues in their connections to obligation, the good, emotions, concerns, abilities, skills, judgments, perceptions, and anything else that's connected with virtue or this or that particular virtue. Deontology and virtue ethics of this kind will support and enrich each other as explorations of different regions of the ethical landscape. At some points in her book, Hursthouse seems to move in this direction. But consider the "reductive" tendencies of two more examples.

She affirms vegetarianism "on the grounds that (i) temperance (with respect to the pleasures of food) is a virtue, and (ii) for most of 'us', eating meat is intemperate (greedy, self-indulgent)" (227). It seems more plausible to ground vegetarianism in animals' right not to be killed for food or caged and managed in ways that cause animal suffering, or that meat-eating cuts down on the world's food supply by feeding one kind of food to another, or that it's bad for the environment. If you don't appeal to any of these consequences or rights, it's not clear how meat-eating, in itself, is intemperate.

She says gangster activity is bad because gangsters are "callous, unjust, dishonest, reckless" (228), and these are vices. But isn't gangster activity bad also because of the havoc it wreaks in society, the misery it spreads there? Because it creates unjust situations?—And violates people's rights? And a theist can say that it's because it displeases God.

Why is being callous, unjust, dishonest, and so forth, a bad thing? It's only the beginning of an answer to say, "because these are vices." In our exploration of the ethical landscape, we will also be interested in what makes these traits vices. The natural place to look for answers to that question will be in the bad consequences, the violations of people's rights, and the betrayal of humanity that they dispose us to. The Christian will say that these vices are corruptions and dysfunctions because we are beings created to enjoy, participate in, and contribute to an order of peace with God and our fellow creatures. Gangsterism's vices are bad because they're contrary to this order of peace, contrary to a truly human way of life.

Instead of making ethical theories the form of philosophical ethical thought, we would have "ethical angles," that is, exploration of the concepts of an ethical outlook from, say, the obligation angle, the social relations angle, the ethical roles angle, the virtues angle, the consequences angle, the moral affections angle. Any of these projects will tend to incorporate insights about related angles; we can expect this because of the web-like relationships that seem to hold among the concepts that govern ethical life and practice. This way of conceptualizing philosophical ethics would provide a non-theoretical sense of "virtue ethics." It would be the exploration of, say, Christian (or Buddhist, or secular liberal, or Confucian, or Stoic, and so forth) ethical concepts from the virtues angle. And since the whole field of ethical concepts is fair exploratory territory, ethics wouldn't be done in a straitjacket, but would roam freely over the field, taking whatever concepts naturally explain or otherwise connect with the thematic concept.

The Schizophrenia of Modern Ethical Theories

In my opinion, one of the finest ethics papers of the twentieth century is Michael Stocker's "The Schizophrenia of Modern Ethical Theories."[17]

---

[17] Michael Stocker, "The Schizophrenia of Modern Ethical Theories," *Journal of Philosophy* 73 (1976): 453–466.

Stocker points out that if you take the kinds of reasons that the ethical theories claim to be fundamental and try to incorporate them into your ethical activities, you will find that each one fits only some of the cases, and if generally so incorporated, will cause moral degeneration in the cases they don't fit. Any of them will fit some of the cases, but if you try to make any one of them supreme, it won't be a proper motive from which to perform some of the most important actions of the moral life. But making one reason supreme is exactly what the ethical theories do. The philosopher who incorporates into her actual motives the overarching and fundamental reason prescribed by her theory will be morally degenerate by often having the wrong motive for action, while the philosopher who (appropriately) disregards her own theory when going about her moral life will suffer from an uncomfortable and inauthentic cleavage between what she says philosophically and the motives that move her actions, emotions, and thoughts.

Imagine someone who buys a tricycle for her child, and then justifies her action by saying that doing so will make the world better; or that it was her duty; or that it was the rational thing to do; or that she did it because it's the sort of thing a virtuous person would do; or that she did it because God commanded her to do it; or she did it because it's what someone in the role of mother does and she wants to be a good mother; or that someone she admires got a tricycle for his daughter . . . (fill in the principle that is fundamental to your favorite ethical theory). I don't deny that someone might have any of these motives in giving her child a tricycle, but they all strike one as less than ideal, and each one is commended by one ethical theory or another as the ultimate properly *ethical* reason for the action. I would think that the mother who gets the trike for her child should be moved by such considerations as, *She'll enjoy it*; *she asked me for it*; *it will make her happy*; *it's a step toward learning to ride a bike*. And so forth.

If you think that duty is the ultimate (fundamental) ethical reason (motive), it seems to follow that if you give your child a tricycle in such a way that it satisfies the demands of ethics, then you must give it to her out of a sense of duty. But if you do that, ethically you do it for the wrong reason. So your ethical philosophy has made you ethically weird. What if your daughter found out that that was your reason for giving her the trike?

Tricycle-age children are perhaps not very articulate with ethical concepts or very choosy about why they are given a trike. Your daughter may just be glad to get it. But if she finds out that you did it out of a sense of duty and thinks about it, she's likely to be disappointed that you weren't moved by love for her, but for that more theoretical reason. Furthermore, whether or not she reflects about it, it may be bad for her moral development to know that you got her the trike out of a sense of duty, or to make the world a better place, rather than because you delight in her delights and her good development.

We might think that pure virtue ethics is exempt from Stocker's criticism of ethical theories. After all, it *is* virtuous of Mom to give gifts to her daughter. But I think the case is subject to Bernard Williams's quip about "one thought too many." If the child (being a precocious three-year-old!) starts wondering what moved Mommy to get her the trike and asks her, and she truthfully says, "Well, it seemed to me to be the virtuous thing to do," Mommy has had one thought too many (and one thought too few). Being a pure virtue ethicist, she thinks that's the right thing to say. But a virtuous Mommy doesn't say (or think) that when she gives her daughter a gift. She acts *as* a virtuous mom, but doesn't appeal to the grounds of her theory (for example, virtue) when being motivated or reporting her motives. The title of Williams's book is *Ethics and the Limits of Philosophy*. I am trying to formulate, both here and throughout the present book, a way that virtue ethics can transcend the limit of philosophy that we've just identified. I propose that philosophy as an ethically serious exploration of moral concepts may contribute to a person's becoming wise and virtuous; but a wise and virtuous person will be one who acts on wise and virtuous motives, not one who acts on the principle that certain actions are wise and virtuous. As we'll see in the next chapter, Socrates practiced philosophy with the goal of becoming wise and virtuous and helping others with whom he conversed to become wise and virtuous.

I agree with Stocker that this mismatch between ethical experience and ethical philosophy indicates that something is amiss with such philosophy. Surely philosophy should follow our ethics, and not our ethics our philosophy. What would good philosophy of ethics be, if it isn't ethical theory? I think many contemporary teachers of philosophical ethics would be at a loss to answer.

The natural arrangement of the ethical concepts—the one we observe if we just *look* at them to *see* how they work, rather than insisting that they work according to a preconceived pattern of monarchical derivation—is that they form a fabric or web of *inter*dependent items, items that relate to one another in a variety of ways. If this metaphor is correct, then an analogous metaphor for ethical philosophy as the activity of tracing the various interdependencies comes into view. It is that of a map that lays the ethical concepts out to view. Just as maps can be specialized for different purposes—say, for a view of the highways, or the rivers, or agricultural production, or political tendencies, or epidemiological distributions—so ethics as a philosophical enterprise can have various themes: as deontological map, or a map of ethical purposes, or a map of ethical exemplars or social roles. Any such "map" will "locate" its thematic concept relative to the other items on the map. A virtue ethics will relate the various virtues to one another, but it may also locate them with respect to ethical purposes, duties, exemplars, roles, and so forth. Furthermore, foci can be selected for special ethical purposes. The virtues, for example, being traits of ethical excellence, might be selected as a philosophical focus for the purpose of guidance in the project of growing into morally excellent persons.

If maps are to promote an understanding of relationships among the things mapped (rather than just to guide the user to the next turn in the route), clarity and vividness are excellences in them. Colors are often used for this purpose. Analogously, the philosophical mapping of ethical concepts promotes understanding better when the thinking/ talking/writing is "colorful," marked by vivid illustrations and compelling metaphors that spark insights. It is important that the map be memorable, especially if it's to function as a guide to getting somewhere intelligently rather than just mechanically. These features of rhetorical "color" improve the map as an instrument of understanding.

Conclusion

Just as, in the United States in the 1910s, it was a social expectation that Black people would be servants and in the 1950s that women would be homemakers and keepers of children, so in contemporary philosophy, it is currently a social expectation that teachers and thinkers about ethics will be ethical theorists. That is why, when we say that someone is a virtue ethicist, we suppose, without hesitation, that she must be in the business of pure virtue ethics. Is it time for an ethicist liberation movement?

We have seen two different but related faults of ethical theories. Both stem from their artificiality in attempting to arrange the ethical concepts in a monarchical pattern of derivation. One fault is that the theories distort the moral concepts by insisting on ordering them hierarchically or derivationally or foundationally. The related fault is that they don't match or help ethical life but distort it or make philosophical ethics irrelevant to it. This is so because ethical living depends on ethical thinking. See Chapters 5 and 10. If we allow our philosophical thinking about ethics to affect our ethical thinking, then ethical theory can only be detrimental to it and we had better prevent the one from touching the other. If our philosophical thinking about ethics is to affect our ethical minds—our deliberations, our moral sensitivities and judgments, our motives and emotions—as the ancient philosophers thought it must, then we need a better way than modern moral theory to do philosophy.

4

Ancient Virtue Ethics

Introduction

I began Chapter 2 by referring to twentieth- and twenty-first-century virtue ethics as a "return." I put the word in quotation marks to cast some doubt on whether the thinkers that chapter was about were really returning to something that flourished earlier. Philosophy as it is practiced in the modern university—and this usually includes what is called virtue ethics—is a different activity from the ancient philosophers' ruminations about virtues and vices. Ancient philosophy of ethics was more connected with moral training and character formation than contemporary ethics is. The ways that connection with moral formation worked, or was thought to work, differed among the different "schools" in ancient philosophy.[1]

In this chapter, we'll look briefly at four: Socrates; the Stoics, with Seneca as our representative; Aristotle; and the wisdom tradition in ancient Israel. These four "schools" represent different ways in which virtue ethics connected with moral training and character formation. In Socrates we will see, through the eyes of some of his followers, how the combination of his "teaching" and his personality directly disturbed people's moral equilibrium, propelling them toward deeper and greater humanity. The Stoics thought themselves to be heirs of Socrates. Somewhat less directly than Socrates, Seneca taught by writing essays and treatises on the virtuous (Stoic) life. His mode of influence on people's character was more like that of an advice columnist, a life coach, or a psychotherapist. In *Nicomachean Ethics*, I would say that Aristotle seeks an even less direct influence, by producing something of a manual for teachers, legislators, and perhaps parents who

---

[1] See Hadot, *Philosophy as a Way of Life* and *What Is Ancient Philosophy?* trans. Michael Chase (Cambridge, MA: Harvard University Press, 2004).

Virtue Ethics. Robert Campbell Roberts, Oxford University Press.
© Robert Campbell Roberts 2026. DOI: 10.1093/9780197848005.003.0006

are more directly in the business of forming people's character. But all three philosophers—and this is true generally of ancient ethics—aim their work at moral formation. And finally, the psalmists (Ps 1, 119[2]) commend meditating with delight on the law of God as the way to become a healthy, fully functioning person.

Socrates

Socrates[3] is, I think, the first practitioner of virtue ethics in the Western philosophical tradition. At the end of his life, he summed up his career:

> the god commands me to [philosophize], and I believe that no greater good ever came to pass in the city than my service to the god. For I go about doing nothing else than urging you, young and old, not to care for your persons or your property more than for the perfection of your souls, or even so much; and I tell you that virtue does not come from money, but from virtue comes money and all other good things to man, both to the individual and to the state. (*Apology* 30a–b)[4]

Many of Plato's dialogues are conversations between Socrates and one or more others, usually focused on a virtue concept like justice, courage, piety, or love, in which Socrates is supposedly trying to get clear about the nature of the virtue in question. But at the same time, Socrates is examining his discussion partners, with the effect that he lays their souls bare to them, putting them in touch with higher possibilities of personal life. This analytical provocation has a moral effect on them. In the dialogue *Laches*, which focuses on courage, the

---

[2] These psalms are representative of the "wisdom" literature of ancient Israel and should be presented as such. This developed into the pastoral function of theology in the New Testament and later the early church.

[3] Scholars sometimes try to sort out the "historical" Socrates from the "Platonic" Socrates. In what follows, I am unconcerned about the distinction. Socrates, for my purposes, is the man who is presented with that name in Plato's dialogues. You could call him "Socrates" if you wish.

[4] Translation by Harold North Fowler, https://www.perseus.tufts.edu/hopper/text?doc=Perseus%3Atext%3A1999.01.0170%3Atext%3DApol.%3Asection%3D30a.

character Nicias bravely comments to another of the participants, Lysimachus, that conversing with Socrates is like walking into a moral trap. Even if Socrates starts on some remote point, he leads you around to answering questions about yourself and your way of living. And he won't let you go until he's given you a thorough workover and brought to your attention your failings to live a really human life. And Lysimachus notes that part of the magnetism is that he takes pleasure in Socrates's company, so that he doesn't quite mind when Socrates pours him through the moral sieve.

> Rather I think that a man who does not run away from such treatment but is willing, according to the saying of Solon, to value learning as long as he lives, not supposing that old age brings him wisdom of itself, will necessarily pay more attention to the rest of his life. (*Laches*, 188b, 673)[5]

The moral distress occasioned by sitting down with Socrates for a discussion of life is a function of attention. The attention has a dual object. Its structure is the "seeing" of one thing in terms of another. One of the objects is the ideal: the concept of the virtue in question (courage or justice, for example). The other object is yourself, your life, your own character. Setting the two objects side-by-side, Socrates's interlocutor gets an impression of himself, an impression he might never get if he didn't have this conversation with Socrates. It is the distressing impression of his own moral shabbiness, the futility and unworthiness of his pursuits. But, painful as it may be, says Lysimachus, this experience is good for you and may help the rest of your life be more worth living. It seems that taking an ethics class from Socrates requires moral courage (and perhaps humility). Let me offer three illustrations from the dialogues.

In the dialogue called *Euthyphro*, which focuses on the virtue of piety (which is sometimes listed as a fifth cardinal virtue along with wisdom, temperance, courage, and justice), Socrates is on his way to

[5] Translation by Rosamond Kent Sprague, in *Plato: Complete Works*, ed. John M. Cooper and D. S. Hutchinson (Indianapolis: Hackett, 1997).

be tried for impiety (disrespect for the gods). He meets Euthyphro who, also on his way to court, is going to prosecute his father for the "murder" of a servant. Euthyphro styles himself a theologian and an expert in piety. Socrates strikes up a conversation about piety, a virtue that is in part a deep respect for one's parents. Socrates ironically offers to learn from Euthyphro something useful for his own upcoming trial.

Through a series of questions about the nature of piety, Socrates shows Euthyphro to be an empty theological blowhard. Euthyphro never admits that he's a fake, but at the end of the dialogue, he flees from the embarrassing conversation with Socrates, still intending to prosecute his father in honor of the gods for a "murder" that seems at worst to be a case of involuntary manslaughter. Ironically, this "expert" on piety has been spotlighted as bent on an act of filial impiety.

Euthyphro's panic to escape from Socrates's improvised virtue ethics class is matched by the reaction of an old man, Cephalos, in the opening pages of the dialogue *Republic* (328c–331d). Cephalos, who has just come from sacrificing to the gods, comments that old people lament their aches and pains, their loss of the powers and pleasures of youth, and so forth. But, he says, what makes old age a time of happiness is being a person of character: in particular, having the virtue of justice. Socrates points out that people say it isn't justice but wealth that shields some people from the worst of old age. The comment is pointed and barbed because Cephalos is a relatively wealthy man. Cephalos responds that money does help, but it helps by allowing the old person to pay his debts—and paying what you owe is justice.

But it turns out that Cephalos doesn't use his wealth to repay the *people* he has harmed in life, but to sacrifice to the *gods*. Furthermore, he is moved, not by the love of justice, but by fear of punishment by the gods. Neither his sacrifice to the gods nor what moves him to it is a mark of the virtue of justice. Like Euthyphro, Cephalos lacks the courage of Nicias to stay in the dialogue and pay moral attention to his shortcomings in the virtue. If he did, he might become more just by humbly undertaking to mend some of the flaws in his character. Instead, he responds to the Socratic hot seat by hastily turning the conversation over to his son Polemarchos and scurries off to the sacrifice (*Republic* 331d) to "pay his debts."

Alcibiades is a conflicted soul who loves the honors and glories of politics, but who also, in a childish way, loves Socrates and what Socrates has to say. In Plato's *Symposium*, a dialogue on love, he comes into the drinking party (the symposium) at the end and offers a drunken speech about his frustrated love for Socrates. In this speech, he offers a vivid testimony to the ethical pungency of Socrates's virtue ethics.

> "You know, people hardly ever take a speaker seriously, even if he's the greatest orator; but let anyone—man, woman, or child—listen to you [Socrates] or even to a poor account of what you say—and we are all transported, completely possessed. . . . I have heard Pericles and many other great orators, and I have admired their speeches. But nothing like this ever happened to me: they never upset me so deeply that my very own soul started protesting that my life—my life!—was no better than the most miserable slave's." (*Symposium* 215d–e)

Alcibiades speaks of taking a speaker "seriously." If Socrates is the ideal teacher of virtue ethics, the teacher would speak in such a way that you would take the teacher seriously. What kind of seriousness is in question here? If a speaker is a comedian, taking her seriously would be paying close attention, following and enjoying the comedy. If a speaker is a history teacher, taking him seriously would be paying attention and following what he says in such a way that you will understand and remember it, maybe for an exam. If a speaker is a Pericles, taking him seriously will be following him attentively and being inspired to something like patriotism, or possibly political opposition.

But none of these ways of taking a speaker seriously describes Alcibiades's attitude to the speech of Socrates. Socrates's speech (and person) catches Alcibiades's *moral* attention, making him evaluate his own life and asking himself whether it is "worth living." Apparently, in Socrates's words about virtues and related matters, Alcibiades is confronted with a vision of what it is to live well as a human being, a vision that is at once intensely attractive and distressing to a person like Alcibiades who "knows" that he won't choose to embrace it whole-heartedly. Socrates's words somehow make Alcibiades think seriously about *himself* and the value of *his* life.

> And yet that is exactly how this Marsyas here at my side makes me
> feel all the time: he makes it seem that my life isn't worth living!…He
> always traps me, you see, and he makes me admit that my political
> career is a waste of time, while all that matters is just what I most ne-
> glect: my personal shortcomings, which cry out for the closest atten-
> tion. (*Symposium*[6] 215e–216a)

All four of Socrates's interlocutors—Nicias, Euthyphro, Cephalos, and Alcibiades—feel effectively invited, by Socrates's comments and questions, to pay moral attention to their "personal shortcomings"—to the ways their lives fall short of being most "worth living." Only Nicias profits from Socrates's conversation. Two out of the four flee nervously from the invitation, while Alcibiades expresses his ambivalence and ultimately, one feels, fails to pay the kind of attention that would bear fruit for his happiness.

> So I refuse to listen to him; I stop my ears and tear myself away from
> him, for, like the Sirens, he could make me stay by his side till I die.
> Socrates is the only man in the world who has made me feel shame—
> ah, you didn't think I had it in me, did you? Yes, he makes me feel
> ashamed: I know perfectly well that I can't prove he's wrong when he
> tells me what I should do; yet, the moment I leave his side I go back
> to my old ways: I cave in to my desire to please the crowd. (216a–b)

Alcibiades is driven by his vain desire for honor, which keeps him from training his love on something worth loving. But the words of Socrates call the bluff on all the glitter of Alcibiades's showiness. Socrates's speech is not in words of eloquent wisdom. It's homely in its references, but powerful in its truth.

> If you were to listen to his arguments, at first they'd strike you as to-
> tally ridiculous; they're clothed in words as coarse as the hides worn
> by the most vulgar satyrs. He's always going on about pack asses, or
> blacksmiths, or cobblers, or tanners; he's always making the same

---

[6] Quotations from *Symposium* are in *Plato: Complete Works*, trans. Alexander Nehamas and Paul Woodruff, ed. Cooper and Hutchinson (Indianapolis: Hackett, 1997).

tired old points in the same tired old words. If you are foolish, or simply unfamiliar with him, you'd find it impossible not to laugh at his arguments. But if you see them when they open up like the statues,[7] if you go behind their surface, you'll realize that no other arguments make any sense. They're truly worthy of a god, bursting with figures of virtue inside. They're of great—no, of the greatest— importance for anyone who wants to become a truly good man. (221e–222a)

Seneca

The Hellenistic period in ancient philosophy is the period after the great classical Greek philosophers—Socrates, Plato, and Aristotle. It encompassed a number of schools: the Cynics, the Stoics, the Epicureans, the Skeptics, and in addition there were Platonists and Aristotelians. After the example of Socrates, all the Hellenistic schools were therapeutic—they expressly aimed to help people live better lives by transforming their attitudes, their character traits.[8] They thought of themselves as discovering and dispensing wisdom about living. The problems of living, according to these schools, could be traced to bad attitudes on the part of the sufferers, who could dissolve or mini- mize their woes by acquiring virtue as the different schools diversely conceived virtue.

For the Stoic, the chief virtue is apatheia (detachment, the absence of pathos). The Stoics thought of Socrates as the founder and a chief exemplar of Stoicism because he seemed to them to be "detached" from things that tended to be all-important to ordinary people: petty things like health, longevity, material possessions, power, and repu- tation. Socrates (*Apology*) had warned the murderous Athenian jury

---

[7] He is speaking of nesting Silenus dolls, figurines that can be opened to reveal an- other figurine inside them, which can be opened to reveal yet another.

[8] One of many excellent books on the topic is Nussbaum's *The Therapy of Desire*. Nussbaum stresses the theme of ethical philosophy as a kind of medical practice aimed at healing pathological belief and desire. This is the "negative" counterpart of the kind of virtue ethics that I am promoting. But these two interpretations are similar inasmuch as virtue ethics, in aiming at flourishing (health, human well-being) has the collateral ben- efit of rooting out vice and distortion from the human soul.

that they would harm not him, but only themselves by killing him unjustly. Death is not clearly a harm, but injustice harms whoever does it. It corrupts the soul; it damages the "heart" of the one who does it. It makes its doer rotten as a person. When the Athenian authorities make him drink hemlock to get rid of him, Socrates turns his execution into an occasion for discussing questions that will tend to teach everyone present the right priorities in life (see *Phaedo*). The person with complete and perfect virtue, whom the Stoics call the "sage," is free from such vanities because she doesn't care much about them—though she does regard some as "preferable" and others as "not to be preferred." Having or lacking them makes no difference to her happiness. Ultimately, the only thing that matters to her is the beautiful rational order of the universe and the intentional reflection of that perfect order in perfected human souls (that is, virtue, apatheia).

The Stoic Scheme

The Stoics' virtue ethics was based on a well-articulated philosophical and psychological understanding of reality.[9] According to this understanding, the universe is a perfectly rational system of physical causes and effects. For each event in the universe, a set of causes makes it happen just the way it does happen; and each of those causes is a physical event that has a set of causes that make *it* happen just the way it does happen, and so on and on for everything in the universe. There are no "accidents" or mere probabilities. The Stoics were determinists, and their determinism applied also to human psychology: Our thinking and choosing and doing of things are also physical events that have causes that make them occur necessarily. But the Stoics thought that we human beings, being rational choosers, are responsible for becoming virtuous. The combination of determinism with human responsibility, which is called "compatibilism," is puzzling.[10]

---

[9] The following summary is loosely indebted to several papers in Brad Inwood, ed., *Cambridge Companion to the Stoics* (Cambridge: Cambridge University Press, 2003).

[10] Dorothea Frede discusses this problem in "Stoic Determinism," in the *Cambridge Companion* (Cambridge: Cambridge University Press, 2003), 179–205.

So the universe is rational in the sense that it is highly—indeed, *perfectly*—ordered. Its order is like that of a mind that has a perfectly good reason for everything it does and can explain everything that it does with a perfectly good and sufficient reason. Naturally, the Stoics thought of this order as God (or god). Since they think every event is physical, they think of god (and therefore the universe) as an animal, a living being. And, appreciating the beauty (and therefore goodness) of this perfect animal, they spoke of providence, as though the order that constituted the universe was due to the benevolence of its (or his) mind (or "mind"). As a whole that is ordered so beautifully, the universe is good. Note that among the events that fit together in this beautiful systematic way are diseases, pain, starvation, earthquakes, extinctions, hurricanes, floods, death, and the like. These are as much part of the beautifully ordered system as health, pleasure, full bellies, tranquility of nature, and gently babbling streams full of healthy, fat trout.

In the universe is another kind of animal that is also basically rational: human beings. We are unique among the animals in our ability to "follow" rationally what happens—to explain the events in the universe by reference to their causes. We can see the order in the universe and appreciate it as order, and thus as good.

I say "basically rational" because we can be irrational in a way that a non-rational creature like a tree or a squirrel can't. In particular, in addition to the rational ability to appreciate that universal order, we have what we might call a localized viewpoint. Thus, when disease, hurricane, hunger, or death touch too closely on our own lives, we tend to become unable to appreciate the beauty of their interlocking with other causes and effects in the grand picture of harmonious interaction. They cease to appear integral to the good of the whole and start looking decidedly evil. Relief of them and protection from them, and health, pleasure, a full belly, and the gently babbling streams start looking good in a way that contrasts with the look of disease, hunger, and so forth. Since the rational harmony of the whole universe is good, this partial view of things, which picks out particular events and labels them good, and labels other particular events bad, is itself arbitrary and bad. Our local viewpoint turns into an irrational protest against the goodness of the whole.

This irrational strand in rational human nature, this narrowness of vision, this local viewpoint that blinds us to the good, is due to our emotions and desires. Emotions like fear, anger, joy, and hope are false beliefs that particular events and states of affairs are bad or good. They are false because only the rational whole (or the state of mind of the rational human being who grasps the rationality of the whole) is good, and only the distorted state of mind of the rational human being who denies the rationality of the whole by thinking that some particular event or state of affairs is good or evil is bad. An emotion occurs, according to the Stoics, when I have an *impression* that something is good or bad (say, that I won the lottery, or that a grizzly bear is charging toward me with the intent of eating me) and, in addition to having the impression, I assent to it (say to myself, as it were, "Yep, that's how it is! It really is gloriously wonderful [or terribly horrible]!"). Both the impression and the assent are essential: Without the combination, the emotion doesn't occur. I may withhold assent from the initial impression, and say to myself, as it were, "It looks good (or bad), but it isn't." Then I have prevented the emotion from occurring, despite the initial impression.

So emotions are false judgments of value, and as such are the root of all evil. They make us consider evil what isn't evil and good what isn't good. The project of becoming a sage or perfectly virtuous human being is the project of attuning our mind to the mind of the universe in such a way that we judge only the rational order of the universe and the rational reflection of that order in a perfectly ordered human mind as good, and only the failure of human minds to appreciate the goodness of the universe as bad.

But among the particular events in the universe, none of which is either good or bad in itself, are ones that are preferable for the conduct of a human life, and others that are not to be preferred. For example, in many circumstances, continuing to live is preferable to death, and health is preferable to illness, and the gently babbling brook full of fat trout is preferable to a stinking cesspool (at least if it's in your yard). Unlike us immature people, the sage is fully aware of the difference between things that are preferable and what is good, and between things that are not to be preferred and what is bad. She never feels negative emotions toward what is not preferable, or positive emotions toward what is preferable, but she does take the difference into dispassionate consideration as she makes choices in life. There are mountains and molehills, and the sage never confuses the twain.

This emotionlessness, or apatheia, is the very essence of the sage's virtue. "There is no surer proof of greatness [of mind] than to be un-provoked by anything that can possibly happen."[11] The sage never confuses what is preferable with what is good by taking emotional joy in it. For example, if she was very sick and got well, she wouldn't rejoice about her restored health, though she might calmly see it as preferable—an option to be selected if possible, though it is ultimately indifferent. The Stoics call this attitude of calmly appreciating what is preferable 'joy' and distinguish it from the emotion or passion of joy. Real joy can be felt only toward the rational order of the universe or the virtue of a sage that reflects that order. In the Stoics' view, true joy is not an emotion (which must be false to *be* an emotion), but a true judgment that something is virtuous. Only the sage experiences this joy. What we ordinary non-Stoics call joy is, according to the Stoics, mostly a result of our moral degeneracy. What the Stoics call joy is an expression and appreciation of perfect apatheia.

What about virtues in the plural? Though Stoic virtue seems to boil down to apatheia, the Stoics do sometimes talk about "the virtues" and mention such standard ones as clemency (see Seneca's *On Mercy*[12]) and justice. He says that philosophically meditating on the concept of a gift " . . . breeds good blood and generous thoughts; and instructs us in honor, humanity, friendship, piety, gratitude, prudence, and justice."[13] But note that a just social transaction, such as a person being paid fairly for the work he does, would not be good in the Stoic's estimation, though it is certainly preferable. And whatever benefit to a wrongdoer resulted from an act of clemency would likewise be merely preferable, not good. Similarly, if the wrongdoer was

---

[11] Seneca, *On Anger* III.6.1, in *Seneca: Moral and Political Essays*, ed. and transl. John M. Cooper and J. F. Procopé (Cambridge: Cambridge University Press, 1995), 82.

[12] In Cooper and Procopé.

[13] *Of Benefits* chapter 1. Translation by Roger L'Estrange, https://www.gutenberg.org/files/56075/56075-h/56075-h.htm.

denied clemency, the punishment wouldn't be bad, but merely not preferable.

Seneca's Virtue Ethics

When Seneca wrote his essays, he assumed that the point of writing them was to improve people's character: to help them integrate Stoic teachings into their lives. Often, the essays take the direct form of moral advice on how to become more virtuous, or what attitude to take to a particular kind of life situation or a type of human activity. The discourse is more like what we call counseling or even sermons than like "ethics" as it is taught in a philosophy class of our time, although the Hellenistic philosophers used conceptual analysis and argument more than most of our therapists and preachers. If they were therapists, they were of the cognitive-behavioral type. As an example of Seneca's practice, we will look at his essay *On Anger*. Anger is a vice, and the corresponding virtue is *gentleness* or *mildness*. It is pretty easy to see how this virtue is a part of apatheia.

In Seneca's virtue ethics, his writings and conversations are also rhetorical. He wants, not merely to make intellectual points about the vice of anger and to convince his interlocutor of what he believes, for example, but to get him or her to change attitudes, to give up the attitudes that make for emotional "disturbance" and to take on the calm and healthy attitude of apatheia. Motivation is crucial to virtue ethics as Seneca practices it, and rhetoric is the art of motivation. The kind of understanding that his virtue ethics is designed to foster includes motivation. He wants to interest his interlocutor in adopting the ideal and life-goal of Stoicism. So he uses lots of appealing narrative examples, striking metaphors, and often writes in rather "emotive" (!) terms. For example, *On Anger* opens this way:

You have demanded, Novatus, that I write on how anger can be alleviated. I think that you are right to have a particular dread of this, the most hideous and frenzied of all the emotions. The others have something quiet and placid in them, whereas anger is all excitement and impulse. Raving with a desire that is utterly inhuman

for instruments of pain and reparations in blood, careless of itself
so long as it harms the other, it rushes onto the very spear-points,
greedy for vengeance that draws down the avenger with it. (17)[14]

We've all experienced anger that is neither hideous and frenzied nor
even excited and impulsive, much less raving and bloodthirsty and
heedless of self-destruction. This is "rhetoric" designed to get Novatus's
attention. Nevertheless, the Stoics are philosophers and philosophical
psychologists, so their toolbox includes careful attention to the nature
of the mental states and traits that make for what they regard as well-
being or its opposite. Philosophers call this careful attention conceptual analysis. In Greek, the word *analusis* means loosening. Analysis is
the loosening or separation of the parts of something so as to understand better how the whole thing works. Thus, it clearly involves putting back together what you've taken apart. The putting back together
(in the sense of seeing the roles or functions of the parts in constituting
the whole thing) is crucial to understanding. I prefer the term conceptual exploration, since it sounds less final, less highfalutin and formal,
and a bit more tentative. In any case, virtue ethics, as a philosophical
discipline that aims at wisdom, requires careful attention to the structural details of the psychological concepts of virtue and vice. This is
what Elizabeth Anscombe called "philosophy of psychology." What
is this deranged state of character that the Stoic calls 'vice'? Seneca's
therapeutic method involves taking the concept apart to put it back
together again with greater understanding. He integrates the analysis
with the rhetoric, or hides the analysis within parts of the rhetoric, or
conveys the analysis by way of the rhetoric.

As a Stoic, Seneca thinks that anger is a false belief, roughly the belief that somebody (or something) has seriously wronged me. Therapy
consists in the effort to persuade the angry person that the belief is
false. To come to believe that the belief is false is to give up the belief and cease to be angry. But this seemingly simple belief includes or
entails or assumes a variety of "background" or constitutive beliefs, as
Seneca's therapeutic practice shows. If the patient can be persuaded

---

[14] *Seneca: Moral and Political Essays*, 17. All following references to *On Anger* are to
this edition.

to give up one or more of the assumptions or background beliefs, his or her anger will be weakened or will even collapse. We won't find in Seneca's text the kind of analysis of anger that I will now present, but we can tease it from his text.

First, here is a short narrative of the situation or episode that has aroused my anger:

> After observing my behavior in a meeting, Rex called me an effing moron, so I'm going to do what I can to make him suffer for it.

The Stoic thinks that my belief that *Rex called me an effing moron* is my anger. But this belief can *be* my anger—an encompassing attitude of mind toward the situation I find myself in—only if it entails or assumes something like the following thoughts (beliefs), which I now present in a more formal analysis:

1 In calling me an effing moron, Rex has harmed me.
2 Calling me an effing moron is very bad (that is, harming me is very bad).
3 Rex is blameworthy for this action.
4 Rex has underrated my importance and demeaned me.
5 Rex is a bad person.
6 Rex deserves to be punished for calling me an effing moron.
7 I know enough to judge in this matter.
8 I am in a moral position to judge.

To say that these thoughts are internal to my anger is not to say that I "tell myself" these things in any explicit way (though certainly I *may* do so); instead, they shape or inform my understanding of the situation I am in when I am in this angry state. Thus, to take any of them away by "refuting" it (or in some other way—say, by causing me to "forget" it or "ignore" it) is to undermine the anger, to change my take on the situation. If this is right, then the Stoic view would have to be that I can "assent" to a thought without the thought coming explicitly into my consciousness. The angry person assents to an impression of having been wronged, and so forth, but need not be fully articulate about what the impression is *of*. However, the therapy can be effective by addressing these implicit assumptions, because to see that they are false will undermine the judgment that constitutes the anger.

Seneca describes the mind of the sage as having canceled all of anger's evaluative thoughts. "A mighty mind with its true self-awareness will not avenge [§5 in the formal analysis], since it *has not noticed the wrong* done to it" [§§1, 2, and 3] (*On Anger* 82, italics added). If I am a sage, I realize that Rex's calling me an effing moron is not a bad thing, and therefore not a wrong, but at worst something not preferable; and a person can't be morally *blamed* [§3] for doing something that is merely not preferable. The insult is a "vulgar triviality" (62), and to react to it as though it is something truly bad is to show that I am "soft." Perhaps I have been made so by a life of pleasure (63).

As a rational being, I am important indeed. After all, I am a mind capable of reflecting the chief good thing, the beautiful rational order of the universe. But it's a false sense of my importance that reacts to an insult by feeling that an injustice has been done to me [§4]: "Who am I that it should be a sacrilege to offend my ears?" (101). As to the fifth proposition—that Rex is a bad person—Seneca advises me to consider two things: the good that Rex has done me on other occasions, and the fact that I am just as bad as Rex. §5 is really comparative (like §8): In seeing Rex as bad, I am seeing him as worse than others, and especially worse than myself. I will weaken my anger by remembering some good things that Rex has done for me. "It will make us milder if we think of the help which we may have had from the person with whom we are angry, and allow the good turns to make up for the bad" (72). "All of us are *bad*. Whatever he blames in another, each will find in his own heart. Why point out the pallor of one man and the gauntness of another? We are faced with an epidemic! [Vice is in us and all around us.] So we should be more indulgent towards one another" (103).[15]

We can weaken our anger by generous and empathic thoughts about what motivated the offending action. "But the motive is what should be considered: was it intentional or an accident, was he forced or misled, was he acting out of hatred or for reward, was he indulging himself or assisting another? The wrongdoer's age and his position are factors

---

[15] We are reminded of Romans 3:23, ". . . all have sinned and fall short of the glory of God," a reminder we would all be wise to remember when we are angry with someone.

which make it humane or prudent to allow and put up with it" [§3, §5] (88). Maybe Rex was just having a bad day, or maybe the statement about me was an involuntary reaction to frustration, and Rex reached a breaking point. Also, maybe Rex just doesn't understand how wise I am and will eventually come around to see my point. Such generous thoughts about Rex's motivation can help me deal with my anger.

Anger involves the desire for revenge—the desire to hurt the offender [§6]—but real human nature, our deepest essence, is inconsistent with the impulse to revenge: "Anger ... is greedy for punishment. That such a desire should reside in that most peaceful of dwellings, the breast of man, is utterly *out of accord with his nature*" (23, italics added). So when, in anger, I desire revenge on Rex, I make myself less human according to the Stoics' understanding of human nature as basically rational.

Seneca proposes that I take seriously some mitigating interpretations of Rex's comment: "Suppose, then, that someone speaks ill of you ... We should think, I maintain, of some not as doing us wrong but as paying us back [that is, we are only getting what we deserve: §3], of others as acting on our behalf [§1 and §2], or as acting under compulsion, or in ignorance; we should think that even those who wrong us knowingly and deliberately are not out for the wrong itself when they wrong us. A person may have slipped into it through delight in his own wit ... " [§3] (66). Whether or not Rex intended to "act on my behalf," I can weaken my anger by considering that he may be right and that I may profit from his insight about my mind: Maybe I *am* less wise than I thought and can learn something about myself from his coarse remark. He is really an inadvertent benefactor!

Seneca notes that we humans are prone to jump to conclusions about other people's misdeeds. In his anger therapy, he recommends that we learn to resist this tendency, practicing a selective skepticism when it comes to accusations. So if someone tells me about Rex's comment, a healthy approach is to suspend my judgment [§7] as long as I can about whether it's true (61).

And then if it turns out that Rex did say that, I can resist my anger by attacking §8, that I am in a moral position to judge: "Suppose, then, that someone speaks ill of you—think whether you did not do so to him, think of how many people *you* speak ill of. ... [A person] can avoid immediate anger, especially if he says quietly to himself at every vexation 'I too have done this myself.' . . . A look at ourselves will make us more forbearing, if we start to consider: 'Surely we too have done something like this? Surely we have made this sort of mistake.'" (66). "No [angry person] ever says to himself: 'What is making me angry is something which I have sometimes done myself or could have done'" (88).

Rebecca DeYoung, following Thomas Aquinas, points out that, among the "negative" emotions, which register badness, anger specializes in the kind of badness that is unjust.[16] Whether or not the situation it takes to be unjust really is unjust, anger "sees" injustice in the situation. It is often unjustified, and then it properly invites "therapeutic" elimination. But sometimes, especially in people of virtue, anger is justified. And then, in attributing injustice to a situation, action, or attitude, it hits a real target and the construal of the situation is to that extent true. Consider Jesus's anger at those who, seizing an opportunity to get him in trouble, were moved to withhold healing from a man with a withered hand (Mark 3:1–6) on the grounds that it was the sabbath. "[Jesus] looked around at them with anger; he was distressed at their hardness of heart and said to the man, 'Stretch out your hand'" (Mark 3:5, altered slightly). Both Christian and Aristotelian virtue ethics, in contrast with Stoicism, distinguish between virtuous and vicious anger.

Seneca's virtue ethics would eliminate *all* anger as inconsistent with virtue. But his examples tend to be of rather stupid, trivial, and irrational anger. His therapy is by and large well taken for the examples he gives. A "cognitive" therapist of our own day might well adopt some of Seneca's strategies for clients who come to her office for "anger problems." But unless she is a Stoic, she will probably not aim her therapy at perfect apatheia. She will allow that sometimes anger is appropriate

---

[16] Rebecca Konyndyk DeYoung, "What Are You Guarding? Virtuous Anger and Lifelong Practice," in *Faith and Virtue Formation: Christian Philosophy in Aid of Becoming Good*, ed. Adam Pelser and Scott Cleveland (Oxford: Oxford University Press, 2021), 20–47, 23. DeYoung compares Aquinas's understanding of anger and its therapy with that of the "desert fathers," Evagrius of Pontus and Cassian. These were Christian leaders in the early church who followed the Stoics in attempting to eradicate *all* anger and other "passions."

and even virtuous. And she might aim at inculcating forgivingness, a virtue that seems to derive from Judaism and Christianity.[17] To the extent that she helped the client be less irrationally angry, she would have improved his character. But Seneca's examples don't support the ideal of eradicating all anger. Many of Seneca's recommendations are relevant to the virtue that Aristotle calls "gentleness," which is a disposition to get angry (only) on right occasions and (only) to the degree that the seriousness of the offense warrants. His recommendations might describe either the semi-automatic workings of a gentle person's mind or strategies of self-management.

Aristotle

Aristotle's ethical treatises look more like what we call philosophy than the conversations of Socrates or the essays of Seneca, but Aristotle tells us that their ultimate point is not "theory," but making people good. In *Eudemian Ethics*, he says, " . . . our aim is not to know what courage is but to be courageous, not to know what justice is but to be just, in the same way as we aim to be healthy rather than to ascertain what health is, and to be in good condition of body rather than to know what good bodily condition is" (1.5, 1216b22–25).[18] And in *Nicomachean Ethics*, he says, "Our present inquiry does not aim, as our others do, at *theoria* [contemplation]; for the purpose of our examination is not to know what virtue is, but to become good, since otherwise the inquiry would be of no benefit to us" (NE 2.2, 1103b26–29).

The Greek word *theoria* doesn't quite translate our word 'theory.' It means something more like *the activity or experience of being a spectator*. It is a looking-at or contemplation, a kind of rapt attention. If we consider the theories we reviewed in Chapters 1 and 3, and ask what their point is—what the philosophers who create these theories seek in

---

[17] "The discoverer of the role of forgiveness in the realm of human affairs was Jesus of Nazareth." Hannah Arendt, *The Human Condition: A Study of the Central Conditions Facing Modern Man* (Garden City, NY: Doubleday, 1959), 212–213.

[18] Translated by H. Rackham in Loeb Classical Library, vol. 285 (Cambridge, MA: 1935).

concocting them, once they realize that the project of saving the world from pluralism and skepticism is hopeless—a plausible answer is that they are seeking something intellectually satisfying, like a mathematical solution or an elegant explanation. The contemplation of the field of ethical concepts through the lens of an elegantly formulated ethical theory, then, would have the character of *theoria* for such individuals. Aristotle is saying that many of his inquiries have exactly this purpose: to enable a satisfying intellectual grasp (a *theoria*) of a subject matter. His ethical inquiries, too, may offer intellectually satisfying views of this or that, but their purpose or ultimate aim is different. It is to guide and move people to live good lives. When it comes to happiness, we want to participate; being a spectator isn't enough! Compared to the great good of living our lives well, getting a merely intellectually satisfying understanding of happiness and the virtues is "of no benefit to us." Aristotle does tell us what happiness and virtue are, but he thinks that if we learned only that, we'd have missed the point of his inquiry.

If we have an impression to the contrary, it's because *Nicomachean Ethics* is less direct than Seneca's essays; he is not so much addressing the person whose character is to be transformed, but rather writing a handbook for legislators or teachers or anyone whose work will influence people's character. *Nicomachean Ethics* is not confrontation of individuals in ethical conversation, like the virtue ethics of Socrates, and not counseling, like Seneca, but it aims ultimately to serve the same purpose: to help people get their priorities right and acquire healthy dispositions—to become temperate, courageous, just, and wise. In other words, to help people become excellent as people, and thus also as citizens.

Aristotle is aware that most people don't live very well. Everybody wants to be "happy"; we all "aim" at this, in some sense, in everything we do. But in the absence of fairly rigorous investigation, we don't know more exactly what we're aiming at in aiming at happiness. Ethics, or political science, is the branch of investigation that identifies the target and figures out how to hit it. The investigation is important because you can hardly expect to hit the target if you don't know what it is and how to do so. We can express this, perhaps, in the paradox that if a person hit the target without aiming, *she* wouldn't have hit the target (maybe "luck" hit the target). But in virtue ethics, she is the center of attention; the point is for *her* to hit the target by *conducting* her life with the target—living a good one—in her sights.

We have noted that Aristotle's ethical thinking is "biological," and we express this fact by putting his question as "What is the good life for *a human being*?" or "How does one live a successful life given that it's a human life?" Many other kinds of living things—animals and plants—can have good or bad lives. They can flourish, or they can just barely make it. For each species, the conditions for a good life are specific to the species. And in his ethics, Aristotle wants to know what the conditions are for human beings to live a good life.

Like the Stoics, Aristotle has an outlook on us human beings. His idea of what we are guides his account of living well. We are rational animals. When Aristotle thinks fundamentally about human beings, he puts us in a schema of species of living things, of plants and animals. Plants differ from animals, and most animals differ from rational animals, and each species of living thing—plants or animals—has its own "function," its own characteristic way of going about life, of sustaining itself, of reproducing, and finally, of *living*. Let's think a bit about the concept of FUNCTION.

The Idea of a Function and the Hierarchy of Souls

Start with artifacts—things we make. When we manufacture something, we have in mind some function or other for it. If we make bricks, we have in mind their function as, say, BUILDING PARTS. If we make a building, we have in mind its function as SHELTER or a PLACE TO MEET or as a DECORATION of the landscape. If we make a computer, we make it for the sake of its various functions. Manufactured things are defined, in large part, by their functions. A house *is* a house only if it's the sort of thing that *might* function as a house, or *once* functioned as a house, or at least was *intended* to function as a house. The qualities of a manufactured thing that make it function *well* can be called its VIRTUES (its excellences).

For example, a good hammer is one that drives nails well. To do this, it needs to have a handle and a driving head, a combination that allows a wielder to swing the head in a controlled arc without its flying off the handle and to hit the nail on the head, driving it into something penetrable. For all this to be possible, the head has to be of a certain weight and shape, made of a material that is hard enough to withstand all the pounding, flat on its face (but not too flat) and neither too light nor too heavy to swing to that end. The handle has to be designed with a shape that allows it to remain in the hand (thus under control) during the swing rather than slip away. For this purpose, it needs to be made of a non-slippery material and/or to be shaped with a little flair at the bottom. These qualities, among others, make a hammer good, and they do so by enabling it to serve its function. The weight of the head and the shape of its face, the shape and length of the handle, and texture of its surface are all qualities that serve the function of a nail hammer. Such qualities, then, are the excellences (virtues) of the hammer.

Hammers, houses, and computers are a good place to start in thinking about functions of things, but only up to a point. Aristotle wants to know what a good *life* is like, and how to find out. Hammers and computers don't have a life. Because they don't have a life, hammers and computers don't have *well-being* even if they have all the hammer virtues and all the computer virtues and thus function beautifully as hammers and computers. We don't speak, except in jest, of healthy or happy computers and hammers.

But natural beings, things that reproduce biologically and grow and have self-sustaining inner resources, do have a life, and so they can have a good life or a bad one; they can have well-being or ill-being. They don't just function well or badly for some purpose external to themselves (like providing food or building materials for another species), but function well or badly *with respect to themselves*, just in their own terms. A tree that has grown from a seed that landed in an arid place and without much soil to hold is likely to be a scrubby, grievous little thing, that doesn't produce fruit according to its kind, and whose leaves are small and wither easily. It's not "doing well," quite apart from the fact that it will never become lumber or a source of squirrel food.

By contrast, in that sense, we don't talk about artifacts doing well or not doing well.

To have a life, according to Aristotle, is to have one or more souls. In fact, to have a soul just *is* to have a way of being alive. Different kinds of living things are differentiated by the kinds of souls they have. If a plant is growing and processing light and water and nutrients from the soil, then it has what Aristotle calls a **nutritive soul**. The activities of a nutritive soul are such things as metabolism, photosynthesis, respiration, and circulation. Plants have *only* a nutritive soul. Animals (insects, worms, rats) have, in addition to a nutritive soul, a **sensitive soul**: They have sense organs that enable them to see, hear, smell, and feel things in their environments and respond to them with movement. They also have within them the power to be attracted or repulsed by things: For example, they are attracted by food, and so tend to move toward it, and are repulsed by predators, and so tend to move away from them or otherwise react defensively to them.

We human beings have both a nutritive and a sensitive soul, but in addition, we have a **rational soul**. The function of the rational soul is to think thoughts. But thoughts come in broadly two varieties. We can think about how to do things and what to do; and we can think, not with any practical purpose, but just to know the truth about things. Aristotle calls these two powers practical reason and theoretical reason. No plant has the power to think about what to do. Some birds and other animals do seem to be able to solve some problems by what resembles human thinking; but we're probably on solid ground in thinking that none of them can do science or philosophy or history, or examine and evaluate their own states of mind and character. The power to do these kinds of things, thinks Aristotle, is HIGHER than any power of the nutritive or sensitive soul; it's an intrinsically *better kind* of power. So reason is both what sets human beings apart from the rest of the biological world and what sets us above the rest of the biological world.

Each of these kinds of soul is a power of functioning and can function well or not so well. Digestion, which is a function of the nutritive soul, can be poor or excellent; as can eyesight, which is a function of the sensitive soul. And no doubt, a human being's quality of life is compromised if her digestion and eyesight aren't excellent. But because human beings are rational animals, they can be functioning very well in their nutritive and sensitive souls, and still not have a good life. To be happy, or to live a truly good human life—to have what Aristotle calls *eudaimonia*—requires that a person's rational soul function properly. The proper practical functioning of the rational soul requires the moral virtues and a social context in which those virtues can be exercised as well as at least a modicum of the intellectual virtue of practical wisdom. The proper theoretical functioning of the rational soul requires the intellectual virtues.

Practical Happiness

I said the rational soul has two functions—practical reason and theoretical reason. Let's look at excellence of practical reason. The word *praxis*, from which we get our word 'practical,' means *action* or *activity*. But action or activity isn't just movement, for example, the movement of blood through the circulatory system, nor is it just behavior as produced by a stimulus such as the movement that the doctor provokes when she taps on your knee with her little hammer. Action or activity has to be motivated. That is, we have to desire something if we are to act; we act for reasons. The desire might be a bodily appetite (say, the desire to eat) or it might be a desire for something non-bodily like respect from our fellow human beings, or money, or the understanding of something. Even when we do what we "don't want" to do, we do it out of some concern such as to avoid the consequences of not doing it, or to fulfill a duty. When a student enrolls in college, she does so for some reason—to prepare herself to earn a living, to cultivate her mind by acquainting herself with science, art, and literature, to please her parents, or to have a ready source of parties. Aristotle thinks that some of these reasons are better than others. Some are more reasonable or rational than others by the standard of what a human being is.

How do you determine which reasons are more reasonable? Aristotle does this, in his ethical and political writings, by drawing a picture of human nature and thus of human well-being. Rational action is action that serves, or at least is compatible with, the human function, the pursuit of a good human life.

We have a good human life, according to Aristotle, when

- Our desires are infused with practical understanding, and our practical understanding is infused with desire for the good (practical wisdom serves this part of our function).[19]
- We satisfy our appetites in moderation and in such ways that they don't disrupt peaceful relations with our fellow human beings (temperance serves this part of our function).
- The higher faculties of our soul are cultivated (practical and intellectual wisdom).
- We have a circle of friends to whom we are attracted because of their excellence as human beings (the capacity for friendship serves this part).
- We prize belongings only to the extent that they serve the excellence of our life (not to such an extent that we have useless accumulation of wealth and become slaves to it) and share it with others freely as occasion offers (liberality serves these parts of our function).
- We get angry with one another only if the other has done something really worthy of the anger (gentleness serves this).
- We live in a society where people are rewarded according to their merits (justice serves this part of our function).
- We face the dangers and threats of life without cringing and falling apart (courage).
- We are self-sufficient and have power over other human beings, and so can think highly of ourselves (magnanimity [greatness of soul]).

You might say that, just as the acorn has it in it to become that magnificent oak tree covered with beautiful green leaves and abundant acorns of its own, if only it's given the right conditions of soil and moisture and sunshine and warmth, so the human embryo has it in it, with the proper education and environment, to become an animal that is living the kind of life roughly described above. According to Aristotle,

---

[19] See the following chapter for more detail.

human nature dictates that kind of life as the ideal outcome of human development, just as the genetic structure of the acorn dictates what the mature oak will be like if it's properly nurtured. And the personal qualities that emerge as the dictates of human nature are satisfied are the virtues: temperance, wisdom, friendship,[20] liberality, gentleness (good temper), justice, courage, magnanimity, and so on.

But this kind of life is necessarily a life of reason, because it's a life of acting for reasons; and because we are able to act for reasons, much of our life is determined by our choices. If your reason for going to college was to cultivate your mind by acquainting yourself with science and art and literature, and to cultivate life-long friendships with like-minded people, then your choice and your action are better and more reasonable, by Aristotle's standards, than if you went to college for the sex and beer. The former action is characteristic of a life in which human nature is at least partially understood; the latter action reflects an unworthy and inaccurate picture of human nature.

Interestingly, both of them reflect a "picture" of human life, a conception of what makes it worthwhile and fulfilling. Even adherents of the playboy philosophy of life have a conception of the good life. They too are rational animals, according to Aristotle, however poorly thought-out their conception of the good life may be. You might say they are irrational exemplars of the species rational animal. You can't be irrational in the way a playboy is without being a rational animal.

Plants have no reasons at all for what they do; animals have desires and perceptions, but don't have thought-out reasons for what they do. According to Aristotle, we human beings alone have thought-out reasons for what we do, and so we have much more potential for error in living our lives than the other biological organisms. But we also have much more control over our lives than the plants and animals. Our lives can be planned, both by ourselves and by our elders and our legislators; they can be shaped by beliefs about what kind of being we are and what kind of life best fits our being human. We can form a

---

[20] Aristotle hesitates to classify friendship as a virtue (see NE 8.1). It is of enormous importance to human flourishing and requires virtues to be practiced well, but is unlike the virtues in being a relationship with a particular other person. Furthermore, you can have several friendships, but not several courages or gentlenesses.

conception of the good life "scientifically," that is, to say, reflectively and critically, so that we can arrange our life according to the results of our science—the good life to the best of our knowledge. This is what Aristotle is doing in his ethical writings. It is "political science."

The shape that a soul takes when it's formed by such thoughts is the moral virtues. According to Aristotle, a virtue is a disposition to choose according to a rational principle. Virtues that enable persons to live good lives and to contribute to the good lives of the others they live with are temperance (proper appetites), courage, justice, liberality, good temper (proper anger), magnanimity, practical wisdom, and others. A person with a virtue responds thoughtfully with proper emotions and proper actions to the situations of his or her life. Such virtues are all forms of thinking right and desiring according to one's right thinking. The good life, according to Aristotle, is not found in the abundance of one's possessions, in maximizing the pleasures of the body, or in having "fun," but in the character of one's mind and heart, active in a well-ordered community of people of such character.

Contemplative Happiness

We've been talking about practical reason and conforming our life to its dictates. This is implied by our nature as rational animals. But Aristotle doesn't suppose that the life we've been describing is the best life for us or the life of highest virtue. Even higher is the life of the purely rational element in the soul (NE 10.6–8). This is the life of *theoria*.

The best happiness we can live, according to Aristotle, is the life of contemplation of eternal objects (*theoria*). It's better than the "practical" life for a surprising reason: because it's a life of fundamental independence or "self-sufficiency." To live the life of practical reason, you have to have other people to interact with: You can't practice liberality or justice all by yourself, and you can't act liberally if you have nothing to give. But, Aristotle thinks, you can think about and appreciate the beauty of mathematical truths and the truths of physics all by yourself, without depending on any colleagues, possessions, or apparatus. Because of the self-sufficiency that the activity of *theoria* affords, contemplative happiness is superior to practical happiness.

With our wind tunnels and colliders and AI software and scientific collaboration teams, we'll probably disagree with Aristotle about the self-sufficiency of the practitioner of theoretical contemplation. But it's an interesting feature of his thought that for him, the ideal of the best life is one in which we depend as little as possible on people and things. How different this is from a Jewish or Christian way of thinking about our nature in which our dependency—on natural resources, on one another, and on God—is fundamental to our being and not a defect that, ideally, could be overcome. Instead, it's the matrix of the good life for beings like us.

Since the proper object of theoretical intellect, according to Aristotle, is things that can't be otherwise than they are (like unchangeable physical laws and mathematics), and God is the highest of such objects, *theoria* is "religious" in a broad sense.[21] It is a contemplation of God and God's ways. So it invites comparison with another ancient picture of the good human life. I have in mind the wisdom tradition in ancient Hebrew thought as represented in many of the Hebrew psalms and the book of Proverbs. Psalm 1 succinctly represents this outlook:

> 1 Happy is the person
>   who walks not in the counsel of
>   the wicked,
>   nor stands in the way of sinners,
>   nor sits in the seat of scoffers;
> 2 but his delight is in the law of
>   the LORD,
>   and on his law he meditates
>   day and night.
> 3 He is like a tree
>   planted by streams of water,
>   that yields its fruit in its
>   season,
>   and its leaf does not wither.
>   In all that he does, he prospers.

[21] John Hare, *God and Morality: A Philosophical History* (Hoboken: Wiley-Blackwell, 2009).

> 4 The wicked are not so,
>   but are like chaff that the wind
>   drives away.
> 5 Therefore the wicked will not
>   stand in the judgment,
>   nor sinners in the congregation
>   of the righteous;
> 6 for the LORD knows the way
>   of the righteous,
>   but the way of the wicked will
>   perish. (RSV, modified)

Like Aristotle, the psalmist compares human well-being (happiness, blessedness, wholistic health) with the radiant health of another biological kind, in this case, a tree. But for the psalmist, we, unlike any other species, depend for our well-being on voluntarily following a law that God has lovingly tailored to our nature. The whole purpose of the law is that we *practice* it. To use Aristotle's phrase, if we don't practice the law, thinking about it will "be of no benefit to us." It's a mark of our kind of agency, special among living creatures, that we must follow it in such a way that we take pleasure even in thinking about it. But that pleasure must be in anticipation of the joy of living it out before God. For the psalmist, the law satisfies two distinct but inseparable concerns: a longing for contact with God and a felt need for guidance of our conduct. God's law is to a human life what water is to a tree: essential sustenance.

The happy person is one whose heart so laps up the will of God that it becomes her sap, nourishing her actions and feelings and giving them a specific character. As if reading a love letter from God, she drinks in the law and the prophets again and again, savoring the details, and it becomes a means of fellowship with God. As she reads, she grows to be "like-minded" with God. To appreciate the contrary, imagine someone who "behaves himself" in accordance with the law. He refrains from stealing, adultery, besmirching his neighbor with lies, and so forth. But his heart isn't in it. He would really like to do all these things. His attitude toward the law is: It's an unwelcome burden, a dead albatross that hangs from his neck. It doesn't "fit his personality." It's "not his type."

The virtuous person is one who spontaneously, with understanding and from the heart, does what God prescribes in the moral law. The deep prescription of the law—what the law really, and fully understood, enjoins—is the keeping of the law *as intended by the law giver*. In this sense, virtue is being of one mind with the law giver, the mind that is reflected in that law. It prescribes not just behavior, but action in the full sense: doing what is enjoined with appreciation of its purpose. And its purpose, since it is God's law, is God's purpose. Our pleasure in the law indicates that our mind and heart are tracking God's. Like the dictates of Aristotle's practical wisdom, the law on which we would meditate is a "rational" construct that prescribes a way of living a human life. It expresses God's understanding of the good life for human beings, and part of its goal is that we understand it as prescribing the good life for us. Jewish or Christian meditation is a consumption of understanding, an eating, drinking, and digesting of God's understanding of what we need if we are to live a truly human life. For the Hebrew, acquiring this condition of the heart/mind—understanding the "mind" of God about the good life for human beings—is the purpose and joy of studying the law. Nothing could be more "practical" than this "intellectual" practice.

Aristotelian practical wisdom is likewise an understanding of the good life. Both the dictates of practical wisdom and the precepts of the law of God are "understated" in the sense that particular judgments that express the understanding fall short of doing so unless processed by an understanding mind that grasps their drift or career—one who has an intelligent feel for their bearing on the good as a whole and toward other judgments in the moral-conceptual array. Aristotle's contemplative happiness, despite its "theological" reference and despite its being a practice, is not at all "practical." The Aristotelian's delight in contemplating the physics of God is purely "theoretical." It's a delight simply in knowing—in knowing something that is quite remote from moral practice.

Yet this very delight is a bridge that allows us to imagine an Aristotelian practice analogous to the Hebrews' practice of meditation on God's law: To experience joy (pleasure) in something is to see it as good. This is why joy is so important for virtue: The virtuous person sees as good what is truly good, while the vicious person construes as good what is not good—and as tiresome what is really life. Your character is the pattern of your dispositions to take pleasure. If you take pleasure in just actions, you are a just person; if you take pleasure in liberal actions, you are a liberal person; and so forth. And if you take pleasure in what is sordid and unwholesome, you are vicious and ill-formed. Moral virtue is the disposition to take pleasure in acting for the sake of human well-being (practical goodness), and virtue in general is the disposition to take pleasure in what is good.

If this is right, then *theoria* too is a perception of a good—the beauty of unchanging truths. From this, it seems to follow psychologically that moral philosophy, which is the study of human well-being (eudaimonia) and therefore a study of practical wisdom, must be delightful in a way that is comparable to the Hebrews' delight in the law. Like the Hebrews' practical delight in God's law, the Aristotelian's activity of thinking the thoughts of practical wisdom must also be a joy that is both intellectual and practical. (Aristotle doesn't say this, as far as I know.) This, too, surely would be a kind of philosophical contemplation. And, because of the deliberative character of human agency, the intellectual and the practical would here be inseparable (NE 6.2, 1139a23–35). The activity of contemplating the judgments of practical wisdom would be intellectual because of the intrinsically "intellectual" (deliberative) nature of human practice, and it would be a motivating contemplation of the good insofar as the understanding of those deliverances was practically pleasurable: a joy in real eudaimonia.

Understanding—this capacity to navigate around the system of judgments—would, plausibly, be enhanced by an activity like the Hebrews' happy ruminations on God's law. Such "Aristotelian" meditation would include both conceptual and logical exploration—the meaning of terms and the examination of possible inferences—and "aesthetic" appreciation (for example, gratitude, hope, and other variants of joy) as fitting the goodness of the projected order of peace.

Aristotle doesn't seem to reckon with any such free-standing activity of meditation on the concepts and precepts of eudaimonia (practical wisdom). Instead, he seems simply to commend "the man of practical wisdom" rather abstractly, as fully formed, and apart from any intellectual developmental exercise. When he does speak of moral development, he stresses habituation—the repetition of actions characteristic of virtues—as though that will be enough, eventually, to engender wise judgment. Charitably, we might note that it's just common sense to suppose that such repeated good actions will often be performed in contexts where the moral learner hears and assimilates bits of wise talk that make sense of his or her growing habits. But still, it seems plausible that a more intentional and philosophical, analytic and synthetic activity of joyfully pondering the deliverances of practical wisdom—an activity similar to the psalmist's happy meditation on God's law—would benefit Aristotelian moral education.[22] In fact, Aristotle verges on this when he says that the ultimate aim of moral philosophy, which surely is *theoria* in some broad sense, is that we become good. A body of thoughts like the *Nicomachean Ethics* itself might function as a vehicle for such moral-developmental philosophical *theoria*.

Conclusion

If contemporary virtue ethics is to be really a return to the ancient practice, it must differ from what Michael Slote calls "pure virtue ethics" (Chapter 3). Its discourse needs to differ markedly from most of what passes as philosophical ethics today. It must be a practice that is at once philosophical (that is, carefully clarifying concepts by asking questions and trying out answers) and ethically transformative of its practitioners and their beneficiaries. Notably, it needs to be sufficiently rhetorical—ethically appealing enough—to "speak" to the deeper and more personal ethical and human concerns of those who practice it. It needs to be, not a technology of reduction, but a craft of induction—a dialectical art that induces ethical character by deepening understanding. Such rhetoric is not a compromise of clarity and precision, but a prerequisite of it, given the final import of ethical discourse.

I agree with MacIntyre that the right "school" to choose is the Aristotelian in a Christianized mutation. But MacIntyre's apparent aspiration to overcome ethical pluralism by developing this tradition seems to me misguided. Ethics in the ancient world was as fragmented and diverse and contentious and pluralistic as it is today. As nearly

---

[22] See Kristján Kristjánsson, *Aristotelian Character Education* (London: Routledge, 2017).

everyone who has thought about it agrees, only parts of Aristotle's teachings, brilliant as they are, can be seriously retained. And Christianity in particular enters the ancient world as a strikingly and self-consciously distinctive *alternative* to other outlooks—including Aristotle's. Christians have a stake in resisting the elimination of ethical pluralism—the differences of what we learn and teach from its various alternatives. The disappearance of alternatives threatens to bode the dilution or dissipation of the distinctive lineaments of Christian character, of Christian ethics itself. An indication that this liability stalks MacIntyre's ethics, despite his fierce defense of Roman Catholicism, is that his ethics makes hardly any appeal to the distinctively theological resources that are essential to Christian ethics.

Philosophical ethics is investigation. It is inquiry. It asks and tries to answer questions. The Hebrew meditator asks, "What does the law say? What is God's mind about us? How does the law bless our community? Show me the glories of the law!" "Open my eyes, so that I may behold wondrous things out of your law" (Ps 119:18). Hebrew meditation on the law is contemplative and exploratory, eager to learn, inquisitive, and all this with the practical bent of seeking to live well. Its questions differ from those of modern ethics. In looking for the grounds of the moral concepts, modern ethics seeks to find them elsewhere than in morality or ethics—in pre-moral pleasure, practical reason, mere human agreement, human sentiments—anything but morality! The psalmist starts with a moral order as embodied in God and expressed in God's law. And his project is not to find their grounding, but to familiarize himself with the layout, the plan, and to rejoice in its beauty.

In Part 2, we will consider in some detail a particular kind of virtue ethics as a case that illustrates the philosophical approach to ethics that I am proposing.

PART 2
CHRISTIAN VIRTUE ETHICS

5
Ethical Frameworks

Introduction

In this chapter, I'll explore the idea of a moral framework or ethical outlook, with special interest in the Christian ethical framework and the virtues that it implies and structures. I'll do so by comparing and contrasting the framework of Christianity with those of Stoicism and Aristotle. I will also begin to set the Christian framework and its virtues in relation to some more general features of virtues, to be continued in Chapter 6. In the present chapter, I'll focus on the relation that virtues bear to human happiness. 'Happy' always needs to be specified, since it means different things to different people. The frameworks all frame happiness in one sense or another, but because each has a different notion of what good character and the virtues are, they have somewhat different ideas of what it is for a human being or society to flourish, to be mature, to be fulfilled. Different frameworks propose different, but often overlapping, lists of virtues. I will argue that Christian virtues and Christian happiness are distinctive but within some features that Christianity shares with other moral outlooks. Christian and non-Christian, we are all human beings, after all!

In Chapter 6, I'll further explore the commonalities among moral outlooks by considering the general psychological elements that go to make up moral character. I'll argue that these elements are dispositions to think and be concerned, abilities to manage oneself, and the incorporation of other minds. In Chapter 7, I'll introduce the notion of virtue ethics as grammatical inquiry and begin to look at the grammar of Christian virtues. I'll explain how understanding can *be* virtues. With that, we'll have revived the ancient virtue ethics in its general aim, though the Christian virtues we aim at differ deeply from the ones that ancient paganism pursued. In Chapter 8, we'll think about the Christian virtues in their relation to the law of God and try

Virtue Ethics. Robert Campbell Roberts, Oxford University Press.
© Robert Campbell Roberts 2026. DOI: 10.1093/9780197848005.003.0008

to figure out where to place virtues in relation to the categories of habit, habitus, and skill. In Chapter 9, we'll continue the discussion of what makes a disposition a virtue and of Christian virtue ethics as a branch of philosophy.

Then, in Chapters 10 and 11, I'll further illustrate Christian virtue ethics by exploring wisdom and humility and some of the many ways they connect with the rest of the Christian virtues. Our aim will be to see if we can, by practicing some philosophy, become wiser and more humble, and at the same time advance in some other virtues, and so in happiness. Our aim will be to acquire a kind of understanding (knowledge, wisdom) that itself is Christian virtues.

Ethical Frameworks

An ethical framework is an implicit or explicit set of beliefs about what human beings are most fundamentally, and so about what it takes for us to reach our state of completeness, success, maturity, flourishing, genuine happiness, full formation, or well-being. The apostle Paul calls the Christian version of this "maturity, . . . the measured stature of the fulness of Christ" (Eph 4:13, my trans.). This notion, which Paul develops at various points in his letters and is sketched in his lists of virtues (Gal 5; Col 3; Eph 4; Rom 12; I Cor 1–2, 13; II Cor 8; Phil 2, for example), can provide a framework for understanding and perceiving the situations of life.

The framework offers to answer the question, What kind of being am I? What is the goal of life for a creature like me? What is the path for reaching that goal? The location of the goal and the path to it are internally related; they are two aspects of the same idea.

'Framework' is a metaphor. Literally, a framework is the structure of something, as of a house, which has a framework made of wood or metal or concrete. A moral framework is made of concepts, thoughts, and ideas. These ideas can constitute a reference point in our walk through life, indicating where and where not to go. When thoroughly integrated with concerns and self-management skills, they can structure character traits such as those that Aristotle explores in *Nicomachean Ethics*, and such as Paul lists in the passages I mentioned.

A moral framework functions as a sort of compass that locates us in our progress toward, or divergence from, that happy maturity. Life is like walking in a dense forest. We're all more or less trying to find our way, and we're looking for well-being, either our own or other people's (or both in the same breath). Without markers, it may be hard to know whether we're walking toward or away from happiness, or just wandering about, groping. A moral framework orients us, gives us a sense of direction, and frees us to choose intelligently the direction of our life. The names of the virtues—'justice,' 'gentleness,' 'generosity,' 'courage,' and the like—are main conceptual parts (perhaps joints?) of the framework.

As beings that live in time, we're ever changing, developing, constantly moving through life, and that "movement" inevitably has a moral direction, one that can be either right or wrong, well-guided or misguided, and about which we may be clear or in the dark. We progress and we regress by reference to the goal internal to our fundamental species make-up. A moral framework is a way of thinking about ourselves—each about himself and his fellow humans and his relations with them and his God—that holds an answer to the question, How do we become real human beings? How do we move in the right direction? What is the shape of a good life for beings like us? What kind of life is most worth living for us? What does real success in our life look like?

Living things are environmental in the sense that we find ourselves and live our lives in an environment, a world, and our well-being depends on our adjusting to and being properly nurtured by that environment according to the standards that our nature as living beings sets for us. It is controversial what, exactly, that environment is or contains, and diverse frameworks have different conceptions of the environment that we navigate in living.

I use the word 'environment' in an extensive sense: It covers not only such things as temperature, environmental air and water, other species, gravitational pull on our bodies, and so forth, but also what kind of universe we inhabit. This last is entailed by the fact that we aren't just physical but thinking beings who conceptually construct our environment. We can conceptualize other people as threats or opportunities, divided into competitors and objects of possible exploitation, as divided into fellows and aliens, us and them; or we can think of others and us as all in the same boat, brothers and sisters in the human family; we can see ourselves as independent individuals or as dependent rational animals; we can conceptualize the universe as cold and indifferent, or as under control by a loving governor. We can conceive ourselves as fully autonomous in principle, or as properly under a higher authority. All such environments are contestable, but we all have to make our way in one or another of them because congenitally, we're thinkers. We can't not construct an environment or world for ourselves in this extended sense. The concepts out of which we construct it constitute our moral framework.

In classical frameworks, human nature is seen as relational in the sense that fulfillment requires that the human being relate properly with people and/or Someone or Something else—other human beings, the order of the universe, or God, for example. Stoics think that our world is deterministic and overall rational and rather coldly good. Christians think the world is ruled by a loving God who is incarnate in a man who lived in Palestine a couple of thousand years ago, but that it has fallen into disorder from which God, in his goodness, will rescue it. Aristotle believes in god, but his god differs from that of Christians and Stoics. An interpersonal relationship with God is not a possibility if our larger environment is what Aristotle thinks it is.

In a sense, every human being begins, at an early age, to be a philosopher. We think about life, and we do so in evaluative terms—with a prejudice for living well. The vast majority of rats and ants and other animals are non-philosophers, who therefore neither have nor seek a conception of what it is to be a successful animal of their kind. Nor (fortunately for the rats and ants) is it part of their being successful to have such a conception. But for us human beings, not only do we conceive our success; we do so well and accurately, or poorly and falsely. And it's a requirement of our being a success that we conceive our success accurately enough, that we aim at what is true success for a human being, real happiness, real completion of our nature. Not just anything in the way of a philosophy of life will do. Some moral frameworks are disastrous. For example, what if somebody thinks that being a success in life—being great as a human being—is measured by your success at bullying other people into submission? What if somebody thinks that to be maximally successful, you have to have more than your fair share of money and luxury? If we're doing moral philosophy, it's part of our work to clarify a conception of human maturity. As an activity in the service of moral character, philosophy—the understanding of the goal of human life—is a significant part of the philosophy's person-transforming character. The conception, when presented clearly, "inspires." It speaks to us by speaking to the philosopher in all of us: We have a natural appetite for knowing where we are in this forest of life. Moral philosophy can be a nutrient that meets this appetite, an activity that satisfies our urge to understand ourselves and what it takes for us to live the life we crave.

The Biblical Framework

According to the overall biblical picture of human beings and our place in the world order, God created us to be free, willing, and obedient stewards of the rest of creation (Gen 1 and 2) and to live with one another, under this task, in peace and mutual helpfulness (Is 58:6–12). God's purpose in this is irrevocable (Rom 11). We human beings were (are) destined to be a kind of royal priesthood, sub-sovereigns who represent God to the world and the world to God. N. T. Wright helpfully proposes the metaphor of an angled mirror in which what is above can have access to (see) those below and those below have access to (see) what is above. "The point of an angled mirror is that it reflects one thing to another: in this case, God to the world (mission) and the world back to God (worship). I now propose that the New Testament's vision of Christian virtue, of the holiness to which Jesus's followers are called and for which they are equipped by the Spirit, can be understood (and is perhaps best understood) as a function of that dual role."[1] We are created to be that mirror, to mediate between God above us and the non-human creation below us. If the mirror is in good shape (not fogged or bent), then when a perceptive creature looks at us, it sees God in the reflection; when God looks at us, he sees a representative of

---

[1] N. T. Wright, *After You Believe* (San Francisco: HarperCollins, 2012), 243.

all creation. We represent creation well when we nurture and care for it as God's obedient proxies. As God's priests, we should lovingly honor God by lovingly nurturing human and non-human creatures.

But, in our freedom, we've shunned this task in many ways, have exploited and spoiled the creation that we were to nurture, have failed to function well as that mirror, have turned to our own selfish purposes, have ignored or crassly exploited our priestly powers, and have divided from one another and competed and fought against one another.

In view of the general corruption of the world, God selected Israel as his representative to the world, thus for a special assignment of royal priesthood. But the history of Israel is almost as much a story of disobedience and rebellion as that of the rest of humankind. Jesus, as the incarnate Son of God and true humanity, is the perfect angled mirror that humankind, and then Israel, was supposed to be. He is the new Adam (Rom 5). He was killed by our iniquity, but God raised him from the dead, making him the "first fruits" of the new creation, a new order of the world. He is the head of the church, which is his "body" in the present era. The church, in its worship of God and its service to humanity and the rest of creation on God's behalf, is an anticipation of the kingdom of God that Jesus has initiated in his ministry, his sacrificial death, and his resurrection from the dead.

In the church's life, the church "breathes" Jesus's Holy Spirit, his personal presence. Christian virtues of **faith, hope, love, compassion, generosity, self-control, forgivingness, boldness, courage, humility, patience, forbearance, gentleness, truthfulness, justice, wisdom, gratitude, kindness,** and **faithfulness** are the traits that "fit" members of the church for the expected new order of the world, and for the life of the church that prefigures that new world in the present generation. These traits make the angled mirror capable of reflecting accurately. The church, as a community, is an anticipation (in hope) of the new earth. So the character traits of the church's members are anticipations of that new social world. Many of the virtues are specifications of love, and specifically of a love that doesn't discriminate among those to whom it is directed: The virtuous Christian loves not just members of our in-group, or people who like us or are like us, or people who are "important," but the "neighbor," the "least of these," and even the enemy! The lists of vices that we find in the teaching of Jesus (Mark 7:21–22) and the letters of Paul (Gal 5:19–21; Col 3:5–9) are all traits or kinds of action that are contrary to, corrupting of, and excluded from, the order of peace called the kingdom of God.

This framework is plainly different from all its competitors in the ancient (and in the modern) world. It contrasts starkly with the frameworks of the ancient virtue ethicists, Socrates, the Stoics, and Aristotle, among others, as well as the secular liberalisms and conservatisms that prevail in our own time. This fact suggests that biblical Christians have little reason to be worried about moral pluralism. In Chapter 1, I argued that the original motivation behind the moral theories was the worry about moral pluralism and possible consequences like relativism and moral skepticism. Christians shouldn't be surprised or dismayed that some or many people have different moral standards than Christians. They should think, "but of course!" Given the peculiarity of the Christian moral framework, differences between our morality, including the list of virtues that we aspire to, and the other moral outlooks are only to be expected. Christianity will always be confronting other ways of thinking ethically. Rather, believers and unbelievers alike should be impressed by how much some of the Christian peculiarities have seeped into secular morality. Jewish and Christian innovations such as inherent human rights, humility, patience, forgiveness, and universal benevolence are now presupposed, in altered variants, by much of secular ethics.

Differences and Similarities Among Frameworks

Moral frameworks are fundamentally controversial or contested. Talk of moral frameworks presupposes moral pluralism, but not relativism or skepticism. Stoics, Aristotelians, Nietzscheans, and Christians who acknowledge that many people don't share their frameworks may nevertheless believe that their moral framework is the true one—the one that matches human nature and the nature of the universe as it is. In this sense, they are "creeds."

Stoicism, Aristotle, and Christianity prescribe different but somewhat overlapping sets of virtues. A set of virtues is a unified character with interlocking parts. Character is the overall shape of the good human being (his or her goodness or excellence as a person), and the parts or aspects of good character are the person's virtues. Here are the sets of virtues belonging to good character according to the three frameworks that we are comparing:

Stoicism: Apatheia, wisdom [justice, mercy]
Aristotle: Justice, Practical Wisdom, Courage, Temperance, Liberality, Magnanimity, Magnificence, Gentleness, Friendship, Theoretical Wisdom
Christianity: Faith, Hope, Love, Compassion, Generosity, Forgivingness, Forbearance, Gentleness, Gratitude, Kindness, Faithfulness, Justice, Truthfulness, Boldness, Self-control, Courage, Humility, Patience, Wisdom

The differences among the Stoic, the Aristotelian, and the Christian characters can be traced to differences in the moral framework—to what kind of being we think we are in the first place and the kind of (social) environment and activities that are therefore optimal for our becoming the best we can be. Christians, for example, believe that we come into a world that God created, that God created us to live in this world, that we are fundamentally "adaptable" to God's kingdom (rulership) and that, given what we are like and what God is like, we must learn to trust and love and serve God and love our neighbor if we are to "succeed" as human beings, that is, to become fully human. The Christian virtues are personal traits that fit us for the roles and relationships prescribed by the framework.

In Chapter 4, we saw that Aristotle's moral framework is "biological": All living things have a species function that determines what it is for members of the species to have a good life. We humans have a function that we must fulfill to have a good life. Aristotle emphasizes more strongly than most moral frameworks the continuities and discontinuities among human beings and other animal species, but every moral framework is "biological" in the sense that it gives or presupposes a conception of what kind of living being a human being is. This includes Stoicism and Christianity. Genesis 1–2, for example, compares humans with other species and gives humans a special role, which is part of our moral imperative. We are created in the image of God in a way that is not true of any other species, but still, we are a kind of living being. The earlier MacIntyre was right to reject *Aristotle's* metaphysical biology, but he later recognized that he'd gone too far in trying to avoid metaphysical biology as such.

In Chapter 2, we saw that MacIntyre initially thought he could make do with the notions of practices with internal goods, a moral tradition, and the narrative unity of a human self. But a little reflection brings to light that these human phenomena presuppose a good deal of human metaphysical biology. To participate in what MacIntyre calls a practice, our mind/heart needs to have a nature that fits it to engage in practices. We are peculiar, among the species of living things, in having the kind of minds that give us the ability and motivation to practice chess, violin playing, natural science, and other practices. A practice, in MacIntyre's sense, requires participating in a tradition of that practice that extends backward beyond our memory and to which contemporary violinists or chess players may contribute as the tradition accumulates historically. The traditional aspect of practices places demands on the human mind/heart that no other species can meet. Furthermore, for practices to support virtues, we must be able to engage in them "for their own sake." Our mind/heart must fit us to love the practice itself, and not just some more primitive advantages it may afford us, such as money or fame or reproductive fitness. As a species, we have moral traditions, and these depend on powers of communal memory that depend on the human kind of language abilities, as well as forms of motivation that transcend self-interest. We must be fit by nature somehow to receive the tradition as an inheritance, but we must also have minds that empower us to understand it and think critically about it, perhaps detect faults and gaps in it, and make our own adjustments and contributions to the tradition. We must both belong to the tradition and be able to step back from it, though in the stepping back, we depend on it. And to have a human self, our mind/heart must enable us to understand (or create) narratives that identify us as ongoing particular individuals and as members of communities such that we can have the kind of virtues that are marked by "constancy" (*After Virtue*, 183, 242). All this is a rich metaphysical presupposing: powers of understanding and memory and will and emotional complexity. Not just any animal out in the forest or down on the farm can do these things. Such powers and penchants presuppose a quite special "biology" or human nature. The earlier MacIntyre tried to reject "metaphysical biology," but he couldn't avoid presupposing one. In *Dependent Rational Animals*, he changed his mind.

In the last chapter, we noticed some rather stark contrasts between the ethical thought of Seneca, who belongs to the Stoic school, and that of Aristotle. Now I want to offer a little more detail and bring Christianity more explicitly into the discussion. The Stoics think of moral character as a reflection or reduplication in attitude of the beautiful deterministic system of the universe. As the Stoics understand us, we are beings whose minds can mirror this system, in all its indifference to particular individual perspectives. Our minds can become mirrors of the perfect order of the universe. And this implies that the chief virtue will be apatheia—emotionlessness—because emotions are judgments that falsely embody our individual concerns about particular situations by making world cataclysms out of minor local incidents and earth-shaking good fortune out of little boosts. In the Stoic framework, wisdom isn't really a different virtue than apatheia. Wisdom is the deeply integrated insight that only the universe and the mind that reflects it matters; nothing else is of urgent importance. And that *is* apatheia. The character that most perfectly exemplifies apatheia is the "sage": the sagacious or wise person. The sage sees ("places," identifies) the vicissitudes of life in the perspective of the good system of causes and effects that is the universe, and in so seeing the vicissitudes, the sage is "OK" with them, thus even-tempered, neither "upset" nor elated about them. Though the Stoics sometimes mention justice and mercy as virtues, their metaphysical biology rules out that it is really good to distribute benefits fairly or to mete out lenient punishments to the guilty, or to be disposed to do so. These dispositions are good only insofar as they express acquiescence in "the benign indifference of the world."[2] It seems to me that the Stoic must view fair

---

[2] " . . . la tendre indifférence du monde" from the last paragraph of Albert Camus's *L'Etranger*. Camus's novella is usually classed as an "existentialist" work, but Meursault, its hero (or anti-hero) can be seen as exemplifying the Stoic virtue of apatheia. Repeatedly throughout the story, he comments that this or that (marriage, advancement

distributions and fitting leniency in themselves as merely "preferable indifferents."[3]

In our emotions, we take a "stand" either for or against the way things are ("Let us rejoice in the abundant harvest!" "I'm angry at him for what he did to me!"), or have been ("I am grateful to her for her love"; "I have regrets about having done that"), or will be ("We're hopeful!"; "I'm scared!"). But if we are the perfectly virtuous person that the Stoic calls "the sage," the only stand we take is for the universe as a beautiful, harmonious, perfectly rational, and in-principle predictable system of causes and effects. Our deepest nature is our ability to mirror the order of the universe. For the Stoic, emotions are extraneous to our basic nature and impediments to maturity. They are more like warts and moles than like eyes and teeth. Emotions are not basic and essential to human nature. We are, *instead*, "rational" beings.

Aristotle, in his metaphysical biology, rejects this notion of our rationality and thinks that desires, and thus emotions, are an essential part of our "biology" and practical rationality and thus must be properly developed—not eliminated—if we are to be "complete" human beings. In comparison with the Stoics, Aristotle is saying that we are beings for whom the situations of life properly matter. It matters to our well-being that people and governments be just, for example; so it's appropriate and virtuous for a person to be angry when she encounters a significant injustice. The virtue called "gentleness" is a proper formation of our disposition to get angry. The fully formed human being gets angry on occasions—but only when it's fitting—that is, when it's "rational."

On this point, Christianity agrees with Aristotle. Paul advises, "Be angry but do not sin. Do not let the sun go down on your anger" (Eph 4:26). Earlier, we cited an incident in which Jesus was angry (Mark 3:5). Both Aristotle and Christianity are "cautious" about

in his work, for example) "doesn't matter" or "has no importance." At the end of the story, as he faces the guillotine, he struggles against a feeling that his impending death is, after all, something terrible and catastrophic; and then his emotional struggle resolves into apatheia and his "authentic" sense of the "benign indifference of the universe."

[3] Richard Sorabji, *Emotions and Peace of Mind* (Oxford: Oxford University Press, 2000), 169–170.

anger: Because our anger is often trivial, selfish, excessive, and irrational, it often deserves a liberal application of self-control—or to be dispelled. But it can also be warranted by the standards of justice and compassion, and so must not be completely ruled out.[4]

Relatedly, in contemporary English, gentleness is usually the contrary of a tendency to be rough or harsh (benevolently or not) or violent with other people. The connection is that angry people often act roughly or harshly or violently. For example, a gentle person usually speaks to others in a way that avoids arousing shame or anger or fear. A harsh person is not careful in this way and may even go out of his way to arouse such emotions in the other. Roughness or harshness is loosely associated with cruelty, and gentleness with compassion.

Thus, apatheia and gentleness are incompatible "virtues"; if one of them is really a virtue, the other isn't. It is logically impossible to be perfectly gentle, that is, to be disposed to get angry on (and only on) fitting occasions, *and* to have perfect apatheia, that is, to be disposed never to get angry. These frameworks are incompatible because they have incompatible conceptions of what it is for a human being to be "rational." The difference centers around the notion of emotion and the importance of the particular situations of our lives. These are differences in "metaphysical biology" and yield incompatible conceptions of what it is for us to be virtuous, mature, and happy.

Stoicism's ruling against emotions also rules out the Christian virtue of compassion, which involves feeling emotional distress on behalf of a suffering human being (or animal). Seneca distinguishes *clementia* (mercy) from *misericordia* (compassion), and says, "mercy and gentleness are qualities displayed by all good men, while pity (*misericordia*, compassion) is something they will avoid. . . . *Misericordia* is 'sorrow of the mind caused by miseries affecting other people' . . . nothing more befits a man than a great mind. But a mind cannot be both great and also grieving, since grief blunts the wits, debases and shrivels

---

[4] A good discussion of this, comparing the Christian desert fathers, who were influenced by Stoicism, with Thomas Aquinas, a sort of Aristotelian, is DeYoung, "What Are You Guarding?, 20–47. Aquinas points out that anger, by its nature, always attributes injustice, so where there really is injustice, anger is justified; but a great deal of our anger attributes injustice wrongly or exaggerates. In such cases, the desert fathers are right to prescribe eradication.

them."[5] Compare this with the parable of the good Samaritan. When the Samaritan saw the wounded man, "he was moved with compassion" (Luke 10:33, altered). The Greek *splangchnizesthai* (feel compassion) means literally something like, "being wrenched in the gut." Jesus clearly recommends compassion, making it "rational" (appropriate, fitting, expressive of deep humanity) for a human being. Also, the apostle Paul recommends that we "rejoice with those who rejoice, weep with those who weep" (Rom 12:15). These emotions express our love for one another. To eradicate them would be to make our love a casualty of our tranquility.

Although Stoics aim to care little about the particular situations of life, they aim to care very much about the beautiful order of the universe, and so they might seem to endorse an emotion, namely, joy that the whole universe is as it is. But they don't call this joy an emotion; emotions, in their understanding, are only about "local" situations, not about the universe as a whole. But then again, they also take joy in the conformity of a mind to the universe, and that conformity, which is just the existence of a sage, does seem to be a local situation—a contingent fact about this particular person. The Stoics define emotions as false judgments, and the judgment that the conformity of a mind to the universe is not false, and so not an emotion, according to Stoicism. We may begin to think that the Stoics' ethical ruling against emotions runs into conceptual problems and that they must admit the importance of proper emotions in the life of virtue.[6]

We've seen (Chapter 4) that self-sufficiency (independency of things and people) is an important part of Aristotle's ideal of human fulfillment. MacIntyre reacts against the idea that dependency is somehow a shortcoming. He prefers Aquinas's Christian view of human life as in significant part a life of dependency on one another. Contrary to Aristotle's drift, we are "dependent rational animals." No doubt practical rationality—the ability to act deliberately and thus for good reasons of our own—affords us a degree of autonomy, but our

---

[5] Cooper and Procopé, eds., *Seneca: Moral and Political Essays*, 161–162. The quotation is from On Mercy II.5.

[6] In *Emotions in the Moral Life*, chapter 2, I have given a run-down of the ways Stoics back-pedal from their theory of emotions.

rationality doesn't rule out dependency from the best, most virtuous, and happiest life. In fact, it enables us to recognize our dependency on one another. Christians gladly see everything in their life as depending on God's grace, and proper church life as life in which they gratefully acknowledge their dependency on one another's contributions. This is a strong theme in the NT, especially in the letters of Paul (See I Cor 12, Rom 12:6–8, Eph 4:1–16). Receiving help from others isn't inherently demeaning, though because of the sin of pride (in its hyper-autonomy variant; see Chapter 11), we often think like Aristotle on this topic.

Aristotle's self-sufficiency theme implies an understanding of self-respect, and thus of gratitude. The drive for self-sufficiency shows up in our natural motivations and interests. On Aristotle's outlook, we naturally and properly aspire to self-sufficiency; the best of us have a strong appetite for it. We lose self-respect to the extent that we depend on others and gain it as others depend on us. In this way, the "good" of self-sufficiency becomes a matter of competition with fellow human beings. We are averse to being treated with "charity," though it's arguable that a willingness to be so treated is a corollary of the Christian virtue of generosity.[7] The aspiration to self-sufficiency and its connection to self-respect come out clearly in the discussion of the magnanimous man's giving and receiving benefits.

Magnanimity (literally, greatness of soul) is the "crown of the virtues" (NE 4.3). Aristotle notes that the magnanimous man likes to give benefits, but dislikes receiving them. The giver of benefits is superior to the receiver, and the magnanimous man wants to be superior. If someone gives him a significant benefit and he can't get even, his dependency on the giver injures his self-respect. So if somebody has the effrontery to try to be his benefactor, he will do what he can to turn the tables on the aspiring benefactor by giving an even greater benefit in return. If he succeeds, he will restore his self-respect. If he simply accepted the gift and remained in the giver's debt, he would show a "slavish" nature. Thus, the virtue of gratitude, which is important in

---

[7] See my "Gratitude, Friendship, and Mutuality: Reflections on Three Characters in *Bleak House*," in R. Roberts and D. Telech, ed., *The Moral Psychology of Gratitude* (Lanham, NJ: Rowman and Littlefield, 2019), 317–337.

the Christian schema,[8] is shameful in the Aristotelian. As an abject admission of personal inferiority, it's a sort of vice.

In this section, I have illustrated differences, and even incompatibilities, among different moral frameworks. They conceive human nature diversely; such difference yields diverging conceptions of the good life for human beings and consequently different ideas about which traits are virtues and which are vices. We will see more of this in the coming chapters. But let us also note some ways that moral outlooks are similar.

They tend to have some idea of what it is to be excellent, not just at some particular skill or role (lawyer, carpenter, violin player), but at being a human being; and correspondingly, to have a notion of a bad or mediocre person. Also, they tend to think that excellence as a person involves caring about the good as the outlook conceives it. Most outlooks divide the excellence of a person into more specific features or traits: compassion, courage, justice.[9] Outlooks have overlapping concepts: Christianity and Aristotle both have concepts of justice, wisdom, courage, self-control, and gentleness. But Aristotelian justice differs from Christian justice: Jewish and Christian "justice" seems to include forgivingness and is for everybody, not just "important" people or fellow citizens. Aristotelian wisdom differs from Christian wisdom. Consider Paul's discussion of 'wisdom' in I Corinthians 1–2, and the "detail" of Christ's being crucified, which Paul says is foolishness to the "Greeks."

An assumption that seems common to all moral frameworks is that we reach our maturity by way of development. We don't spring fully formed, either physically or morally, from our mothers' wombs. We have to undergo (and undertake) a process by which we go from having a potential for living well to actually living well. And that's a process of change *in us*. We require certain conditions in the physical

[8] Seneca's *On Favors* (or *On Benefits*), a long treatise on generosity and gratitude, is in my opinion one of the great works on the topic in the history of ethics. Since the book is largely about the joy of giving and receiving finite benefits, it's hard to detect the Stoicism in it. But at least apatheia would protect a person from the Aristotelian concern to beat out the competitor at beneficence and the consequent grief at being a helpless beneficiary.

[9] In *Protagoras*, Socrates tries to buck this trend by arguing that all virtue is wisdom: "virtue is one."

and social environment, and also have to contribute our own action, effort, and attention to reach full formation as human beings. This will be true of Aristotelians, Christians, Stoics, and many others. Most of us get part way there, perhaps, but most of us fall short of the full realization of the goal. Given the kinks in our formation, we don't live as well as we might.

Virtues and Concepts of Happiness

Though moral outlooks have different concepts of happiness, they tend to have *some* concept of well-being, maturity, happiness, shalom, peace, flourishing, success, eudaimonia, and so forth, and to associate it with having the virtues. Moral outlooks all seem to aim at happiness in a generic sense.

To the kind of goal that moral frameworks propose for us human beings, I have given a rather long list of possible names. Each of these carries different associations and will vary in reference depending on which moral framework is appealed to. We can add a couple of others. An ordinary human being who is flourishing Aristotle calls *eudaimōn* ['of good spirit'], but a god in ideal condition he calls *makarios* (blessed). This last is the same Greek word as in the biblical beatitudes (see Matt 5:1–11: the "beatitudes" or blessings). Thomas Aquinas uses the Latin *beatus* (blessed), where Aristotle uses *eudaimōn*. Several English translations of Aristotle's *Nicomachean Ethics* use the word 'happiness,' but they sometimes simply adopt 'eudaimonia' as an English word, because 'happiness' can be confusing in this context.

Let's think again about how we use the word 'happiness' in English. Five-year-old Isaiah got in a fight with his sister and was unhappy for a few minutes, but then his Oma found him some chewing gum and he's been happy for the last while. This is a natural way to use 'happy' in English; in fact, it's probably the main way we use the word. 'Unhappy' is shorthand for more specific states like sad, frustrated, angry, anxious, disappointed, grieving, in despair, and so forth. In this sense, happiness is a state of feeling good—or at least of not feeling the distress of anger, frustration, anxiety, disappointment, or whatever. Somebody gave the drunk a $5 bill, and he's now sitting on the curb happily drinking his cheap wine; he'll be sorry when it's gone, but he's happy at the moment. I submit, however, that we wouldn't say he has a happy *life*, or that he is a happy *person* (or is happy *as a person*, or *as a human being*). He's "happy" at the moment, but his life is miserable; he's an unhappy human being.

With this last sense of 'happy,' as qualifying a whole person or a life, we're entering virtue ethics territory. It's natural to speculate that the drunk's troubles may go back to problems in his character. Did he lack courage or perseverance or self-control at crucial earlier turning points? Did he have a problem with making and keeping healthy relationships? Was he unreliable in the workplace? Was he an unforgiving or unfaithful spouse? Did he tend to alienate his friends and colleagues because of his self-centeredness and ungenerous inflexibility and unwillingness to forbear others' flaws, or tend to injure them because of his invidious competitiveness? Isaiah is happy with his chewing gum, but the jury is still out on whether he'll have a happy life. And if he does have a happy life, according to the kind of ethical thinking we find in Aristotle and Psalm 1 and the New Testament, a large part of the explanation will be that he developed the kind of concerned thinking and thoughtful concerns characteristic of generosity, compassion, justice, truthfulness, gratitude, and the like, and the kind of self-management powers that make up self-control, perseverance, patience, and courage. And that he was reasonably humble—was not much given to envy, domination, arrogance, and vanity.

These virtues have a variety of connections with human happiness, flourishing, well-being, blessedness, or whatever you wish to call it. Perhaps the most important is social: As the apostle Paul so often stresses, a Christian virtue of love, as well as all its variants or consequences such as patience, forbearance, humility, compassion, generosity, and forgivingness, make it possible for us to live together in friendships, fellowships, work relationships, neighborhoods, and most importantly marriages and families, and to do so with grace and joy. And such living makes for a happy life. It stands to reason, therefore, that all these virtues are friends of the happy life, and the social disabilities are associated with the vices contrary to these virtues—Paul mentions selfish ambition, conceit (Phil 2:3); covetousness, malice, envy, murder, strife, deceit, craftiness, gossip, slander, hatred of God, insolence, haughtiness, boastfulness, invention of evil, rebelliousness toward parents, foolishness, faithlessness, heartlessness, ruthlessness (Gal 5:26; Rom 1:29–30); cursing, haughtiness, repaying evil for evil (Rom 12:14–19); fornication, impurity, passion, evil desire, and greed (which is idolatry), anger, wrath, malice, slander, abusive language, lying (Col 3:5–9); impurity, licentiousness, idolatry, sorcery, enmities, strife, jealousy, anger, quarrels, dissensions, factions, envy, drunkenness, carousing, and things like these (Gal 5:19–21). All of these vices, attitudes, emotions, actions, and ways of relating to one another make for personal unhappiness and the misery of the people whose lives our lives touch.

We have distinguished episodic personal states such as feelings, impulses, actions, and perceptions from dispositional personal traits. A feeling of compassion or a compassionate action is not the same as the virtue of compassion. The virtues are dispositions, not episodes of action, impulse, or emotion. Such episodes arise out of the virtues and express the virtues, but they are not virtues. In a similar way, the happiness of a person or a life is a complex of the dispositions of the person, a readiness or tendency to do certain things and feel certain things in specific kinds of circumstances, rather than the actual doing or feeling of those things.

What the happy person feels as a result of her virtues are not always "happy" feelings. Even in her griefs and regrets, the happy person can express her well-being, her flourishing, her maturity. Paul's anxiety about the churches and his grief at the Jewish resistance to the gospel are as much indications of his well-being as the joy he takes in the friendship of the Philippian church. This is because, according to the Christian framework, to love what is good is at the center of virtue, and such love brings pain when frustrated, as it often is in this present, ailing world. The well-formed Christian not only rejoices with those who rejoice, but weeps with those who weep (and weeps at those who cause the weeping of those who weep). When a compassionate Christian looks at the destruction, disruption, and pain that the Russian army inflicted on Ukraine starting in early 2022, she feels emotional pain. Like the Samaritan seeing the wounded man in the ditch, she feels a "wrenching in the gut." The experience is not a "happy" one, even though compassion, as the virtue from which her emotion arises, is an aspect and condition of her happiness as a person and the happiness of those whose lives are touched by her mind and actions.

Ethical Outlooks and Ethical Theories

In Chapters 1 and 3, we were preoccupied with ethical theories as a form that philosophical ethics can take, and with what differentiates the various theories from one another. The theorists pretty much agree that any ethical theory has to have a place for "the good," "the right," "obligation," "virtue(s)," "contracts," or "promises," and perhaps a few other items. And each assumes that its chosen foundation is univocal in meaning. Practical rationality, for the Kantian, purports to be what any reasonable person would regard as human rationality; happiness (the good), for the utilitarian, purports to be a state that everybody should be able to agree is human happiness. The differences among the theories are their claims about which part of the ethical conceptual array is the foundation for the rest of the parts. The difference is supposedly not so much in the elements as in the way the elements are "arranged," to use John Rawls's word.

The concept of an ethical framework may seem similar to that of a theory, but I want to distinguish them sharply. No such simple answer as the one about the arrangement of the concepts will tell you the differences among Stoics, Epicureans, Cynics, Skeptics, Platonists, Aristotelians, Jews, Muslims, Buddhists, Hindus, Sikhs, and Christians. These are not ethical theories in the way the modern theories are; they are more or less complete ethical frameworks or "worldviews." They embody alternative, though often overlapping, understandings of what we humans are and the nature of the world we inhabit (for example, whether reality is deterministic, whether God exists, and if so, what God is like, the place of autonomy or dependency in fulfillment, the specific grammars of the particular virtues, and so forth). Outlooks don't differ by which element is foundational for the rest, because they don't have a foundationalist form. Instead, they differ in what the elements are. For example, Stoicism places at its center the idea of the universe as a system of causes; for Aristotle, the city-state is a crucial element; and Christianity has at its center an atoning death and a community that is the risen body of the One who died, animated by His spirit. These frameworks have different conceptions of the good: For the Stoics, it is the harmoniously structured system of causes and effects and the minds (god's and ours) that can grasp it. For Aristotelians, it's the life of civic virtue pursued in a well-constituted city-state. For the Christian, it's life in a social order of peace ruled by God. Stoics, Aristotelians, Christians, Muslims, and Platonists have different concepts of God, and the different concepts of God function in different ways in the lives of the persons who occupy the outlooks. Aristotelians and Stoics don't worship or obey God, but Jews and Christians and Muslims and Socrates do.

Access to One's Ethical Framework

How do we get access to the moral framework in which we seek to be complete human beings? This may seem an odd question: If a framework is *ours*, then surely it's "in our bones," isn't it? It's *our* way of thinking ethically, and surely we must know it perfectly well. So there can be no question about our access to it. But the word 'ours' is ambiguous here. An outlook can be ours in the sense that it is the prescribed outlook of our community, while we as individuals are less than clear about how the framework goes: the nature of the virtues it prescribes, the kind of happiness it offers, our own nature and the nature of our fellow human beings, and the nature of the world into which we need to fit, as they are seen in our framework.

In Aristotle's discussion of eudaimonia (his version of happiness or well-being), he says that everybody seeks happiness, but many don't know what it is (NE 1.4, 1195a14–30). Some wrongly think that eudaimonia is being wealthy; others that it is indulgence in physical pleasures. In fact, the whole of *Nicomachean Ethics*, which ranges over such topics as pleasure, action, pathos, courage, justice, temperance, wisdom, philosophical contemplation, and friendship, is about eudaimonia—the good life for human beings. He seems to be suggesting that it takes all that subtle discussion to make eudaimonia really clear—to people who share the very framework that he's expounding!

Aristotle says that, though everybody aims at eudaimonia in some sense, if people don't know what it is, they'll miss the target. And he formulates *Nicomachean Ethics* so that people will know what to aim at, and thus how to aim at it. The knowledge of eudaimonia is nothing less than a formulation of Aristotelian ethical wisdom. *Nicomachean Ethics* is an example of what I call philosophical exploration of the good life for human beings. Philosophical exploration is an important kind of access to a moral outlook. It brings out features of the moral outlook that can't otherwise be brought out.

Church people share the Christian ethical framework. But I think many church people are as much in the dark about the exact nature of that framework as the people for whom Aristotle wrote *Nicomachean Ethics* were about *their* own framework. If we often hear good biblical preaching and regularly study scripture and theology, we will be well informed, but even in that rare case, many questions of a philosophical kind about the good life by Christian lights will remain unasked and unanswered. If so, then to some extent our access to our own ethical framework will remain blocked. There will be important things we don't understand about it. And even if we're pretty enlightened about our framework, we may find room for improvement, and specifically room for improvement *by philosophy*. Philosophy has its own special light to shine on the ethical life, as I hope we will see clearly in the next three chapters. Wisdom admits of degrees. A person can be *more* or *less* wise than he used to be; one person can be wis*er* than another. But only God is *absolutely* wise—as wise as possible. If the purpose of virtue ethics is growth in ethical wisdom, we can all profit from thinking philosophically about the good life.

Like *Nicomachean Ethics*, Christian virtue ethics will be a philosophical exploration of the good life for human beings—an exploration of the Christian framework. But how do we get at the Christian framework? If we were immersed in a church where it was perfectly reflected in action, emotion, and thought, then perhaps morally and intellectually mature members of the community could just consult their intuitions about what the moral framework is. The framework would be the structure of their minds, of their thought, feelings, and motivation. Sometimes an individual like this emerges, but unfortunately, our communities are not usually entirely well-formed. We can't presuppose that we already think in such a perfectly wise Christian way that we need only consult our own intuitions, ones we have picked up over the years in sharing the life of the church, breathing in the pure breath of the Holy Spirit. To all of us, I dare say, the Christian conceptuality is to some degree alien and needs to be intentionally adopted, studied, and constantly re-adopted, continuously appropriated. We need to be constantly correcting and refining our moral intuitions and responses. This is a place of the virtue of self-control in Christian ethics and a way that self-control interacts with the virtue of wisdom in the activity of Christian virtue ethics.

Our moral framework has been revealed to us by God, and the record of that revelation is in the Bible, especially the New Testament. For this reason, we constantly check our intuitions against what the Bible says they should be (and would be if we were perfectly catechized). So there are two senses of 'have access' to the Christian framework: (1) the understanding or fitness of an individual in knowledge of the framework and (2) the resource from which that fitness can be derived. In the first sense of "have access," we have access to the Christian framework to the extent that we have the Christian virtues, and thus Christian wisdom. In the second case, we have access to our moral framework through careful study of the Bible and the discourse (theology, interpretation, literature, teaching, and other sources) that reflect biblical thought. Virtue ethics is nevertheless a *philosophical* practice. It goes beyond consulting texts that mention virtues and the practices they enable (and in which they are learned) and attempts to dig helpfully into their inner nature and peculiarities. It reads the Bible, but it does so with philosophical questions. Here are some examples of philosophical questions about the Christian moral framework that are not to be answered by simply consulting the Bible or teaching about the Bible:

—What are the kinds of traits? And how do they work? What does each contribute to the overall good life?

—Which virtues are "defined" by their motivation (the reasons for acting on them or for the emotions they engender), and which ones are "defined" in some other way?

—What aspect(s) of excellent human functioning does this or that virtue enable? For example, what kind of trait is wisdom? If it's a kind of knowledge, what kind is it, and how is it related to other kinds of knowledge? How is wisdom related to such other virtues as compassion, self-control, and truthfulness?

—What does the fact that such-and-such a trait is a virtue imply about what we take human well-being to be?

—What is the "grammar" or conceptual outline of this or that virtue, for example, generosity or self-control? That is, what is its affective, motivational, and thought-structure and relation to the other virtues in these regards?

—What are the kinds of situations that elicit, say, a wise person's generosity, compassion, or self-control? What are the characteristic expressions of this or that virtue?

—How is this or that vice related to specific virtues?

—How do the Christian virtues resemble and differ from their counterparts in other frameworks? How does Christian compassion differ from secular compassion?

—How does the distinctiveness of the framework make for the distinctiveness of the various Christian virtues?

—Why are forgivingness, gratitude, and humility absent from Aristotle's list of virtues? What is it about his framework that makes these virtues unwelcome, and what makes other frameworks receptive to these virtues? Is there a Christian counterpart of the Aristotelian good of self-sufficiency?

—How does this or that virtue support other virtues, and how do other virtues support it? For example, how are compassion and forgivingness related to love? to wisdom? to humility? to self-control?

—Given that virtues are interrelated and interdependent, what makes for their differentiation from one another, their "individuation," each one's deserving a name of its own?

—How is character constituted of the virtues? (In this or that outlook? In general?)

The above is just a sampling of possible philosophical questions.

Conclusion

In this chapter, I have tried to develop and clarify the idea of an ethical framework as a conception of human nature in its setting in the world (reality, the universe, being, society). Ethical frameworks, it seems, are perpetually contestable, partly because the nature of reality and human nature are perpetually contestable. The idea of a virtue (an excellence of character) is set within that of an ethical framework, inasmuch as the framework lays down what it is to be an excellent specimen of one's kind, and a virtue is an aspect or dimension of such excellence. All the virtues taken together and interlocking with one another constitute excellent character. Different frameworks yield different sets of virtues and thus different ideals of character. Christianity is a rich ethical framework and yields a specific and unique set of virtues.

In the next chapters, we'll look at the psychological constitution of the virtues, the different kinds of virtues, and how they interlock in Christian character. We'll consider how the virtues are related to the law as God has promulgated it, and the role of philosophy (and thus of Christian virtue ethics) as a discipline of moral formation.

6

The Psychology of Character

Introduction: The Psychological Composition of Virtues

We've reflected about ethical frameworks, how they imply sets of virtues, how they differ from one another, and how they're related to human happiness. We've distinguished them from ethical theories. We've considered how we access them. We've considered philosophy as an important means of access to our ethical framework. In the present chapter, we will go a little deeper into the nature of moral character and the virtues of which character is made up by reflecting about the psychological elements of character—thoughts, concerns, powers, and the indwelling of other minds.

Let's review as a way of moving ahead. Virtues are good features (traits, qualities) of a person as a past and ongoing being. They aren't momentary and passing states of the person, like dizziness or euphoria or an emotion like anger or fear or gratitude. Nor are they performances of any kind. The virtuous person acts virtuously, but her good actions are a different kind of thing: *expressions* of virtues, but not virtues themselves. Virtues are more or less permanent traits (qualities, dispositions) of the person. If you're a kind person, you'll be kind whether asleep or awake, whether you're having intercourse with your spouse or giving a speech at a political rally or disciplining your child. If you're a courageous person, you'll be courageous whether or not you're currently *doing* anything courageously. Your kindness may be expressed in actions like having intercourse or giving a speech or dealing with your child's waywardness, as well as in emotions like feeling good about another person's pleasure or success or hoping for his future success. If you don't really feel much like having intercourse, but do so because it will please your spouse, your action may express your kindness and generosity; and if, in giving that political speech, you risk your safety or peer acceptance by speaking a truth, the speech

Virtue Ethics. Robert Campbell Roberts, Oxford University Press.
© Robert Campbell Roberts 2026. DOI: 10.1093/9780197848005.003.0009

may be an act of courage, as well as an act of truthfulness. An action is kind if and only if it's motivated in a certain way, and an action is courageous if and only if it's knowingly performed in the face of some threat. Thus, different kinds of considerations determine that an action is kind than determine whether an action is courageous. Kindness is not just a different virtue from courage, but a different kind of virtue, as I'll try to show. But both are excellent traits of a person.

Most virtuous actions are virtuous in more than one way. The courageous action of risking your own job by standing up for a poor person's rights will just as much express your virtue of justice. And that act of justice may be compassionate, as motivated by your compassion for the person you defend. When we call the action courageous or just or compassionate, we're picking out dimensions of the action, probably because a dimension is especially prominent or we want to call special attention to it. In the case of justice and compassion, each of the virtues supplies a different reason for the action: justice because it's just for the poor person's rights to be honored and would be unjust if they weren't, and compassion because the violation of his rights might occasion his suffering. By contrast, what makes the action courageous is not a reason for which it was performed, but the fact that it was performed in a situation that was threatening in some way, you were aware of the threat, and the scariness of the situation didn't deter you from acting. As far as I know, there's no limit to the number of virtuous dimensions that an action can have.

I don't think you have to have a perfect track record to have a virtue. Our virtues have limits and are sometimes "specialized" for certain kinds of situations. For example, you might care quite a bit about justice, and yet in some circumstances be tempted to cut corners on it; or you might be a courageous person where the threat is social, but fear heights to the extent of being paralyzed by them.[1] We are merely

---

[1] Robert Adams, *A Theory of Virtue: Excellence in Being for the Good* (Oxford: Oxford University Press, 2009), supports this opinion, but Christian Miller, *Moral Character: An Empirical Theory* (Oxford: Oxford University Press, 2013), disagrees. The issue is discussed in the literature on "situationism," and both Adams and Miller are contributors to that discussion. I have assessed situationism in the light of the New Testament concept of the heart in "Situationism and the New Testament Psychology of the Heart," in *The Bible and the University*, ed. David Lyle Jeffrey (Paternoster Press [2008] and Grand Rapids: Zondervan [2007]), 139–160.

human, and just as our physical strength has limitations even though we may be very strong, so our character traits have limitations even though we may be known for our virtues.

Your height and the color of your skin are also traits or features or qualities, but they aren't the kind of trait that virtues are. If you're physically strong, we can attribute that quality to the muscles and bones, and a physiologist can say which qualities of the muscles and bones make for your strength. Again, if you have the attribute of health, we can attribute it to your circulatory system or your immune system, or whatever part is in question. Health and strength and height and skin color have "locations" that we can identify. But what kind of trait is a virtue? Broadly speaking, character traits—virtues and vices—are psychological, not physical traits, though they are certainly related to the brain, and in some sense may be, or be loosely correlated with, brain "states," maybe networks of neurological connections. But can we be more helpfully specific? Psychologically speaking, what are virtues composed of? What specific psychological dimensions of us have to be excellent for them to be virtuous and to warrant attributing virtues to us?

I propose that moral character is composed of *concerns*, *powers* (abilities), *thoughts* (understanding), and *"fellowship"* (communion: your mind harboring other minds by way of "being with" or "incorporating" them). The traits, or specific dimensions of this character, will be adaptations to typical features of a human life— adaptations by concern, thought, powers, and incorporation of others' minds. If these adaptations are good and proper, they'll be virtues.

Concerns, thoughts, and incorporations of others' minds can also comprise vices, which are bad adaptations to typical features of a human life. That is, our vices are evil thoughts and concerns, and the possession of our minds by evil spirits (including, but perhaps not limited to, bad people). I will argue that abilities can't be bad or evil. They can, of course, be weak, that is, smallish as abilities; and if they are strong, they can be misused for evil; but taken just in themselves, the very fact that they are abilities—capabilities—gives them a kind of goodness (not a directly moral kind).

The thoughts that constitute virtues and vices are not just ideas that flit across our minds at one time or another. Instead, they are what we might call entrenched understandings—rooted ways of thinking about ourselves, the world, and our fellow human beings by which we make sense of ourselves, our world, and our fellow human beings. Of course, in the case of the vices, the thoughts, concerns, and being possessed by others' minds don't constitute understanding proper— real or true understanding. I assume that real understanding at least approximates the truth. But vices do constitute *an* understanding, *a* way of construing and making sense of the world, however unrealistic and confused the understanding may be. As traits, cruelty and vengeance are understandings of the good. For example, that it is good for me to get revenge on my enemies for ways in which they have harmed me or deprived me of the good as I see it. Examples of evil thoughts and concerns, by Christian lights, are the vices of pride, greed, vengeance, and the hatred of individuals and groups (race, gender, ethnicity, nation, and so forth).

Let's consider what each of these four things is and the contribution that each makes as an ingredient of the virtues.

Concerns

A concern is a caring, a desire, a love. Concerns can be momentary (a craving, an impulse, an interest that arises in you for a time and then goes away). But to be a virtue or vice, a caring must be a quality of the person. It will be a concern that belongs to a person's general psychological profile, her character. She's concerned for truth, for other people's well-being, for the physical environment, for justice, for doing her duty, for peace, and so forth. In short, a virtuous person cares about the good. These concerns for good things "define" her in a way. They are who she is. They are her truth, and she is true to them.

She is reliably moved by those considerations. Though such a virtue isn't itself a momentary desire, given the right trigger, it will give rise to desires of the moment. For example, if what you love is absent, your concern can be manifested in a felt longing for it, an emotion-laden preoccupation with it. In a world that can seem hopelessly out of joint morally, happy are those who hunger and thirst for righteousness, even if what they feel in the moment is frustration. Also, we actively seek what we care about, whether this be money, fame, crafting skills, or the kingdom of God. What we care about is our "treasure": Where our treasure is, there will our heart (mind) be also (Matt 6:21). So a virtuous concern can be manifested in seeking: Seek first the kingdom of God (Matt 6:33). What we treasure gives us pleasure when our concern is satisfied. As Aristotle comments,

> to each . . . that which he is said to be a lover of is pleasant; e.g. not only is a horse pleasant to the lover of horses, and a spectacle to the lover of sights, but also in the same way just acts are pleasant to the lover of justice and in general virtuous acts to the lover of virtue. (NE 1.8.10, 1099a8–12)

Being a lover of horses isn't a matter of the moment, but a continuity, the make-up, the identity, the psychological profile, of a person. Yet a concern of this kind manifests itself in emotions. If you love horses, your emotions (positive *and* negative) will be tied up with seeing, owning, nurturing, riding, propagating horses. When a beautiful foal is born, you rejoice; when one of your horses is sick, you become anxious. The lover of the good likewise takes joy in things that are good, like just laws and rectification of injustices, and the well-being of people more generally: peace, healing, virtue, and real successes of all kinds. But the same love of good evokes distress when the good is opposed and frustrated by conflict, harm, vice, and real failures of all kinds.

When the good Samaritan sees the injured man in the ditch, he feels a painful emotion that we call compassion, an emotion he wouldn't feel if he didn't care about the man in the ditch. And his concern manifests itself in actions: Because he cares, he patches the man up as best he can and generously takes him to a place of refuge where he can be further cared for. He does so at his own expense. He has the virtue of love for people. Apparently, he is seeking the kingdom of God: It's his treasure. He finds a bit of it in the comfort and recovery of this man in the ditch. This seeking, this treasuring, amounts to the virtues of compassion and generosity. Love—for God, for fellow human beings, for the creation more generally, and for the renewed creation that God has promised in Christ—is the basic virtue in the Christian framework. If your concerns are good (and rightly ordered[2]), *you* are also good; to the extent that your concerns are bad (vengeance, greed, pride, selfish ambition) or not good (only for things of indifferent value), you are bad or not good. In general, good character consists in truly good things mattering to us; and bad character consists in bad things (vengeance, invidious put-downs, destruction of competitors) mattering to us or good things (justice, well-being of fellow human beings) not mattering to us, or relatively unimportant things like money and fame and power and immediate pleasures mattering to us so much that better things are neglected or destroyed.

Thoughts and Understanding

We don't think much about things that don't matter to us in any way. If we're required, somehow, to think about things that don't matter to us, we need to use self-control to keep our minds on task, and this may involve finding some way to make the thing that doesn't matter to us matter to us, say, by considering the distasteful consequences of *not* thinking about this thing that doesn't matter to us. On the other hand, it comes naturally to us to think about the good fortunes and misfortunes of what we do care about. In fact, if we want to know what we care about, we do well to ask ourselves what we think about a lot. Whatever "occupies our minds" is probably what we care about—or is instrumental to or a threat to what we care about.

It also works the other way around: We can't care about something without having some thoughts about it. To care about something, we have to understand it in such a way that it seems valuable to us. Caring is always *about* something, and for our caring to have an "object," our minds have to be set on it. Try to imagine caring about your hobby, but never having any thoughts about it—never bringing it or anything connected with it to mind, never paying it any attention. Only by our thinking is it possible for our caring to be about something.

---

[2] I thank a reader for Oxford University Press for suggesting this qualification.

And the value of what we care about determines the value—positive or negative—of our caring.

Consider the Christian virtue of joy (Gal 5:22). Joy as an emotion can be about a great diversity of things, including both trivial and bad things. You can take joy in baubles, and there is also schadenfreude, which is joy in somebody's misfortune. But the Christian *virtue* of joy takes as its object what is most worthy of joy. As we pray in the Collect for the 5th Sunday of Lent, "Grant your people grace to love what you command and desire what you promise; that, among the swift and varied changes of the world, our hearts may surely there be fixed where true joys are to be found."[3] The "fixing" of the heart on something truly worthy to be cared about and desired requires thinking about it, paying attention to it, and doing so in a "fixed" (established, unremitting, regular) way. The Christian virtue of joy has a particular and encompassing object: the promised kingdom of God, in which all is (will be) peace and wellness and righteousness (justice, the rightness of things) and generosity and the honoring of God and his creatures, especially his human creatures. So far, this joy is hope. But the Christian also rejoices in present indications and instances and anticipations of that kingdom, and in remembering past faithfulness. In rejoicing in this object, in feeling it to be beautiful and excellent and worth celebrating again and again, Christians show what they value, what they care about, what preoccupies them, where their heart is.

The Christian virtue of joy illustrates how virtues are kinds of caring or loving (in a broad sense); but it also illustrates how the Christian virtues are a matter of thinking: The thinking focuses the caring; it fixes the heart and mind on what you care about. So we can't really care about anything without understanding it in some way or other.

It also illustrates, as the Collect suggests, the importance of truth in such thinking and understanding: In matters having to do with evaluation, at least, we don't understand unless we *care correctly* about the object of understanding. If the object is deplorable (for example,

---

[3] *The Book of Common Prayer* (New York: The Church Pension Fund, 1928), 219, https://www.bcponline.org.

Russia's attack on Ukraine in early 2022), its deplorability needs to be registered in the understanding. That is, it needs to be appreciated *as* deplorable—rightly *felt* to be deplorable—for example, by the emotion of horror. If you don't feel bad about Russia's attack on Ukraine, there's something you're not "getting."

I HAVE A BEAN is a coffee roaster in Wheaton, Illinois. The company is dedicated not only to excellent coffee but also to employing people emerging from prison who would have a hard time finding employment. Its idea is to help people get their lives back together after prison and live good lives. An onlooker might understand the company in the sense that she can tell you how it works. She understands how it acquires and roasts its bean, and how it trains its staff. She sees that it provides interesting work and income for people who might be regarded with suspicion by other employers. It provides training in useful skills. Our onlooker sees how you apply for a job, what the interview process entails, and so forth. She "understands" I HAVE A BEAN, but she isn't especially glad that it exists. So she fails to understand I HAVE A BEAN. There's something important she doesn't "get." In its ethical dimension, she can't be said to understand I HAVE A BEAN unless she sees the glory in it, the beauty, the excellence, the worthiness. Joy is this part of understanding.

This is true in ethics, broadly speaking. In virtue ethics, whose aim is to understand the good life and the virtues that support it, it is important that the philosopher be growing in his or her emotional appreciation of the virtues and of virtuous actions and passions, and thus of the surpassing value of a good human life. Otherwise, the philosopher will suffer from a deficiency of ethical understanding. It will be a philosophical deficiency because it will be a deficiency of wisdom. Emotional sensitivity to the virtues and vices is essential to understanding them and is itself an expression of the virtues the philosopher is seeking to understand and of the wisdom the philosopher needs as she seeks further wisdom.

Testimonies to the intimate connection between thoughts and love (desire) in the working of the human spirit are found in both pagan and Christian philosophy. Aristotle notes that virtues are dispositions to make good choices, and in choice-making, thought (reason, understanding) and desire are integrated:

> Since moral virtue is a state of character concerned with choice, and choice is **deliberate desire**, therefore both the reasoning must be true and the desire right, if the choice is to be good, and the latter must pursue just what the former asserts. . . . Hence choice is either **desiderative reason** or[4] **ratiocinative desire**, and such an origin of action is a human being. (*Nicomachean Ethics* 6.2.2, 1139a23–26; 6.2.5, 1139b5–6, p. 139 Ross, slightly altered)

When Aristotle speaks of deliberate desire, he is talking about desire that results from deliberation. Deliberation is thinking about what to do. It is a desire for something where the desire has resulted from thinking through the options. For example, if you are trying to decide which kind of computer to buy, you might consider your various needs and desires, and how well the various computer models would satisfy them. After this comparative thinking or deliberation, you decide on a model that best satisfies your most important concerns. All this thinking is encompassed within, and guided by, your desire for a computer and your interest in the tasks you can accomplish with it. The Ross translation from which I quote, unlike some other translations, nicely reflects Aristotle's syntax in the expressions that I have put in bold. It suggests that the thinking and the desire are not separate mental actions but a synthesis of thought and desire. The thought is desirous and the desire is thought out. Aristotle's point is that for your choices to be consistently good and virtuous, you need to desire the right kinds of things (justice, the well-being of your city-state, the "noble," your own and your fellow citizens' eudaimonia) *and* you need to be able to think accurately about them—to know what they are and what it takes to get them. When the wise person makes a choice, it is that thought-through desire—a desire that is shaped and focused by accurate thought and a thinking that is soaked in virtuous desire.

Reasoning and desiring can come apart, and when they do, it can be a sign of immaturity. It's possible for the reasoning to lead in one direction without the original desire following it. I might be led, by correct reasoning, to the conclusion that I should, for some noble purpose,

---

[4] This 'or' is not disjunctive, but substitutive: It connects two alternative ways of saying the same thing.

take a job that pays less than I am now making. Perhaps, before I go through the reasoning process, I feel that I want to do whatever is the most noble thing; and let's say that that desire is a mark of true practical wisdom. But when I get to the conclusion, my desire doesn't match my reasoning: I resist the conclusion because I like money too much. In this case, no matter how good a "reasoner" I am, I don't exemplify practical wisdom, because my desires (or perhaps we should say "desires") don't follow my reasoning. The root of my problem seems to be that I care too much about money and too little about noble ends. Here, the reasoning, and my failure to follow it, may reveal something about my character: I think I want to live a noble life, and so start reasoning apparently guided by that end, and then the reasoning reveals to me that I didn't actually desire sufficiently to live a noble life. When I see the entailments of what I took to be my desire, they (and my reaction to them) reveal to me that it was actually not my desire, or that the feeling of the desire was abstract and unrealistic. This mismatch between concern and thought is a sign that I'm not yet perfectly virtuous.

Another scenario, perhaps more common, is that if my logical acuity permits it, I see the conclusion coming and abort the reasoning or divert or distort it in some way by rationalization. Perhaps I say to myself, "So-called noble desires are really just hidden forms of selfishness anyway, and so keeping my lavish income is morally on a par with taking the more 'sacrificial' job." Or maybe I say to myself, "I already make a lot of sacrifices in my current job. I'm the only one in the department who makes arrangements for outside speakers. I need to start caring for myself more, and I think I'll start by not considering this current offer." Thus, just as faulty reasoning can lead good desires to the wrong conclusion, immature desires can short-circuit the reasoning. Desires direct thought, *and* thought directs desires.

Christians, too, who think about spiritual character, have emphasized the intimacy between thought and desire in the life of virtues. Elder Thaddeus of Vitovnica was a wise monk in twentieth-century Serbia. His biographers note that

> Fr. Thaddeus tirelessly taught all the Christian men and women who came to him at Vitovnica the truth of the centuries-old experience of the Church—so easily forgotten and ignored in our day and

age—that man is a creature of energy and thought, a being of noetic energies. He taught that most of the thoughts which torment us
from the inside are not ours at all, but come from the demons, that
every one of us has the God-given power and freedom to refuse such
thoughts, and that our lives depend on the quality of the thoughts we
nurture in our minds and hearts.[5]

This report about Fr. Thaddeus's teaching touches helpfully on all
four of the elements of virtue: concerns, thoughts, powers, and the incorporation of other persons. But our present topic is concerns and
thoughts.

'Energies' here means motivating forces, and 'noetic' means having
to do with thoughts and understanding. Thus, "noetic energies"[6]
are thoughts that move us: the occupants of the mind that move us
to action and emotion, for better or worse. This is why it's important to think thoughts that direct us to the good. For example, well-
disciplined Christians think frequently about God's grace to the world
(and to themselves) in Jesus Christ. They turn their minds to the works
of holy people, people who have forgiven us some transgression, or
to acts of generosity or courage on behalf of the order of peace and
the community, or about the attitude of a friend who is able to see the
good in even the most wayward persons. We think about Dorothy
Day's ruthless practice of respect for the poor. Even thoughts about
evil can direct us to the good if they direct us *against* it (seeing the
evil *as* evil and so shunning it) or *despite* it (as in forgiveness), or as
attributed with sorrow to ourselves (as in repentance). But in these
cases, the thoughts about evil are oriented by morally good and healthy
thoughts: Thinking of the evil *as* evil implies setting one's mind on the
good to which the evil is contrary. And in forgiving him who has offended us, yes, we think of the offense, but we also think of how precious the offender is in God's sight. In his created beauty, the offender
is one of the "things of the spirit" (Rom 8). And in confession, we bring

---

[5] *Our Thoughts Determine Our Lives, The Life and Teachings of Monk Thaddeus of
Vitovnica*. Compiled by the St. Herman of Alaska Brotherhood, trans. Ana Smiljanic
(Platina, CA: St. Herman of Alaska Brotherhood Press, 2012), 46.

[6] Greek: *Energein* = to work, to be active. *Noēsis* = thought, intelligence.

our own evil and misery before God who is merciful and kind and learn to see ourselves as objects of God's love and concern, despite our waywardness. So this isn't just the power of positive thinking, which unrealistically ignores what isn't "positive." It's moral realism.

Psychological "energy" (desire, concern, drive) needs to be harnessed and directed. Thoughts are the harness and directors of the mind/heart, while its desires and loves are its energy. The virtuous Christian thinks healthy, virtuous, humanly worthy thoughts, while the vicious person has perverse thoughts, thoughts that direct the moving forces wrongly, contrary to the proper goal of human life, the life of the kingdom of God. For example, the vices of pride are concerns ("energies") that are structured by such misdirected thoughts. Here are four of them:

> *Domination*: I am important if I dominate other people and am diminished if others dominate me.
>
> *Envy*: I am important to the extent that I am superior to others and unimportant to the extent that others are superior to me; life is a contest for superiority.
>
> *Arrogance*: I am important to the extent that I have privileges and entitlements that other people don't have; let me claim them, whether or not legitimately.
>
> *Vanity*: I am important to the extent that I am the object of other people's admiration and envy, and especially if I am more admired and envied than others.

Note that in each case, a concern—the concern to be important—is misdirected by a false conception of what it *is* to be important as a person. These false thoughts about personal importance corrupt us and make us miserable, even if we don't notice that we are miserable. Using the false standards, we may even rate ourselves as successful. If the concern to be important is directed wisely, it leads to good living; if it's directed perversely, it leads to destruction, disease, and death; though this may not be immediately apparent. More on the vices of pride in Chapter 11.

Practical wisdom, according to Aristotle, is a virtue that binds together all the other virtues. It is the interested understanding of the good life for human beings. To say that practical wisdom is "interested" is to say that the practically wise person cares about the good life, for himself and his community, as he understands it. He has a personal stake in it. He desires the good life; in his practices, he intentionally pursues it. It is of more than "academic" interest to him. If Aristotle, as a practically wise man, had identified the vices of pride as contrary to the good life (he didn't), he would have seen their eradication as a moral goal and would have undertaken to root them out of his life and the life of his community. This motivation would have been a consequence of his wisdom. A "wise" person who was not interested in rooting out the vices of pride would show a deficiency of understanding (an "intellectual" deficiency, a "blind spot," though of course not a complete blindness).

We might be tempted to think of mind and heart as two different faculties with distinct functions: The mind is the intellect and its functions are thoughts, reasoning, and understanding, while the heart is the faculty of desires, interests, concerns, and emotions. But the New Testament doesn't bear out such a division of our faculties.

On the "mind" side, the relevant words in Greek are *nous* (intellect, understanding), *logos* (thought, reasoning), *dialogismos* (a thought), *dokein* (think, suppose, consider, imagine), *dokimazein* (think something through, assess, test), *phronein* (think, reason), and a few times *enthumēsis*, and the cognates of all these terms; on the "heart" side, we have *kardia* (heart). But it turns out that the *kardia* has thoughts and the *nous* has concerns, interests, and desires. The "cognitive" and the "conative" functions of the mind don't belong to separate faculties yielding different kinds of mental events but are aspects of what we might call the "heart/mind." The yielded mental events can have both aspects at the same time, just as choice does, according to Aristotle. For example, Jesus responds to the scribes who mentally grumble about his readiness on the sabbath to heal a man with a withered hand. He says, "Why do you think (*enthumeisthe*) evil in your hearts?" (Matt 9:2). It is "from the human heart (*kardias*)," says Jesus, "that evil thoughts (*dialogismoi*) come: fornication, theft, murder, adultery, avarice, wickedness, deceit, licentiousness, envy, slander, pride, folly" (Mark 7:21–22, altered). Simeon foretells that the baby Jesus will reveal "the thoughts (*dialogismoi*) of many hearts" (Luke 2:34, NKJV).

In the passage from Mark's Gospel, the NRSV has 'intentions' where I have written 'thoughts.' My dictionary doesn't give 'intention' as a possible translation of *dialogismos*. The evil of the *dialogismoi* surely doesn't require that they rise to the level of intentions to act. It is sinful even to wish or fantasize the action: to contemplate it with pleasure and approval. I doubt that when Jesus says that whoever lusts after a woman has already committed adultery in his heart (*kardia*; Matt 5:28), he supposes that the man must actually intend to commit the act; and the same for murder. The man's evil thought might be: "What delicious fun it would be to do that, but of course I won't." I think that in translating *dialogismos* with 'intention,' the translators were rightly trying to capture the idea of the motivational engagement (the "energy") of the heart. But in doing so, they connect the evil of thoughts too closely to the evil of actions. This temptation could result from being in thrall to a philosophy of ethics that makes actions (rather than virtues and vices) the central focus. Even if it isn't a full-fledged intention, a bad *dialogismos* needs to be more than just a floating "thought." It needs to be soaked with desire.

The other way around, we have the "interestedness" of *nous*, *phronein*, *dokein*, and the other "cognition" words. Romans 8:5–6: "Those who exist in a fleshly manner set their minds (*phronoûsin*) on fleshly things; but those who exist in a spiritual manner set their minds (*phronoûsin*) on what is spiritual; for the fleshly mindset (*phronēma*) is death, but the spiritual mindset (*phronēma*) is life and peace." Each "mindset" is a way, not just of thinking, but of living, of being guided in life by such a way of thinking, and therefore being moved to act and feel accordingly. Romans 12:2: "Do not be conformed to this world, but be transformed by the renewing of your minds (*nous*), so that you may discern (*dokimazein*) what is the will of God—what is good and acceptable and perfect."[7] This verse and the six that follow it are about the Christian mind: how to *think* about oneself and the church, and how to be and become *discerning* about the will of God and what is

---

[7] Romans 8:27 "and the searcher of hearts (*kardiōn*) knows the mindset (*phronēma*) of the Spirit because he pleads for the saints in concert with God." (my trans.) When Paul says, "We have the mind of Christ" (I Cor 2:16), it wouldn't be right to translate, "We have Christ's intellect." To have the mind of Christ is also to have his heart. It is to have something of his wisdom, his integrated thinking and love, his practical intelligence.

truly good. But surely the good, if rightly apprehended, is an object of concern, of caring, of cherishing. It is, as Jesus says, a "treasure." So if it isn't seen as a treasure, it isn't properly discerned. For example, discernment about what is good for the church involves loving the church and so caring about what's good for it. A person who had perfect "thoughts" about self, fellow church members, God, and the world (maybe she was able to write a perfectly orthodox sermon about them), yet didn't care about them in the right way, wouldn't be discerning about the good. Maybe she deploys all this flawless thinking to build her reputation as a leading theologian or does it to fulfill the terms of a grant. What *she* treasures—reputation or the grant—is not the good by Christian lights. Her heart is blind to the truth about the good because her treasure isn't the real one. She talks well about discernment, let us say, but with defective understanding.

Powers

Being human comes with special abilities. We can think, and we can intentionally select what we think about. We can evaluate and approve or disapprove of our own beliefs, desires, and emotions. We can turn our attention to chosen objects and fix our attention on them; we can divert our attention from other objects, for moral reasons or other reasons. We can deliberate—engage in trains of reasoning that improve our decisions and actions. We can decide on courses of action. We can execute many of our decisions. When we get "good at" these abilities, and if we use them for the right purposes, they become an aspect of virtuous character. The abilities can be deployed as self-control, patience, steadfastness, courage, forbearance, and perseverance. This kind of virtue has had different names: "structural," "executive," "auxiliary," "virtues of willpower." Let's borrow a term from both Aristotle and the New Testament, the Greek word *enkrateia*, which just means "strength." Let's call these "the enkratic virtues." These powers are characteristic of us humans regardless of our moral outlook. Even the Stoics, who are determinists, acknowledge these human abilities, despite the fact that they seem to be powers of freedom. Powers like patience, perseverance, and courage become moral virtues to the extent that we deploy them within a moral framework and for moral purposes.

Father Thaddeus "taught that most of the [vicious] thoughts which torment us from the inside are not ours at all, but come from the demons, that every one of us has the God-given power and freedom to refuse such thoughts."[8] Some of us have a better record of refusing them than others, and a very few of us have refused them so regularly and for so long that the vicious thoughts don't constitute much of a challenge anymore. They've become feathery and fleeting. They float by without threatening damage. The serious Christian will regard sinful thoughts such as the vices of pride, temptations to cheat and deceive, vengeful impulses, episodes of lust and gluttony, impatience, discouragement, anger and irritation, fear and anxiety, obvious folly, and so forth, as alien to our true selves (see Rom 7:17). Clearly, these thoughts are not mere thoughts, but thoughts that give shape to concerns: They are thoughts that direct our concerns toward perverse and unhealthy objects. For example, if my concern is the kind that we call envy, then I am concerned about besting another person (my rival) in a contest for self-importance. My thought is: *Let me best this person, and so increase or maintain my importance.* That is the identity of my concern; the thought determines which concern it is. It is a concern to become or stay important in a certain vain way. Since such thoughts are not characteristic of our renewed selves, they are "not ours at all," and we are committed to "refusing" them. And the human abilities that I mentioned in the previous paragraph give us much power to do so. We can often snuff out, or at any rate disable, our perverse concerns.

How do we do it? We do it by turning off the thoughts that shape them—the thoughts that give their concerns their identity and seem to give them their point. Paul suggests that we turn off the thoughts that give sinful concerns their targets by "setting our minds on" (see Rom 8:4; Col 3:2, Phil 4:8) something incompatible with them. If people who are "in the flesh" set their minds on things that kill us morally, like the self-importance that envy cherishes, those who are in the spirit of Jesus set their minds on the things of the spirit—things like God's

---

[8] *Our Thoughts Determine Our Lives*, 46.

love in Christ for our "rival," things that are "above" like forgiveness, generosity, and compassion, examples of saints, the fact that every individual we meet, however corrupt or rough and threatening he may appear, is a precious and unique soul. We have this God-given power.

OK, so if we control our concerns by controlling our thoughts, how do we control our thoughts? Do we do so *by* doing something else? Yes, in part. Let's distinguish direct control of our thoughts from indirect control and say that both kinds belong to the abilities that we call the enkratic virtues. Attention is an essential part of thinking. Whenever you think about something, you're paying attention to it in a particular way. So we can say that our power to direct our attention intentionally and for a reason (including moral reasons) gives us direct control over our thoughts. For example, we can decide to think about a particular math problem and then set about doing it. We can decide to stop thinking about revenge against someone who has wronged us or stop thinking of someone as a rival and think instead about his well-being or his excellence as a creature of God. We can stop "comparison"-thinking and start thinking about another person as a fellow human being. And so forth. To change our thoughts about something is often not to pay no attention at all to it, but to stop paying attention to it in one way and start thinking about the same thing in another way. The thesis that this basic human ability to direct and fix our attention can become a virtue is that we can get good at controlling our attention, and thus our thoughts. It can become a form of self-control, a habitus of self-management, an intelligent and morally important ability.

So, one basic way to control our thoughts is to do so directly, by redirecting our attention. But we can do so indirectly as well—by doing something else that will cause our emotions and concerns to become better. A major indirect way to control our thoughts is to put ourselves in circumstances where we're more likely to have the good kind of thoughts and thoughts that will "refuse" the evil thoughts. For example, if we're being tempted sexually, we might pick up the phone and call our spouse. Or if we are tempted to cheat on our income tax, we might switch to an accountant we know to be scrupulous. Such strategies of situation change will tend to lead to setting our minds on the value of chastity or of honest dealing, and this change of mind-focus will tend to help us refuse the evil thoughts.

Thus, a certain practical wisdom is to be learned, a wisdom that serves virtues like self-control, patience, and courage. We learn how to manage impulses like lust, cheating, impatience, anger, and fear. As we exercise this wisdom, which is a kind of knowing our way around our motives, it becomes stronger, more skilled, and more second nature. And we will have grown in the virtues of self-management, the enkratic virtues.

Fr. Thaddeus says that most of our evil thoughts are not really our own but are planted there by demons (some of whom are no doubt living in our friends and colleagues). But Jesus observes that it's the evil thoughts that come from within the person's heart that defile him or her (Mark 7:20–23). Thaddeus says the evil thoughts are not our own, and Jesus says they come from within. Can we square these statements? I think we can, and that doing so will deepen our insight into the working of these vices and of the enkratic virtues.

The mere presence of a thought that would give a bad target to a concern or would cause a concern to be evil is not itself an "evil thought." If someone shows you how you can cheat on your taxes and you understand what he says, then you have the thought about cheating on your taxes, and the thought comes from your informant. Perhaps you work for the IRS and need to learn ways that people cheat on their taxes. So far, this thought doesn't come "from within" because it doesn't move your heart toward cheating on your taxes. You understand what cheating is and know how it's done but have no personal interest in doing it. The thought becomes evil only when it's taken to heart, not when it's merely understood (and so in *that* sense "taken in"). That a thought is taken to heart in this sense is perfectly compatible with Fr. Thaddeus's claim that most evil thoughts don't originate in the individual's mind but are contributed from outside.

In the course of daily reading, listening, and conversations, we have many thoughts that never come to be "within" us in the sense in which Jesus speaks. Many of them come from outside in the sense in which Thaddeus speaks. Such thoughts don't call for self-control or any other enkratic virtue. These virtues are needed only for thoughts that supply targets of bad motivation. And such thoughts get to be from within by our actively acquiescing in their attractions, letting them have their motivational way.

Think of the man lusting after the woman and so committing adultery with her in his heart. He could look away and turn his attention elsewhere, but he indulges himself and so *acts* with guilt, though he makes no move to touch her and doesn't intend to. Think of the man fantasizing revenge against his "enemy," cruelly indulging his delight in the thought of the other's agony, though he is afraid enough of the consequences of carrying out the fantasy to forswear resolutely to perform the action. And yet there *is* action: In both cases, we speak of "indulging" the fantasizing desire. Such self-indulgence is optional, and the opting for it comes from within. And it's the taking it to heart that makes it evil and defiling.

We can say something similar about virtuous thoughts like those of generosity, compassion, or forgiveness. Certain thoughts are constituent aspects of such virtues. Forgivingness, for example, is marked by such thoughts as that *I have been forgiven much*, that *all have sinned*, that *this offender is my brother or sister*, that *to forgive is to follow Jesus*, that *God has forgiven this person*, and so forth. If such an idea merely flits across your mind without getting any purchase on your heart, it won't constitute virtue, no matter how virtuous the thought may be in itself. The thought needs to move you by inspiring and shaping desire. And eventually, the desire needs to do this "habitually." To constitute a virtue, it needs to be, not just a one-off impulse at an odd moment, but characteristic of you. Your mind needs to be *set*[9] (Rom 8:5; Col 3:2) on the thoughts that shape the forgiving attitude. The thought needs to belong to a mindset. And setting our mind on such thoughts is something we *can do*.

Incorporation of Others' Minds

As constituents of our moral character, our concerns, thoughts, and powers can be affected for better or worse by our interaction with the

---

[9] We meet here an ambiguity in the notion of setting the mind. A single setting of the mind on something doesn't constitute having a mindset with respect to that thing. We have seen that Paul makes this distinction in Romans 8 by distinguishing *phronein* (the action of setting one's mind on) from *phronēma* (the psychological state that results from repeated or habitual *phronein*).

minds of fellow moral agents, and thus of their concerns, thoughts, and powers as properties of their persons.[10] We form mental constructs of our colleagues' minds, as we do of our own, and these constructs—these souls in our souls, as it were—look at us, so to speak, and we look at them, and they accompany us on the way. In fellowship with another, we are not merely "external" to one another. We are intuitive mind-readers. We participate in others' minds, and they participate in ours.

Most of us have experienced being inspired and built up morally by working alongside a virtuous colleague, mentor, friend, or fellow church member. We take in part of the "mind" of the other. It's a gradually built-up wholistic impression of the other, a sense, or perception, of the companion's character—his concerns, his ways of thinking about persons, relationships, and life, and his powers of self-mastery. If these dimensions together constitute a person's moral agency, then the impression we have of the companion, by way of our association, co-ordination, and co-action with this other person, becomes a breathing of the virtuous other's agency.[11] It's a person-infusing breathing, and not just a disinterested impression. We take it "in." Because we are concerned, we import its concerns. It inspires us. It blows into our heart, our moral identity, our self-respect. Our mind/heart and our abilities to recruit our moral powers are the better for it. Acting in concert with this virtuous other, we become, at least for the nonce, better than our usual selves—more compassionate, more generous, more patient, more courageous, more truthful, because the other's mind is present in our moral consciousness.

The effect is probably most powerful when the other person is currently interacting with us, but through memory, a residue of this presence can linger when the person is away or even dead. If the relationship is intense or has lasted a long time, it may have left a lasting

---

[10] In writing this section, I have profited from Steve Porter and Brandon Rickabaugh, "The Sanctifying Work of the Holy Spirit in Virtue Formation," in *Faith and Virtue Formation: Christian Philosophy in Aid of Becoming Good*, ed. Adam Pelser and Scott Cleveland (Oxford: Oxford University Press, 2021), 123–145.

[11] In imagination, we may even "consult" the other's mind, so to speak, the way we might consult a moral rule in deciding what to do. But even without explicit "consultation," the other's mind has bearing in our thoughts and decisions, just as we often follow rules without consulting them.

impression on our character. A few particular episodes of interaction may stand out as particularly formative for us. Communion with the other tilts what's already in us toward the good and away from evil. It steers us. But it can have that effect only if we're receptive. If our character is very bad, an inspiring person may not move us at all. Similarly, if we are already well formed, an evil character may find no inroad to our mind.

How does the other's character get access to our mind? We get a clear view of the other's mind by learning what the other cares about, what he does, how he feels about things, and the kind of adversities he has transcended. Much of this would be opaque to us if we didn't talk with one another about what we're doing and how and why we're doing it. Both elements—the doing and the talking—are important to the phenomenon of communion. We get into each other's minds by talking to one another as we act and by acting as we reveal our minds to one another. We don't get as far if we merely talk, not acting together; nor do we get as far if we merely act together, not talking. Why is acting together so important to our getting into each other's minds? I think it's because of the general importance of the engagement of action and the granularity that engagement in action requires of our understanding. It's also because the kind of thinking that engages is typically the kind that involves personal concern for what we are engaged with. Engagement can enhance concern for what engages.

To put the point another way, in intensive fellowship with someone who is morally out of our ordinary (for better *or* worse), we're subjected to a moral current that may take effort to resist, depending on where we are on the moral spectrum. If we don't resist it, either spontaneously (say, by way of disgust or fear) or with effort, it tends to carry us in its direction. If the person with whom we're fellowshipping is more virtuous than we, the current will tend to carry us to greater virtue if we don't resist it. "He's inspiring. I'm a better person when I work with him." If the associate is unusually bad, then the undertow will be away from virtue, and we will drift in vice's direction if we don't resist.

An uncle showed me some shoddy but superficially attractive work on some real estate he intended to flip. I commented that it wouldn't last very long. He said, "you sell it and then run like hell." I was not much more than a teenager at the time, but I thought, "What about the one who buys it?" If I had respected this uncle more, my mind would have been less inclined to put up this resistance. A recent public case is that of Rudolph Giuliani, mayor of New York City at the time of the 9/11 attacks. He was then admirable enough to become "America's mayor." But in close association with Donald Trump, his character degenerated, and his life became a disaster.[12] People ask, "What happened to Rudy?" Mark Shields once commented, in a rather mild expression, that all who get close to Trump are "diminished" (as human beings). When his inexplicably magnetic soul gets inside yours, it works havoc with your character, exploiting any weaknesses. For people with a compromised moral immune system, his corruption is virulently contagious. He's a super-spreader of moral infection.

So another natural human power, and one we didn't mention in the previous sections, is the power of reading and absorbing another's moral mind/heart through fellowship with that other. In fellowship, we share our minds with others. We exchange ideas. We act in concert. We explain our actions. We come to "see," in the other's contributions to the common action, the other's goals and understanding thereof, and we share those goals and feel them, feeling common pleasure in successes and frustrations in misadventures. We communicate our goals, our reasons for doing and feeling what we do and feel. Fr. Thaddeus speaks of evil thoughts that come from the demons, and he's optimistic about our ability to resist: "every one of us has the God-given power and freedom to refuse such thoughts, and . . . our lives depend on the quality of the thoughts we nurture in our minds and hearts." If we are in league with the demons, resisting the order of peace to which God has destined us—if our hearts and minds are bearing us along in their direction—then of course our resistance to those evil thoughts will be weak or nil. But if we've been nurtured and well established by the mind of the Spirit, cultivating the Spirit's thoughts by regular fellowship with him, then Fr. Thaddeus's optimism will apply to us.

Our language reflects the phenomenon of mental-moral intercourse. We speak of moral *influence* (the "flowing in" of one person's

---

[12] See the account by Caroline Giuliani in *Vanity Fair* for September 30, 2024.

mindset upon another's) and of drawing *inspiration* (breathing in another's spirit, his or her moral breath; we breathe in what the other breathes out). Our minds are permeable in the context of fellowship. The in-breathing and in-flowing are emotionally conditioned: We tend to breathe in the character of people we respect, love, and admire, and to resist the influence of people we find disgusting and appalling— or I should say, we resist *the imitative kind* of influence that we see affecting their devotees. Revulsion is also a kind of influence—or per- haps we should say, exfluence. We cough appalling spirits out. If by love we breathe some spirits into our character, by contempt we expel others from our minds, and so become confirmed in our virtuous contrariness. This too can be a positive contribution to our character, though I think it's a less important factor in our moral development.

Christians speak of the fellowship of the Holy Spirit (II Cor 13:14; Phil 2:1) and with Christ (I Cor 1:9) and with the Father and the Son (I John 1:3), of Christ being "in" us (Col 1:27) and being "in Christ" (Phil 4:7; II Cor 5:17), being "filled" with the Spirit (Eph 5:18), of having the mind (heart) of Christ (I Cor 3:16), and of "God's love [that] has been poured into our hearts through the Holy Spirit that has been given to us" (Rom 5:5). The Holy Spirit is the Spirit of Jesus Christ, and that Spirit has the traits of justice, respect, generosity, compassion, wisdom, humility, and forgivingness, among others. At Pentecost, the Holy Spirit of Jesus invaded and occupied the minds of the apostles and thus transformed them. We have fellowship with Christ and the Holy Spirit as we join him in worshipful, prayerful service ("liturgy" Greek: *latreia* [also *leitourgia*] = service, ministry, worship; see Rom 12:1) informed by knowledge of Jesus's ministry, both broadly under- stood and in particular stories of his work among us. We work along- side other Christians with whom we share and learn Christ's mind. We practice the fellowship of the Holy Spirit, being "of one mind" with the Holy Spirit. And this one Spirit, pervading the community, unifies the human community that is the church. The cases of congregational disunity that Paul deplores and addresses in some of his letters are all kinds of "disagreement" that come from inattention to God's mind, the Holy Spirit.

What is a spirit? When we speak of "a (particular) spirit," I think we refer to two things: (1) a spirit is a generalized *attitude* and thus

(2) a *subjectivity* (a "seat" of attitude(s)). Attitude here is a personal disposition toward (something): For example, a spirit of love, a spirit of compassion, a spirit of enmity, a spirit of rivalry, a spirit of suspicion. A spirit is not an act or any other kind of episode, but a disposition of a certain character that gives rise to acts, urges, emotions, and moods within the range set by the generalized attitude. But an attitude or set of attitudes must be "seated" or "located" somewhere, and the "where" must be some kind of mind or subjectivity—somebody or some group that *has* the attitude. Only a spirit can have a spirit.

The seat of subjectivity can be individual or communal. A political administration can have an attitude: a pragmatic spirit, a divisive spirit, a domineering spirit, a defensive spirit, or a compassionate spirit. A church can have an attitude (say, of warm welcome or of aloofness); a mob can have an attitude or spirit (we speak of an "angry" or "vengeful" mob). A spirit is a contagious moral character. A person who isn't angry may acquire an angry spirit by joining an angry mob. In Greek (*pneuma*), Hebrew (*ruach*), Latin (*espiritu*), and English, 'spirit' is associated etymologically with breath, and therefore with a living being. That breath is a vitality, but a vitality with a distinctive quality or character, the vitality of a living being. A spirit of love, a spirit of malice, a spirit of calm inquiry, a jubilant spirit—it can spread like a blessing of peace or a destructive infection.

A spirit is like character. In the case of the Holy Spirit, it *is* a character. It's the character of God. But it can also be temporary in a way that character can't. The Christian ideal is for a congregation's spirit to be the Holy Spirit; in this case, the attitude of the congregation is the indwelling Spirit of God. By its fellowship with Jesus, the congregation has taken on his character. The congregation is "in" Christ, and Christ is in the congregation. God and the congregation are "of one mind"— in agreement by virtue of their fellowship. They are of one mind, but that is not to say that they are the same mind. They are two minds, but their attitude toward the world (say) is the same attitude. They share an attitude, and in that sense are of one mind.

When we are with another person whose virtuous attitude we share as we interact with her, the incorporation of *her* attitudes is real: that is, we are really *sharing her attitude* as we understand it. This is made possible by the fact that the other is literally present with us, and we are deriving our attitude to some extent from the course of the co-action and interaction with her. It's the ongoing activity of fellowship (happy, respectful interaction) that makes for the presence of the other's mind in one's own. The experience may leave an impression on our character such that even in her absence, we continue to have her attitude or something like it. In that case, we are no longer literally sharing her attitude, even though our attitude is the same one as hers (a spirit of gentleness, let us say). But unlike human spirits, the Holy Spirit is always present, and the difference between fellowship and no fellowship with the Holy Spirit is made by our attention to it, our awareness of it, and our co-action with it. The sense in which the virtuous human's mind continues to inhabit ours after she is dead or gone from our life is different from the sense in which the Holy Spirit indwells the mind of the practicing Christian.

This is not to deny that the Spirit can work in secret from us, conforming us to Christ's Spirit without our awareness. Attention can be voluntary, as we've seen, but I'm not saying that this attention must be voluntary from our side. The Holy Spirit can impose it, as it seems to have done at Pentecost (though the apostles were primed to receive it by their experiences of Jesus, both before and after his resurrection). We are not in perfect and complete control of our fellowship with the Holy Spirit. The Spirit comes and goes as it wills (John 3:8). Sometimes, when it comes by imposition, our attention to it is aroused, as it was on the day of Pentecost.

Conclusion

In this chapter, we've sought to improve our understanding of virtues by asking what kinds of psychological qualities they are. I've proposed that some virtues are mostly composed of concerns whose identity as concerns for the good is determined by our thought-dispositions— the ways we are inclined to conceptualize, imagine, think, and talk about the good that we care about, the "terms" in which we care about and seek the good in its various permutations. Our moral caring and our moral thinking are thus inseparable. Among such virtues are justice, generosity, truthfulness, and so on. By contrast, the enkratic virtues—courage, self-control, patience, perseverance, and the like—are not a matter of concerns qualified by thought but are instead powers of self-management and thus self-possession and self-constitution. Less noted, perhaps, than concerns, thoughts, and powers as elements of virtues, are the ways that we incorporate other minds into our moral dispositions by way of fellowship—common projects, friendships, church, and so forth. In Christian practice of the virtues, this element is exemplified most perfectly in the fellowship of the Holy Spirit of Jesus. We will return to this element, as well as to the others, in the last two chapters.

7
Christian Virtues and Vices

Introduction

In this chapter we'll briefly survey some of the Christian virtues and some vices that are opposed to them. To highlight the distinctiveness of the Christian virtues, we'll compare them with Aristotelian virtues. I'll argue that the Christian virtues fall in three general categories: *agapē* and its variants, self-control and its variants, and humility. Wisdom is the knowledge of the gospel, the practical theology that pervades these three classes of virtues; it is the knowledge of the virtues in the moral framework that structures them, an understanding of the "world" in the terms of that framework, including souls and their moral psychology. In clarifying the idea of virtue ethics, I'll explain the notion of the grammar, or conceptual structure, of a virtue and connect it with the famous and controversial idea of the "unity" of the virtues. One distinguishing feature of Christian virtue ethics is the role of grace in the constitution and formation of the virtues. Indeed, it gives rise to an objection to the whole enterprise: the Protestant objection that preoccupation with virtues—and especially their dimension of agency—turns them inevitably into "glittering vices."

The concern with the distinctiveness of Christian virtues is not just a reaction to the threat of the virtues being or becoming glittering vices. For some people it may be such, but another reason for wanting to protect Christian distinctiveness by carefully examining their grammar is the wonderfulness of Christianity. We wouldn't want to be tricked into accepting a secular substitute. And we see plenty of those on offer in our society. A reason for wanting to protect Christian distinctiveness may be our observation of degenerate spirituality whose practitioners

Virtue Ethics. Robert Campbell Roberts, Oxford University Press.
© Robert Campbell Roberts 2026. DOI: 10.1093/9780197848005.003.0010

think they are practicing Christianity.[1] A third reason for stressing the distinctiveness of Christian virtues is to display, for virtue ethicists more broadly, some overlooked resources for the discipline.[2]

Virtue Ethics as Grammar

In the activity of virtue ethics, we attempt to make the concepts of the virtues clear to ourselves both in their structure and in their importance for us. In the final two chapters of this book, we will go deeper in virtue-ethical exploration, but here and in the following chapter I want to indicate in a general way how virtue ethics explores the virtues. It does so by noting what the virtues are, how they're related to one another and to our emotions, actions, and thoughts, and to the vices, and how all these features of the moral life are implied by the ethical framework to which they belong. All such structural considerations can be packed into the notion of a virtue's "grammar." Just as the grammar of a word in English is the way it fits into and functions in the larger grammar (rule structure) of the practice of English, so any particular virtue has its nature and importance in relation to the whole of the moral life and its unity.

When we speak of linguistic grammar, we index our remarks to a particular language—for example, to English grammar or Mandarin Chinese grammar. I suppose that all languages have some features in common: they all need to have some way of referring to things and actions, for example, and some way of attributing qualities to things and actions. But the ways they do this may differ from one to another. Even closely related languages, say, English and French, will differ in grammatical details. A book of French grammar is no substitute for one on English grammar. Similarly, the grammar of virtues will differ in different moral frameworks while sharing some features across

---

[1] This is a key theme in the writings of Søren Kierkegaard. See my *Recovering Christian Character: The Psychological Wisdom of Søren Kierkegaard* (Grand Rapids: Eerdmans, 2022).

[2] I'm grateful to a reader for Oxford University Press for this observation.

frameworks. We might call the exploration of a single virtue framework the "internal" or "special" grammar of a set of virtues. When we do specifically Christian virtue ethics, that's what we're doing.

The fact that virtues have a grammar implies that virtues follow rules. But at the same time, exemplifying a virtue is not phenomenologically the same as "following a rule," if we mean 'following' to involve consulting the rule's formula. This is like speaking a language: The grammarian finds a regularity and formulates the rule for it, but people have long been following it without consulting its formula. They didn't even have its formula until the grammarians came up with it. Learners (especially foreign ones) consult the rules for this or that as they learn to do this or that in the language. Imagine someone referring to an instruction booklet for assembling one of the more complex pieces of Ikea furniture, or a cook consulting a written recipe. But mature practitioners follow the procedure without consulting the rules. They act in an orderly or regular way; and in so acting, they improvise. Perhaps an observer couldn't perfectly coordinate their moves with the instructions or the recipe. I will propose that the Jewish law is like a recipe for virtue, whose real point is not to follow the recipe, but to internalize the procedure, to become a full-fledged intuitive practitioner. "Hearken to me, ye that know righteousness, the people in whose heart is my law" (Isa 51:7 KJV).

We make some of the features of English grammar more salient to ourselves by comparing it with Chinese grammar. Analogously, a useful practice in specifying the conceptual structure of the virtues in a given framework is to compare the virtues in that framework and the framework itself with their counterparts in other ethical frameworks. This activity might be called comparative grammar. Since the whole interrelated array of Christian virtues is implied by the understanding of ourselves and our world that I have called the moral framework, a different framework will yield a different set of interlocking virtues, with somewhat different relations to concerns, emotions, and abilities. Such comparative grammar will be important if our goal is to understand the practice and the qualities that make its practitioners proficient. For comparison, consider again Aristotle's idea of the virtuous person.

Aristotelian Virtues

Aristotle expounds about a dozen so-called moral virtues in his *Nicomachean Ethics*: justice, courage, temperance, liberality, magnificence (being a "big doer"—a doer of public works: Benjamin Franklin comes to mind), magnanimity (having a "big soul"), mildness, ready wit, proper ambition, and two nameless virtues that a translator calls friendliness and modesty. Aristotle classifies practical wisdom as an "intellectual" virtue, but it is the conceptual power of moral understanding. The person who has all these virtues and lives in a city-state whose political structure supports their formation and maintenance, and provided that he also has a minimum of material goods and some friends, is a "happy" (*eudaimōn*) person. These moral virtues are distinct from the so-called intellectual virtues (intuitive reason, understanding, and philosophic wisdom) and from the virtue of "art" (*technē*: craft) which is excellence in the capacity to make things.[3] Aristotle gives the lion's share of discussion in *Nicomachean Ethics* to justice, courage, temperance, and wisdom, which are traditionally known as the "cardinal" (or "hinge") virtues. Justice gets a whole book of eleven chapters, and courage, temperance, and practical wisdom get several chapters each. Most of the other virtues get one chapter.

For Aristotle, the disposition to moral shame (NE 4.9) is a quasi-virtue: if you do something shameful, it's good that you're disposed to feel shame about it; the sensitivity is in the direction of virtue, but your inclination to do something shameful in the first place rules out its being a virtue. In marginalizing shame for its taint of unrighteousness, Aristotle shows what Christians will think of as morally naïve over-optimism about the human potential for perfect virtue. For Christians, a readiness to confess sins penitently is actually virtuous. We are "hopeless" sinners (hoping only in God's generous mercy). Aristotle's over-optimism is visible also in his unwillingness to regard self-control

---

[3] The inclusion of art (craft knowledge) and practical wisdom among the intellectual virtues shows that what Aristotle means by 'intellectual' isn't what we typically mean when we call someone an intellectual. For Aristotle, "intellectual" virtue is excellence at thinking and reasoning. A person with the virtue of art knows how to make things excellently, and the person with practical wisdom is morally perceptive and good at ethical reasoning.

("continence") as a full-fledged virtue: it implies impulses that need to be controlled (NE 7.1). The corresponding virtue, in Aristotle's thinking, is temperance (NE 3.10–11), which is the disposition to have only virtuous impulses with respect to food, drink, and sex, so that no self-control is needed. In contrast, Paul calls self-control a fruit of the Holy Spirit (Gal 5:22) and has no category that corresponds to temperance.

Justice, as the disposition to give people the good or evil that's due them, neither more nor less, seems to be at the center of Aristotle's ethical thought. It seems to rule out forgiveness as a virtue and it affects the character of practical wisdom and liberality and compassion. (Compassion is not officially a virtue in *Nicomachean Ethics*; but see *Rhetoric* 2.8.) Justice is premised on the idea of equality—for example, equal treatment of persons—but since Aristotle has no idea of *general* human equality—for example, that "all people are created equal"—he has no idea of justice as the equal treatment of all humans, human beings as such. He believes that some people are naturally slaves (*Politics* 1.2). We might say that Aristotelian justice, despite the centrality of equality, is elitist in that only certain kinds of people warrant it. By contrast, Christian justice is for everybody—with special compensatory attention to the poor and downtrodden—and includes mercy, generosity, and forgivingness as constituents of "righteousness" (*dikaiosunē*: justice). But mercy, generosity, and forgivingness are, in their different ways, mitigations of strict justice.

Aristotle devotes two whole books to friendship—more than to any of the virtues proper—indicating its ethical importance to him. But he's ambivalent about whether it's a virtue: friendship is "a virtue or like a virtue" (NE 8.1). A friendship is, after all, a relationship with a particular person—the friend—and no standard virtue is particularized in that way. Friendship, he says, involves justice in the sense that if you're friends with someone, you are deeply motivated to treat that person justly (NE 8.1). Friendship is permeated by justice also in that it depends on the parties being approximately equal, and to keep the relationship just, any inequality of the two parties needs to be compensated in the interactions of the friendship (NE 8.7). This seems to imply that a child and his father can be proper friends only if the child rebalances the inequality by loving the father (the superior) more than the father loves the child. To a Christian, this condition seems niggling, unrealistic, ungracious, unfriendly—not virtuous. This intuition stems from the grammar of Christian love and its commitment to the fundamental equality and worth of all persons, with its implications for the nature of justice in the Christian framework.

The non-personal character of Aristotle's god, the unmoved mover, rules out such personal attitudes as faith and worship, not to mention gratitude. We have seen (Chapter 4) how his ideal of self-sufficiency rules against gratitude and humility as virtues. His virtue of magnanimity (greatness of soul), which involves a passion for superiority measured by autonomy, rules out gratitude as a virtue of great people. In contrast, Jesus teaches that to be great is to have the attitude of a loyal servant (Matt 20:25–28). Aristotle's conception of justice rules out forgivingness. These are some ways the Aristotelian framework yields virtues strikingly different from the Christian ones, even when the names of the virtues ('justice,' 'liberality,' 'courage,' 'wisdom') are similar.

Christian Virtues and the Spirit of Christ

In the apostle Paul's writings we find lists of Christian virtues, and on one occasion he calls nine of them fruit of the Holy Spirit. "the fruit of the Spirit is love, joy, peace, patience, kindness, generosity, faithfulness or loyalty, gentleness, and self-control (Gal 5:22–23). I make no distinction between fruit of the Holy Spirit and Christian virtues that Paul lists elsewhere but doesn't mention in Galatians 5—for example, hope, compassion, gratitude, forgivingness (a disposition to forgive, Col 3:13), humility, bold confidence, peace, holiness, justice, courage, and wisdom. All the Christian virtues are fruit of the Spirit of Christ, and all the character traits that are fruit of the Holy Spirit are virtues.

Jesus is less inclined than Paul to offer lists of virtues, but he too strikes virtue-congruent themes and uses the metaphor of fruit. Like trees that bear fruit according to their kind, different "kinds" of human beings bear fruits according to their kinds. In general, good people bear good fruit and bad people bear bad fruit (Matt 7:15–18). Whereas Paul's fruit of the Holy Spirit consists in human *traits* that reflect the traits of God's Spirit when that Spirit dwells in a person, the evil fruits of which Jesus speaks are *actions* that come *from* the "inner" character of a person or the "heart"—from the person's desire-laden thoughts and thought-laden desires (Mark 7:14–23). In Jesus's criticisms of the legalists, he stresses the virtue-ethical theme that real righteousness and holiness is a disposition of the "heart" (*kardia*—thought-filled desire and appetitive thought) from which good actions come, rather than merely behavioral conformity to the law.[4] Apparently, good behavior can coexist, though perhaps rather unstably, with bad attitudes.

The "Unity" of the Virtues

I propose that, for purposes of exposition, we can usefully divide the Christian virtues into four kinds. It would be a mistake in moral psychology to suppose that since self-control, generosity, and humility are all virtues, they must have the same kind of psychological profile. To be virtues, they need only be excellent human traits of *some* kind, not the same kind. Examples of this mistake can be found in Zagzebski 1996:137, and Russell 2009: 177. The kinds I have in mind are caring, understanding, ability, and purity. These are represented, respectively, by love (*agapē*), wisdom (*sophia*), self-control (*enkrateia*), and humility (*tapeinophrosunē*). Love is the central Christian virtue (I Cor 13:13), and has several variants (compassion, generosity, gratitude, gentleness, forgivingness, kindness). Wisdom (morally relevant understanding) is embedded in all the virtues, and so, in a sense, has many variants (the wisdom of forgivingness, the wisdom of gratitude, the wisdom of self-control, and so forth), though without having distinct names. Self-control also has several variants (perseverance, patience, courage). Its primary claim to be virtue is that it enables love to resist or overcome various possible psychological impediments such as fear, discouragement, and the emotion of impatience. Love is a kind of concern and self-control is a kind of ability. Thus both love

---

[4] See the discussion of virtue and the Jewish law in the next chapter.

and self-control are kinds of positive moral psychological attribute or condition.

Wisdom is the thought or understanding aspect of love and self-control. When love is directed toward what is genuinely lovely (God and fellow creatures, for example), then it's wise, and only if it's wise is it a virtue. Love of things that are not lovely, for example, revenge, other people's inferiority or pain, self-importance, limitless power and wealth, and so forth, is vicious. Thought (understanding), as I argued in Chapter 6, is what gives love its direction or target and its "content," what it's "about."

Wisdom in love is the recognition and appreciation of the lovable. The wisdom in self-control is of another kind: it's a "how-to," the wisdom of a skill. Being *self*-control, the skill is directed at oneself, and its chief goal is to be and stay loving toward God and God's creatures. But the wisdom of love comes into the practice of self-control in that it determines when and why self-control's skill-wisdom will be applied. So wisdom comes in two kinds, one kind for love and another kind as the know-how of self-management.

Finally, humility is a *contrary*, namely the contrary of the numerous vices of pride: arrogance, vanity, envy, grandiosity, haughtiness, hyper-autonomy, pretentiousness, selfish ambition (competitiveness with other people for importance), presumption, and so forth. In Christian thought, the vices of pride are all variants of the desire to be more important than some other people. They are not just too much of a good thing (say, excessive self-esteem), but any amount of a bad thing (invidious self-concern). As a contrary of these forms of invidious unlove, humility is a negative corollary of love. Where love is, none of the vices of pride will be; and thus will humility be, as a state of purity from them. Thus, **Love** (caring) MOVES or PROPELS; **Wisdom** (thought) DIRECTS or AIMS; **Humility** (emptiness) FILTERS OUT (excludes), as it were,[5] ego-pollutants (of love); **Self-control** (powers) RESISTS impulse-obstacles. By its nature, wisely directed love excludes the vices of pride. So love in its purity and goodness entails humility. But if love

---

[5] I say 'as it were' because 'filter' and 'exclude' suggest positive action, while humility as I understand it is simply an absence of the vices of pride, a state of purity of or freedom from this kind of pollution.

is unwise or weak in "energy," then the aspirant to humility needs to recruit self-control against the impulses of the vices of pride.

This fourfold categorization of kinds of virtues already shows the necessities of connection among the kinds. While self-control, thought of in abstraction from its place in the Christian framework, may have some claim to be thought a virtue even if it's misused (after all, the thief whose self-control makes him a better thief has an admirable quality, a kind of "strength" and self-know-how), it will not count as a *moral* virtue in abstraction from the framework. To be a moral virtue, self-control needs to function as an auxiliary to love. Similarly, the virtue of love in Christianity can be attributed only to someone whose love is "owned" (so to speak), whose love belongs to him or her as an agent. Christian love is agential and not merely a feeling that comes over you or a pattern of behavior that you somehow emit. This implies that love as a human virtue depends on some degree of self-control—some ability to turn love on or off at will. So even if strengths and concerns can be thought of as in principle separable psychological attributes, they aren't separable within the Christian framework. As for wisdom and humility, we have seen that because love is Christian only if it has a correct target and because the target is properly targeted only through some degree of wisdom (understanding), wisdom is "internal" to love; and that Christian humility is simply love's state of purity from the vices of pride. For elaboration of these points, see Chapters 9–11.

The very presence of self-control among the virtues suggests that Christian virtues can be attributed to imperfect persons. You can be wise without being perfectly wise and loving without being perfected in Christian love. Virtues are all subject to a "more or less." The threshold that must be met to warrant an attribution is not well-established or clear-cut. Nevertheless, it does seem that the unity of the virtues makes it impossible to have Christian wisdom without having Christian love and self-control, nor Christian love without some humility. And so forth.

What about the variants? Can a person have perseverance without courage, or generosity without compassion or gratitude? To formulate these questions seems already to sow doubts about the possibilities. It is true that perseverance is about discouragement and courage about fear; and you might be better at managing your discouragement than at managing your fear. But then fears come in varieties as well: social anxiety, fear of heights, fear of death, fear of sin. And surely you don't have to have mastered every kind of fear to qualify as having some courage. The commonality among the kinds of self-control is that they all presuppose a sensitivity to one's adverse impulses and an ability to suppress or redirect them. It seems plausible that the application of these powers to diverse kinds of adverse impulses would have some generality, for example, that the power or strategy for managing sex-urges would overlap somewhat with the power or strategy for managing impulses of impatience. Impulses of impatience and sex-appetite might both be recognizable as adverse *to* the love of one's neighbor. Love of one's neighbor would then be the common sensitivity by which the two kinds of impulse are recognized as adverse. Likewise, both strategies of control might employ selective attention, which seems to be a generalizable skill. So, while recognizing that persons can be better at controlling their sex-urges than they are at controlling their impulses of impatience and that you might have good mastery of physical dangers while falling short of perseverance in tasks that lack immediate appeal for you, I suggest that the two abilities have much in common and will *tend* to co-occur.

Agapē and Its Variants

Agapē is a kind of love that is directed toward God and in being so directed is directed toward God's creatures. So it can be thought of as love for God *and* love for creatures, especially the ones God created in greatest likeness to himself.

Agapē for God is a disposition to "see"/desire/cherish God as incarnate in Jesus Christ. It is thus faith and hope and service to God as self-revealed in Jesus. *Agapē* worships God *as* one who loves and lifts up the poor and downtrodden, *as* one who created the earth good, *as* one who forgives sins and has compassion on the repentant, *as* one who desires fellowship with loyal and obedient creatures, *as* one who humbled himself out of love for his creatures. This connection between *agapē* for God and *agapē* for human creatures is plausibly the reason (or at least a reason) that the apostle John declares (1 John 4:20) that a person who doesn't love his brother and sister can't be a lover of God. *Agapē* for God rejoices in and celebrates God in this way as the sovereign in relation to his creatures.

Jesus says that the commandment to love your neighbor as yourself is "like" the greatest commandment, to love the Lord your God with all your heart and mind. It is plausible that the former commandment is like the latter commandment because human beings are like God in a relevant way. *Agapē* is the disposition to see this quality in the other person, and to be ready to see it in *every* other person without exception. This "seeing" of *agapē*, like all virtuous seeing, is wise and concern-laden.

Agapē for human beings is a proneness to see every other human being as of great value, indeed, as of the same value as yourself (to the extent that you have a healthy respect for yourself). It's a readiness to be in awe of the deep creaturely excellence, the mysterious wonderfulness, the respect-demanding nature, of the other. It is a readiness to "see past" outward and obvious features of a person that are likely to put us off: grumpiness, anger, vice, garish tattoos, disability, commonness, foul odor, craziness, drunkenness, filth, crudeness of speech, and so forth. And what we "see" beyond these things is a God-like being, a soul formed in the image of God.[6] We have the word 'respect,' which refers to a kind of cautiousness something like the caution that Moses felt when he recognized that he was treading on holy ground (Exod 3:5). *Agapē* for human beings involves something like that tender caution vis-à-vis their awesomeness.

Some readers may know that I have said (1988, 2003, 2013) that emotions are concern-based construals. And someone might infer from that, in combination with the present observation, that I take *agapē* to be an emotion. I am not saying that. I say that *agapē* is a "*proneness . . . to see.*" A proneness or disposition is not an event, but a tendency for some kind of event to occur. A disposition to see underpins actual seeing, but it's not the same as actual seeing—and the actual seeing is what I say an emotion is. As I noted earlier about compassion,

---

[6] This power of "seeing beyond" is one of the functions of wisdom, one of the ways that love makes for wisdom. See Rick Anthony Furtak, *Wisdom in Love: Kierkegaard and the Quest for Emotional Integrity* (Notre Dame, IN: University of Notre Dame Press, 2005). It turns knowledge into sight. It puts the "heart" into the "eyes of the heart."

a number of different emotions can be outputs of compassion: anger, fear, relief, compassion, sadness, hope, and so forth. And the same is true of *agapē* more generally conceived. All the variants of *agapē* involve the disposition to see the other as in the image of God and thus as having great, awesome, and ineradicable worth, but they differ from one another in the circumstances in which the other is seen as being.

Agapē is at the same time a caring about the person you see. We have noted that it is a perception of something that is surpassingly good, so it stands to reason that it would involve caring about what is perceived. The good Samaritan, in loving the injured man, wants to help him, and carries through on that desire. It is an exercise in virtue that we stop regularly to admire one another in this way (with this "thought"), to admire one another as extraordinary works of God. For the sake of our virtue and happiness a particularly helpful exercise is to stop to admire in this way people whom we might be a little inclined to hold in contempt, for whom we are inclined to feel disdain or toward whom we tend to be indifferent. Here is a *habitus* that would be an aspect of *agapē*: we become "habitually" alert to the feeling of disdain as a signal that it is time to "stop" for this exercise in meditation. If any thought such as the following crosses your mind, it would then trigger the kind of meditation we are looking for: the other

is a silly person,
is a disgusting person,
is a vicious person,
is not quite human,
is a low-life,
is highly underdeveloped as a person,
compares badly with myself,
is a morally immature person,
is a misguided bigot,
is an ignorant person,
is a nasty liberal,
is a nasty conservative,
is an ungrateful person,
is a snob,
is a bully.

Any of these thoughts might be true of the person you're thinking of. But they aren't the only truths about him or her, nor are they the most important truths, and to dwell on them in isolation from those more important truths is likely to harm you and anyone with whom you share them (explicitly or implicitly). These are all concern-laden demeaning or enraging "thoughts" that are in friction with love. So the Christian-in-training turns them into triggers for vice-contrarian admiration. And this admiration will be a participation in some variant of *agapē*: generosity, compassion, gratitude, forgivingness, gentleness.

I spoke of "stopping" to admire the other. Think about what it is to "stop." It doesn't mean stop interacting with the other, but rather, stop thinking as I was thinking and be reminded of the more normative way to think about the other: to awaken the disposition to appreciate the glory of the other. In fact, to "stop" in this way is to continue interacting, but in a new mode, a mode triggered by the alert. It is brought about in the course of action-interaction. It's a gestalt-switch, or the notice that one is called for.

Among the variants of *agapē* are compassion, generosity, forgivingness, gentleness, kindness, and gratitude. They differ from one another in how the other person is "seen." There will be as many variants of love as there are loving ways of "seeing" another person. The variants of *agapē* are the various ways you see (feel about) the other, or yourself, or the situation as impinging on your concern for the other. In compassion, *agapē* sees the other as suffering; in generosity *agapē* sees the other as warranting a gift of some sort. In the good Samaritan, compassion and generosity come together, as they often do: the warrant for the gift is the injured man's suffering. In gentleness *agapē* sees the other as fragile or vulnerable, and this may be despite the other's crankiness or hostility (gentleness is associated with [lack or moderation of] anger). In forgiveness *agapē* responds to the other's significant wrong or injury against oneself or something associated with oneself. Closely related to forgivingness is love of enemies. Often, when we see a person as our enemy, the background is some perceived grievance: we *identify* him, for ourselves, as the one who has committed a personal offense against us or against something we identify with, such as our family or tribe. If, in our thinking and imagining, we can loosen him from that identification and construe him instead as a fellow human being, as one with loves and joys and problems like our own, we will have softened or removed the enemy-element from our perception of him. We may know that he still regards *us* as *his* enemy, but in our *agapē* for him he will no longer look like an enemy to us, but more like one of us.

Self-control and Its Variants

We humans have, as original equipment, a set of capacities by which we can manage our thoughts, habits, emotions, and impulses. We are, no doubt, passively subject to all of these: thoughts "come to us," habits "dominate us," emotions "move us," impulses "impel us." But that's not the whole story. We can also turn our attention toward some thoughts and away from others. Within limits, we can "look at things" in a chosen way rather than according to a default. And depending on which way we look, we can be moved and impelled in one way or another. For example, alternatively by anger or by tender sadness or hope. What is it about us that enables us to do this?

We can evaluate our thoughts and habits, classing one kind as healthy and another unhealthy for us, one kind as admirable and another despicable. We sort our angers, fears, joys, and hopes into ones that do us credit and others that are shameful or of indifferent value. And, with a little practical wisdom, we can implement strategies for changing our habits, our patterns of thinking, our emotions, and impulses.

Let's call these capacities *powers of self-transcendence*: we rise "above" our immediate states of thinking, habit, emotion, and impulse; we evaluate them from that higher standpoint. Armed with a bit of wisdom (or folly, as it may be) we see some direction to take them and get ourselves in position to take them in that direction. The perspective from which we evaluate ourselves can itself be wise or foolish. For example, we might draw on the Christian tradition for this perspective, or alternatively, we might draw on the vices of pride for our "wisdom": we might be so ashamed of losing an election as to summon our courage and perseverance and patience to steal the next one. Morally, the "higher" standpoint may be pretty low.

These three basic human capacities of self-transcendence—self-evaluation, adoption of a direction of self-change, and devising of a strategy for achieving self-change—can be developed and refined. We can become better at transcending ourselves (honest consciousness and focus is relevant); the standpoint of our self-transcendence can itself become more refined and ethically sophisticated (wiser); and we can become better *at* altering our thoughts, habits, emotions, and impulses with reference to the higher standpoint (more skilled, more disciplined at self-management).

The moral development of these basic human capacities into virtues is perhaps the most important avenue by which we contribute to our own character. They are ways that we become, to the limited extent that we can become, our own moral authors. We become not only agents, but agents of our own agency. I speculate that the apostle Paul presupposes these developments of our basic mental capacities when he writes of *setting your mind on* the things of the spirit (Rom 8:5–8) or the things above (Col 3:1–4); *putting on* compassion, humility, and so forth (Col 3:8–9); *walking in* the good works that God has prepared for us (Eph 2:10), and *putting to death* the works of the flesh (Rom 8:13, Gal 5:24). Plausibly, these exhortations make sense only if we can do what's enjoined. The development of these moral capacities is the power by which we can do this.

Psychologists refer to these capacities as self-regulation (Baumeister and Vohs 2016). The biblical writers and Aristotle refer to the developed capacity as self-control (*enkrateia*: strength; Gal 5:22, 2 Pet 1:5). I will treat generic self-management powers as self-control. Self-control, as I understand it, has variants with virtue-names: courage, patience, perseverance, and steadfastness. Self-control applies to the whole range of psychological states or events that may need managing: If you have a bad habit, breaking it may require you to resist the impulse to implement it (smoking, overeating, touching your face, ogling girls, using vulgar language, nursing grudges, envying peers more famous or capable than you, and so forth). The variants of self-control are specialized with respect to the kinds of states they control. Courage controls fear; patience controls the emotion of impatience;

perseverance controls discouragement; steadfastness controls impulses to deviate from commitments; loyalty controls impulses to disloyalty; and so forth.

A note about 'control': To control your fear is literally to affect the emotion itself: at the moment, the emotion is a property of *you*. To control it might be to mitigate it, so that the fear, for example, is less intense; or it might be to shift its object, so that instead of fearing those who can kill you, you fear to betray the one whom to betray is to betray your deepest self; or it might be to root out fear altogether, to become "fearless." Such would be cases of literally controlling *the fear*, and thus, I think, your *self*. Alternatively, to control your fear might be to control your behavioral response to the fear, while leaving the fear—and your self, to this extent—unchanged. All this is a bit abstract, since the control of your behavior tends to affect the fear; indeed, controlling your behavior in response to the threat is a chief tactic for managing the emotion. Similarly, shifting the object can be a tactic of mitigation, or even of becoming fearless, in case the fear of the new object is swallowed up in love.

In the case where courage is or becomes the trait of fearlessness, the whole idea of control drops out; it is neither control of emotion nor control of behavior against the influence of emotion. It's action in circumstances that would inspire fear in many or "normal" people. But it isn't simply that, as is shown by Aristotle's example of sailors who, unlike the passengers, appreciate that the present storm presents no real threat and therefore do *not* exemplify courage (NE 3.8). So it seems that even the courage of the fearless applies only where the subject appreciates, in some sense, that he is under real threat. I think that courage as fearlessness requires to be thought of historically. That is, it is really courage only if, at some earlier point in the individual's moral development, he actually did feel fear in circumstances like the current ones and overcame it by controlling his fear. This would be a way of preserving the classification of courage as a species of self-control.

While it is extremely unusual, and perhaps even unheard of, for the virtues of self-control to be exemplified entirely without self-control, let's allow that, in principle, acts of any of them—patience, loyalty, steadfastness, perseverance—might in some cases need to be explained with the historical explanation. Self-control itself seems, because of its name in English, not to be possible without an element of active self-control. This problem doesn't arise in Greek, where it is just called strength or enstrengthenment (*enkrateia*); but Aristotle has a distinct name for the analogous virtue that requires no agential intervention: temperance (*sōphrosunē*).

The ethical life in human beings can be thought of as having two positive elements. These might be called passion and action, motive and agency, caring and doing. The first of the pair is a matter of being pushed or drawn from outside oneself, the second of undertaking or originating from within oneself. Both depend, in different ways, on thought (understanding). Human agency is an integration of these two modes, so it's fitting that the mature human being has both kinds of virtues. Aristotle thought that virtues were mean-states with respect to passions and actions. A human being is neither a pure agent nor a pure patient (inanimate objects are the latter, with animals having various degrees of agency short of what humans have; perhaps only human beings have the kind of agency afforded by the power of choice, in case only we, among the animals, deliberate).

We have now looked briefly at two kinds of virtues that are named in the various lists of Christian virtues, first at the virtues of *agapē* or love, and then at the virtues of self-management. Both kinds are permeated by kinds of wisdom—correct understanding of the good and practical understanding of how to manage one's mental states. We'll turn in a moment to humility, which I take to be different from either of the first two kinds. But let us pause first to consider a Christian objection that may be triggered by the discussion of the enkratic virtues.

Excursus: A Protestant Objection to Virtue Ethics. In discussing the virtues of self-control, I've stressed their role in the consolidation and deepening of human agency—the power to be what Aristotle calls an "origin" of action—and I've discussed their role in making it possible for us to become "agents of our own agency." Such talk makes some Protestants uneasy. They feel that virtue ethics' focus on human excellence of character, and now even our being somehow an *origin* of the excellence of our character, threatens God's sovereignty in our salvation and the all-sufficiency of God's grace. Intrinsically, says the critic, virtue ethics underrates our status as sinners. We are hopeless of righteousness apart from God's generous forgiveness. Virtue ethics encroaches on the freedom of God's grace. It gives human agency far too great a role in the economy of salvation. It is paganism in Christian disguise.

I think this objection is misplaced. Here are four considerations to the contrary.

First, the biblical evidence: Paul, whose writings are the main source for the doctrine of justification by grace, repeatedly calls on his churches to *act* in conformity with their justification by grace, often using the language of the heart and speaking in virtue-terms: compassion, gentleness, love, humility, patience, forgiveness (being forgiving), and so forth. The acts to which we are called in Christ are acts *of virtue*, acts arising out of our transformed mind, heart, spirit—our character. In Chapter 8, I'll argue that the purpose of the law received by Moses is to form a people on whose hearts the law is written. This is the biblical idea of a people who are formed in genuine humanity—which *is* the idea of virtue. In the New Testament the goal hasn't changed, despite a highly specific emphasis on grace in the way that genuine humanity is to be transformed.

Second, Paul's concept of the believer's role as responsible agent in his or her sanctification is distinctive and incorporates the idea of grace in a way that, say, Aristotle's concept of agency doesn't. But it's still a concept of agency. In Chapter 6, I claimed that an aspect of virtues is the incorporation of other virtuous persons' minds into the mind/heart/soul/spirit of the virtuous person. Good people carry other good people's minds around in theirs, expressing them in their daily actions and interactions, emotions and perceptions.[7] We don't just imitate good people's behavior, but by a mechanism of empathy (sympathetic mind-reading) we adopt the other's concerns and patterns of thought. Love and respect for the model person catalyze this incorporation. Christianity lays special stress on this feature because the mind/heart of Jesus Christ which, to put it mildly, is friendly to the believer, is central to the formation of the Christian mind. Christ is more than a teacher; he is very God and lover himself, so the incorporation

---

[7] Sadly, bad people's minds are similarly absorbable, causing moral infections.

of his spirit is the incorporation of God's spirit. Worship is an attitude and practice analogous to love and respect that we are forbidden from having toward any object other than God. In worship, the Christian incorporates the righteous and holy mind of Jesus into the Christian's own spirit. Or, to put the matter in the passive voice (where it fits well), in the distinctively Christian virtues the spirit of Jesus is "infused" into the spirit of the believer through the interaction of worship, which is a special *koinōnia*, a participation, a taking-part. Working on behalf of Jesus as his assistants in ministry (I Cor 4:1) further promotes the incorporation of Jesus's mind into that of the believer.

The issue of the relation between the active and the passive in this transaction, or rather the relation between the believer's action and the action of God, is axial for the Protestant objection to virtue ethics. When Paul talks about the role of human agency in the acquisition of the Christian virtues, the language he uses reflects the fact that the Christian's virtues are derivative from or parasitic on the virtues of Christ. Because they are transferred to us by infusion from another, our role in their acquisition is to "yield" (submit) our powers of agency ("members") to God as instruments of righteousness (Rom 6:13); we are to "put on" a pre-existent compassion, kindness, humility, gentleness, and so forth (Col 3:12; Eph 4:24; Rom 13:14); we are to "walk by the Spirit" (hand in hand, following like a child crossing the street with her father or like a partner in a dance, who follows her partner's lead) (Gal 5:25); "For we are his workmanship, created in Christ Jesus for good works, which God prepared beforehand, that we should walk in them" (Eph 2:10, RSV), like footprints in which we have only to put our own feet. Each of these metaphors suggests mitigated, secondary, or derivative agency—agency, to be sure, but not quite, or not fully, our own agency. Or rather, yes, our agency, but with a boost and a guiding hand. All "practicing" Christians are on assisted living. Steering a very heavy vehicle (say, a truck) would be arduous without power steering, which is assisted. Some people couldn't even do it. But still, with the assistance of power steering, even the diminutive, weak-armed driver of such a truck does steer.

I think that advocates of Christian virtue ethics have no stake in denying the passivity of the believer in this interaction, but neither must we admit that the believer's activity has no role in it. *All* of human agency is shot through with elements of passivity—conditions of our responsiveness over which we have little or no agentic control. One of the most important passivities in our moral development is our taking in, by a kind of osmosis or absorption or in-breathing, the attitudes of people with whom we have communion—working together, praising one another (admiration), giving and receiving gifts (generous motives, gratitude), eating and drinking together, confessing to one another, rejoicing and lamenting together, sharing stories and our philosophies of life, singing together. Earlier (in Chapter 6) we discussed the supposed tension between Jesus's saying that evil thoughts come from within (Mark 7) and the teaching of Father Thaddeus of Vitovnica that most of our evil thoughts are planted in us by the demons. Our resolution of that supposed tension is that both are true, in different senses of 'come from within': as father Thaddeus emphasizes, most of our evil thoughts come from outside us, planted there by other spirits, though we have powers to resist them; and as Jesus emphasizes, to become genuinely evil (or good), those thoughts have to come from within us in the sense that we have to have "owned" them, taken them to our hearts as targets of our desires, loves, and concerns, thus making them expressions of our character.

A third response to the Protestant objection is that the denial of human agency implies an absurdity. Let's say someone hears Paul or a Pauline preacher exhort her to *put on* Christ's compassion or to *walk* in the works of generosity that Christ has prepared for us, or to *yield* in justice to the command of Christ. As a fervent Protestant, she believes that works righteousness is a major misstep in the Christian life, a human arrogance to be avoided at all costs on pain of dishonoring Jesus and his all-sufficient grace and falling into pride. So she responds,

> I can't, in good Christian conscience, take it upon *myself* to *put on* virtue, to *walk* in virtue, or to *yield* to Christ's directions to act virtuously. In humility, *I* can't be the one to *do* that, because not I, but Christ lives in me. So he'll have to do it. I have no responsibility in the matter. As an agent, I'm not in the picture and have no contribution to make. As a believer in the all-sufficiency of Christ's grace, I *refuse* to trespass on Christ's sovereign agency.

This seems to be a misguided inference if Christ lives *in her* in the right sense of 'in.' Presumably, Christ lives in her by her having the "mind" or "spirit" of Christ, that is, by the intelligence of Christ directing her to act intelligently, not by a kind of puppeteering causation. She acts in consultation with Christ. In fact, her refusal to act seems self-defeating inasmuch as taking a stand against these actions is itself an action, a resolute refusal based on her theology. As such, it is *acting* (actively forswearing action) *for a reason.* Maybe agency is inescapable for human beings.

Here is a fourth consideration. It is true that, while we were still sinners, Christ died for us; his generous love isn't *conditional* on our transformation. God loves us though we are not yet transformed. Yet our transformation is the *goal* of that grace. It is part of Christ's good will toward us that he aims for us to become gracious in response: generous, forgiving, compassionate, patient, and so forth. If our character isn't transformed by his grace, then we miss many of the joys intrinsic to that transformation; we miss the blessings of being able to bless the world. We miss the *life* that Christ promises. Protestants distinguish forensic righteousness, which is God's judicial declaration that we are righteous because of Christ's righteousness, not our own, from moral righteousness, which is the believer's excellent spiritual maturity (Eph 4:13) of character. But the Christian notion of forensic righteousness depends on *somebody's* being morally righteous (namely, Christ), so forensic righteousness is secondary to intrinsic (moral) righteousness, and can't avoid having the wish and goal that the believer be morally righteous. It would be incongruous and a misunderstanding for the believer to accept Christ's grace without sharing Christ's goal for it.

Humility and Its Variants

Christianity stresses a virtue that was hardly mentioned or noticed in paganism,[8] due to the pagan unawareness of sin. Humility, which

---

[8] But see Plato's *Laws* (4.716a–b) and Socrates's deflection of credit in calling himself a mere "midwife" of ideas (*Theaetetus* 149a–151d). I'll discuss the passage further in Chapter 11.

historically speaking really comes into its own in the New Testament, is a virtue that seems to be neither a matter of motivation-attraction-passion, nor a matter of control or agency. The key sin that paganism overlooked is pride, and the virtue thereby hidden from pagan view was humility. This is perhaps why the church fathers said that the pagans' virtues were glittering vices:[9] The pagans often took their courage, their justice, their temperance, their wisdom, as occasions for self-importance and superiority to fellow humans who were less perfected morally. In this way, they spoiled what would otherwise have been human excellence by attaching a vicious motive to it. This is vividly illustrated in Aristotle's account of the great-souled man (NE 4.3). The vices of pride, which we will examine in more detail in Chapter 11, are conceit, arrogance (presumption), vanity (pretentiousness), snobbery, domination, envy, grandiosity, self-righteousness, haughtiness, and hyper-autonomy (self-sufficiency). The concern at the root of all these variants of sinful pride is the desire for a kind of personal importance that I call "self-importance." This concern is in ferocious opposition to *agapē*. Where it is present, *agapē* is polluted if not entirely eradicated. The virtue of humility is thus a kind of purity in a person's love, and the chief salutary function of humility among the virtues is the protection of love (*agapē*).

I suppose there are as many variants of humility as there are distinct kinds of vicious pride, and as many kinds of pride as there are ways of pursuing self-importance. But unlike the variants of *agapē* and self-control, the variants of humility are short on special names. They are mostly just called 'humility,' though sometimes we specify the kind by saying, "he's unvain" or "unpretentious" or "unarrogant," or "he doesn't have an envious bone in his body." We also give the specialized name of "modesty" to the humility that is contrary to vanity and pretentiousness: vicious pride manifested in self-display.

---

[9] T. H. Irwin calls the phrase "pseudo-Augustinian." See "Splendid Vices? Augustine For and Against Pagan Virtues," *Medieval Philosophy and Theology* 8 (1999): 105–127.

The Christian Vices

In contexts of the lists of virtues in the New Testament, we also find lists of vices, and of actions, practices, and ways of relating to one another that express vices. A locus classicus is the list of "works of the flesh" in Galatians 5 that accompanies the list of fruit of the Spirit:

> Now the works of the flesh are obvious: [adultery],[10] fornication, impurity, licentiousness, idolatry, sorcery, enmities, strife, jealousy, anger, quarrels, dissensions, factions, [murders], envy, drunkenness, carousing, and things like these. I am warning you, as I warned you before: those who do such things will not inherit the kingdom of God. (19–21)[11]

Not everything in this list is a vice in the classical sense of an unhealthy and morally substandard character trait. Adultery, fornication, and carousings are kinds of actions; sorcery is a practice; an enmity is a relationship with another person or persons; dissensions are interactions; and factions are divisions within a community. Nevertheless, these actions, practices, relationships, interactions, and divisions can be characteristic of the persons who perform, foster, or participate in them. Some people's moral character can be a tendency to perform the dysfunctional actions or foster the relationships, and then the traits of that character will be vices. Such traits all have in common that they are at odds with the traits and ways of life and human happiness that are characteristic of the new world order founded and anticipated by Jesus Christ. They are contrary to the character of the Spirit and of people who breathe deeply and regularly the Spirit of Jesus Christ. Such traits show a lack of love, or perhaps even contempt, for God and his good creation, especially as that creation is exemplified in humanity.

---

[10] Adultery and murders are not included in the NRSV but are found in some Greek texts.

[11] Other such lists, not perfectly identical with this one, are at Romans 1:29b–31 and 12:16–19, and Colossians 3:5–9. And Paul mentions and warns against vices at various other places in his writings.

Conceptual exploration of the vice-concepts can be an important dimension of virtue ethics, since we are all beset with vices and our understanding of the virtues is fostered by considering these traits that are incompatible with the virtues.[12] In Chapter 11, we'll explore Christian humility by considering the vices of pride to which humility is opposed.

Conclusion

I have offered an overview of Christian virtues, and in doing so a broad outline of the activity of Christian virtue ethics. I have suggested that virtue ethics can be thought of on analogy with the grammar of a language, a set of implicit rules that can be made explicit with effort (by grammarians) and which articulate the special character of the language under investigation. As such an articulation, a grammar can foster understanding of the language and even, possibly, enhance the practice of it. Similarly, virtue ethics can foster understanding of the practice of Christianity, and perhaps even help people in their efforts to be wiser and better people. In the next chapter I will continue this investigation into the rules of thought governing Christian virtues (and therefore virtue ethics), by reflecting about the relation of Christian virtues to the Jewish law, by considering virtues as habits or competencies, and will finish with reflections about the place of philosophy in the enterprise of virtue ethics.

---

[12] For years, my colleague Robert Kruschwitz taught a very successful ethics course oriented by the "seven deadly sins" using the text of Thomas Aquinas's *On Evil*.

8

Virtues, Regulations, and Regularity

Introduction

In this chapter and the next we will consider four questions connected with the rationality or "normativity" (the "intelligence" or regularity) for the concept of a virtue. First, how are virtues related to commandments or laws? In particular, how are the Christian virtues related to rules like the ten commandments that Moses received on the mountain? I shall argue that the Bible understands the goal of the commandments as the virtuous life. The commandments specify and enjoin key life-features—practices and abstentions—that are characteristic of persons who satisfy certain norms of personal formation. The enjoined actions, omissions, and attitudes are underwritten and given their import by the moral framework that they presuppose. They indicate the framework for living, but their brief expressions in commandments offer only slight indications of the wisdom that upholds them and gives them their meaning. Mature understanding of the commandments requires wise construal of them within the framework to which they belong—in the case of the Jewish law, Jewish wisdom. Often the discourse surrounding the commandment adds detail. The ways the best-formed members of the community understand and conduct themselves within the framework fill out the meaning of the commandments.

Second, in Chapter 6 we said that virtues are dispositions: regularities of concern, thought, powers, and fellowship. What *kind* of dispositions are these? Some people say they are habits. Others liken virtues to skills. While habits are essential to virtues, I will argue that *habit* is not quite the concept we are seeking. This is so because of what we might call the intelligence of the virtues. Virtues are mindful, creative, and improvisatory dispositions. Skills are "intelligent," and while skills are involved in virtues, and the virtues of willpower are more

Virtue Ethics. Robert Campbell Roberts, Oxford University Press.
© Robert Campbell Roberts 2026. DOI: 10.1093/9780197848005.003.0011

purely skill-like than other virtues, skill is also not quite right as a general category for virtues. I will suggest that Aristotle's notion of a *hexis* (Latin: *habitus*) is the right one and that the substantive virtues are a special kind of habitus that is based in concern for the good.

Our third question, to be addressed in Chapter 9, will be to evaluate Aristotle's famous idea that we can determine which traits are virtues by calculating a mean between two extremes, which are vices. And fourth, in the latter half of Chapter 9, we'll return to the theme of the proper nature of moral philosophy that we began discussing in Chapter 5.

Christian Virtues and the Jewish Law

We have leaned pretty heavily on Paul's letters to the churches for our lists of the Christian virtues. Despite the prominence of these lists in Paul and other New Testament authors, Christianity is often regarded as having an "ethics of law" or a "divine command theory" and is thus contrasted with Aristotle, who supposedly has an "ethics of virtue." Even Elizabeth Anscombe, who is herself a Christian, in an essay commending a return to something like an ethics of virtue, says that Christianity has a law ethic. "Between Aristotle and us came Christianity, with its law conception of ethics. For Christianity derived its ethical notions from the Torah."[1] Paul is ambivalent about the law. On the one hand, he tells the Christian congregations at Rome that the law was a confederate of sin and an agent of death from which we are now free:

While we were living in the flesh, our sinful passions, aroused by the law, were at work in our members to bear fruit for death. But now we [who believe in Jesus as our redeemer] are discharged from the law,

---

[1] Anscombe, "Modern Moral Philosophy," 5. See Chapter 2 above. See also J. B. Schneewind, "The Misfortunes of Virtue," *Ethics 101* (1990): 44–45, where Schneewind says that because of its law conception of ethics, Christianity is one of the historical misfortunes of virtue.

dead to that which held us captive, so that we are slaves not under the old written code but in the new life of the Spirit. (Rom 7:5–6)

On the other hand, Paul seems reminiscent of Jesus, who while perhaps appearing to rewrite the ancient Jewish law, warns that he came not to abolish the law, but to fulfill it (Matt 5:17): "So [says Paul] the law is holy and the commandment is holy and just and good" (Rom 7:12), and "Christ is the end [that is, the goal, the point: the *telos*] of the law" (Rom 10:4). So our philosophical question—one of the questions of Christian virtue ethics—is, How are the commandments of the law related to the virtues of the well-developed Christian? I shall argue that these rules aim ultimately at character, that they are therefore a blessing, that practitioners of Christian ethics need to understand their ethical status, and that Christian virtue ethics, as involving meditation on them, is an aid to this essential understanding. The point of the Torah was and is to form people's character as the people of God, not just to secure compliance with God's "dictates."

Commandment and Character

At the end of *Nicomachean Ethics*, in his transition to *Politics*, Aristotle connects the laws of the city-state with the character traits of the happy members of the community that he has been exploring in the previous ten books. The connection between the traits and the laws governing the community is that the latter will inculcate in the citizens patterns of understanding, acting, and feeling joys and distresses characteristic of mature human beings. He doesn't expect mere behavioral conformity to the laws by itself to yield eudaimonia. The laws will have this desired effect only by way of a psychological development in which the spirit of those laws takes root in the character of the people.

A commandment names a type of action or attitude or abstention, which it enjoins or prohibits. Such action or attitude or abstention can be merely episodic or in other ways abstracted from an agent's character; but what it enjoins or proscribes can also be construed as expressing or representing a character and way of life. Plausibly, implicit in the commandments of the Jewish law is some qualifier to the effect of "always," "never," or "generally, in relevant circumstances." The commandments are not one-off like "*Esther*, please shut *the back door now*!" The word 'generally' brings the commandment into alignment with the dispositional character of virtues—the fact that they characterize a personal regularity over extended time. The fact that the commandment not to covet your neighbor's property implies this "never" corresponds to the fact that a generous, property-respecting person is *reliably* generous and just, and that this is a disposition of his thinking and desiring. I have said, though, that this generality is not absolute: imperfect reliability is compatible with the attribution of a virtue.

The deep and temporally extended character of the virtues raises the question whether virtues can be commanded, and thus whether the commandments can be properly thought of as commanding the virtues. It might seem that virtues, in their nature as character traits, can't be commanded because they aren't responses we can undertake; only responses we can undertake can be meaningfully commanded. But the premise might be doubted. Perhaps responses we can indirectly undertake can be meaningfully commanded. And this seems to be assumed in many biblical commandments, for example, the commandments to love. Furthermore, a commandment that commands an action, an attitude, or a refraining from a kind of action can be directly commanded and can be at least a step toward acquiring a character trait. The command, "Don't look at it that way. Look at it like this!" seems sensible. Even a person without the trait of chastity can begin to practice chastity by the intentional redirection of his attention—away from the object of lust and toward the reasons that chastity is good for him and those he loves.

Briefly, the law as a whole is a more or less detailed or general linguistic enshrinement of the thought characteristic of a moral framework such as Judaism or Christianity.[2] The detail is necessarily limited. The form of a commandment is not a very rich articulation of the moral framework to which it belongs. The commandment form only hints at the reality—the richly articulated character with its passions,

---

[2] For an analogy, see *Nicomachean Ethics* 5.1–2.

emotions, nuances of reasons for action, complexities and depths of understanding, and its perceptions of situations. The articulation of the grammar of a virtue is a richer presentation of what is merely indicated in the commandment. Bringing this out is a philosophical task and is a main business of Christian or Jewish virtue ethics. The psalmists' comments (Ps 1, 19, 119) about the glories of the law give voice to an appreciation of its deeper grammar of the implied virtues. And Jesus's comments about the inwardness implications of the law (Matt 5:21–22, 27–28) do the same kind of thing. So we have the bare commandments, as written, for example, in the decalogue. But they are surrounded by comments, both in the decalogue (Exod 20) itself, by speeches of Moses, by wise psalmists, by further elaborations as in Leviticus 19–20, and by wise people such as the prophets, Jesus, and rabbis.

So we can think of each of the ten commandments of Exodus 20 as indirectly enjoining one or more traits of character that are aspects of the excellent communal life lived before God (*shalom*):

1 have no other gods before the Lord (trait: ultimate reverence for God and only God)
2 have no idols (trait: ultimate reverence for and loyalty to God and only God)
3 don't abuse the Lord's name (trait: ultimate reverence for God and only God)
4 keep the sabbath (trait: good sense about work and rest)
5 honor your parents (trait: excellent filiality (filial "piety"))
6 don't murder (trait: reverence for human life, respect for people, justice)
7 don't commit adultery (trait: chastity, justice, family loyalty)
8 don't steal (trait: honesty[3])
9 don't testify falsely against your neighbor (trait: honesty, respect, compassion)

---

[3] Plausibly, honesty is a combination of truthfulness and justice (including respect for others). See Robert Roberts and Ryan West, "The Virtue of Honesty: A Conceptual Exploration," in *Integrity, Honesty, and Truth Seeking*, ed. C. Miller and R. West (New York: Oxford University Press, 2020).

10 don't covet what isn't yours (trait: honesty, generosity, gratitude)

The traits are broader than the commandments, at least if the commandments are thought of as focusing on particular kinds of actions and attitudes. Reverence for God is far more than not abusing his name, and reverence for human life more than not murdering people, and honesty more than not stealing. From the multiplicity of other commandments in the Pentateuch we can infer that the ten commandments are only a summary or sampling of God's will for his people. Much more detail is possible.[4] But no number of specific commandments would match the richness of the virtues they indirectly enjoin.[5]

If we think of an action, as in contrast with mere behavior, as getting its identity from the reason or motive for which it is performed, then we have a less abstract view of action. For example, let us say that I criticize someone's argument. What did I do? Yes, I raised objections to an argument, but I did this for a reason. My reason might be that the truth has high stakes in this case: perhaps people could be endangered by accepting the argument. In that case, my motive is to guard against harm, and my act of criticizing seems to be morally good. What was I doing in criticizing?—Avoiding harm. But maybe my motive was malicious—say, to humiliate the proposer of the argument. What was I doing in criticizing?—Trying to humiliate someone. There's a big difference between these two actions, both of which can be performed by criticizing somebody's argument. And the difference in reason or motive might also be dispositional: my concern to guard against harm might express my virtue of compassion, and my desire to humiliate might express my cruelty.

---

[4] In her essay "Open Thy Hand Wide: Moses and the Origins of American Liberalism," Marilynne Robinson cites a number of commandments from Leviticus which she takes as enjoining the generosity that is an aspect of loving one's neighbor. In *When I Was a Child, I Read Books* (New York: Farrar, Straus, and Giroux, 2013), 59–82.

[5] The Book of Proverbs, with its focus on wisdom, righteousness, holiness, and the fear of the Lord, approaches ethical guidance in a somewhat different way from the Pentateuch (but see Leviticus 19–20, which also makes clear that it is enjoining holiness, and not just behavioral compliance). Proverbs' form seems to be that of identifying an action-type along with recommendation of it or warning against it by reference to its tendency to affect flourishing.

Consider an example. The seventh commandment, "Do not commit adultery," can be construed as ruling out having sexual intercourse with somebody else's spouse or with someone other than one's own spouse. Many people manage to accomplish this abstinence on many days of their life. If you're accused of violating the commandment, it's not much of a defense to reply, "I haven't violated it yet this month." Such an accomplishment is not plausibly what the commandment is enjoining, because it's compatible with being an adulterer. More plausibly, the commandment is really ruling out being an adulterer. Not being an adulterer seems closer to being a character trait than merely abstaining from behavior. It might be thought that not being an adulterer is being *consistent*, across time, in refraining from acts of adulterous intercourse. A Christian might pride himself or herself on having a perfect record of this kind. But Jesus rules out this interpretation when he says (Matt 5:27) that lusting after someone counts morally as adultery. So the Christian should think twice about feeling that pride. Jesus's gloss on the seventh commandment not only shows that the "end" of the commandment against adultery is chastity (a character trait), but that the character trait in question is a disposition of the mind and heart, not merely a habit or policy of behavioral abstention.

Presumably, the raging appetite that you sometimes feel for your spouse doesn't count as lust. This is a conceptual point about the nature of lust, but it's also a psychological point if you are beginning to acquire the virtue of chastity. Desires involve construals (ways of "seeing" the object of desire),[6] and in sexual desire chaste people construe their spouses in ways that lusting after strangers, mere acquaintances, or even friends cannot involve. For example, you construe your spouse as the parent of your children, or the possible or future parent of your children, or the partner with whom you've had many experiences in common, or the partner to whom you are committed for life. Even if such thoughts aren't salient in the moment of desire, they form a background that affects its phenomenology.

---

[6] On the nature of construals, see Robert Roberts, *Emotions: An Essay in Aid of Moral Psychology* (Cambridge: Cambridge University Press, 2003) and *Emotions in the Moral Life* (Cambridge: Cambridge University Press, 2013).

Compliance and Life in the Family of God

It can seem that God's aim in promulgating commandments is compliance, and that God will reward those who comply by giving them a good life in exchange. The relation between compliance and reward, to this way of thinking, is external, or it's internal just to the extent that it's fair: do this, and you get that; pay, and I'll give you the goods. But this isn't the most sympathetic reading of the relevant texts.

> If you heed these ordinances, by diligently observing them, the LORD your God will maintain with you the covenant loyalty that he swore to your ancestors; he will love you, bless you, and multiply you; he will bless the fruit of your womb and the fruit of your ground, your grain and your wine and your oil, the increase of your cattle and the issue of your flock, in the land that he swore to your ancestors to give you. You shall be the most blessed of peoples, with neither sterility nor barrenness among you or your livestock. (Deut 7:12–14)
>
> Choose life so that you and your descendants may live, loving the LORD your God, obeying him, and holding fast to him; for that means life to you and length of days, so that you may live in the land that the LORD swore to give to your ancestors, to Abraham, to Isaac, and to Jacob. (Deut 30:19b–20)

The real point of the law is the beauty of family life. In calling for obedience, the Lord is seeking everybody's well-being, the happiness of God's family.

'Israel' is the name of a people, but originally it was the name of an individual man, the father of a family (Gen 35:9–10). The descendants of that family, and therefore Israel's extended family, became the agents of God's ministry to the people of the world who were not descended from Israel the man. Believers who are not Israelis by ethnicity have been incorporated into Israel's family by adoption (Rom 8) and encouraged to call God father, as Jesus, who is God's son, himself did when he taught his disciples to pray. The apostle Paul regularly addresses fellow members of the churches as "*adelphoi*" (siblings, brothers and sisters, family).

The members of a healthy family love one another, and so they support one another; bear one another's burdens, weep when fellow members weep and rejoice with those who rejoice. The way of family life is love. Whether or not the "way" or "how" of family life is articulated and set out in a code, family life must *have* a way and a how. In a family, not just anything goes; some kinds of conduct are disruptive, causing rifts in the family, and others promote family life, deepening ties and enriching the fellowship. So it may be handy to regulate the way and the how by having some rules, especially for the less mature members. But the basic rule, the one of which all the rest are specifications, is "love one another." Family life goes on best if everyone understands the import of the rules, "internalizing" them in mind and heart by seeking, for self and the others, the internal goods of family life. And that seeking is a good part of love.

This explains what might otherwise seem the extravagant enthusiasm of some psalmists for a bunch of rules: "the precepts of the Lord . . . rejoice the heart." "More to be desired are they than gold, even much fine gold; sweeter also than honey, and drippings of the honeycomb" (Ps 19:8, 10). "I delight in the way of your decrees as much as in all riches." "I find my delight in your commandments, because I love them." "If your law had not been my delight, I would have perished in my misery" (Ps 119:14, 47, 92). I think these poets speak in such affectionate, even passionate terms about the glories of the law because they take it to be an expression, in some detail, of God's fatherly heart for his people. It reminds and assures them of God's guiding love. The faithful Israelite who delights daily and nightly in meditating on the Lord's law (Ps 1:2) is thinking with gratitude and admiration about God's disposition toward him and his people. To him, the law isn't a bunch of rules, but more like a fatherly letter expressing the Lord's heart for him and his people, well-wishing instructions for their happiness and peace.

The psalmists' attitude is a far cry from the grim look and the gritted teeth of compliance in Ogden Nash's poem, "Kind of an Ode to Duty,"

> O Duty,
> Why hast thou not the visage of a sweetie or a cutie?

> Why displayest thou the countenance of the kind of consci-
> entious organizing spinster
> That the minute you see her you are aginster?[7]

Judging with the psalmists, such a reading of God's central rules for family life is a symptom of something going badly awry in the human heart. It marks a shift in the sense of 'due' from a setting of family love to a setting of moral coercion. 'Due' in the context of family love is found in the prayer of General Thanksgiving: "And, we beseech thee, give us that due sense of all thy mercies, that our hearts may be unfeignedly thankful."[8] 'Due' here means 'appropriate,' 'fitting,' and is the kind of fulfillment that's shown by the well-nurtured child who fittingly loves her good Daddy with the unimpeded affection that is 'due' him. It is the kind of 'due' found in the duties of gratitude.[9] By contrast, the 'due' of moral coercion is shown in the notice: "The rent is due at the beginning of the month." You pay, perhaps with grim resignation, what is due because you want to keep living in your apartment. To treat God's directions for family life as creating duties in this second sense is morally to opt out of family life.

The Downside of the Law

The ideal relation of the specific rules of the law to character traits is that the rules commend types of actions, attitudes, and omissions that are marks of the character traits of a morally fit member of God's people. They thus represent the virtues somewhat indirectly (by way of the concept of one of the virtue's characteristic "outputs"—for example, the concept of honoring your parents or abstaining from adultery or murder or coveting your neighbor's property) and in an imperative mood. Furthermore, obeying the behavioral or attitudinal

---

[7] https://www.poetrynook.com/poem/kind-ode-duty#google_vignette.

[8] *Book of Common Prayer*, 33.

[9] Some papers objecting to the idea of duties of gratitude may suffer from confusing these two senses of 'due.' They belong to different moral-conceptual worlds. See, for example, Claudia Card, "Gratitude and Obligation," *American Philosophical Quarterly 25* (1988): 115–127.

orders may carry a person somewhat in the direction of the corresponding character traits by way of "habituation." These facts about how keeping the commandments supports the virtues of God's people contribute to the glory of the law.

Another issue, however, is the moral state of the persons to whom the law is addressed. If you are infected with sin and so read the commandment through the lens of sin, the association of the commandment with character is likely to be one of the first casualties. Sinful passions become lenses through which we sinners view the commandments in relation to ourselves, our neighbors, and the situations of our lives. It seems to me there are at least four related ways that a sinner can take the law as an "opportunity" (*aphormē*, Rom 7:11)—for the satisfaction of sinful self-concern. The first is basic to two of the others. It is *legalism*. Legalism is the interpretation of the law as enjoining simple outward compliance in transactional exchange for the favor of God: literally, just don't commit the act of adultery, the act of murder, and so forth, and do tithe your income, wash your hands on the required occasions, fast twice on the sabbath, and so forth, and you'll be OK before the Lord.

A legalist's approach to the law is like that of people who rely on GPS to get where we're going. Turn right here, then go straight, then take a slight left while staying in the center lane, and so forth, and you'll get where you want to go. Obey the commands, and you'll get there. The more we rely on GPS rather than a map, the less understanding we gain of the layout of the area. For people not interested in geography, this cost in understanding may not be much of a loss. But given the crucial place of wisdom in our character, legalism is an impoverishing reduction of the glory of the moral life. If we're to be mature agents, understanding where we're going and why is a *crucial part* of "getting there." This is why virtue ethics is a *grammar* of the *virtues*, and not just a set of instructions on what to do and not do. It's an exercise in gaining orientation through exploration of the lay of the whole land. So legalism is a lazy short-circuiting of the kind of understanding exemplified by Moses and Jesus.

This misinterpretation of the law is itself sinful for an educated Jew or Christian, who should know better, but it may be used for purposes that add sin to sin. It allows you to present yourself falsely as righteous before others, or at least to feel impenitently secure in your moral status. As presentation to others, it serves *vanity*, and as presentation to self, *moral complacency*. Jesus calls this *hypocrisy* (Matt 6:1–6, 16–18; Matt 15:7–9 Matt 23:23–28; Luke 12:1–3). Possibly worse yet, legalism provides opportunity for you to exalt yourself by comparing yourself with less fastidious others to their disadvantage (Luke 18:9–14). This is called *self-righteousness*. Or, if you sense the deeper requirement of the law, it may spark *rebellion* so that you say, as it were, "don't fence me in; I shall do as I please!" This is the response that Paul identifies in Romans 7:7–12. It's akin to the attitude of the Nash character. In a moral sense, legalism, vanity, moral complacency, hypocrisy, and self-righteousness are all forms of rebellion.

All these missteps are expressions of bad character (moral unseriousness and evasiveness) and, it appears, are not corrigible by our own efforts. If that is our strategy, sin always wins out and we fall back into it. The missteps can be corrected only by life in the Spirit of the one who is the "end" of the law. We attach ourselves to him, and to the greatest extent possible in this life live hand in hand with him and under his moral protection. And so we too in this way fulfill the commandments in our lives, though "this way" means that it is only in one sense *we* who fulfill the commandments. In a sense, *he* in his love fulfills the commandments "in" us. In our halting way we follow Jesus and if we are earnest in our faith, we persevere in doing our best, but in the end, *we* always fulfill the law only because he does and we are his. And the fulfillment of the law is the virtues of love—his above all, but also ours.

Virtues as Habits, Virtues as Skills?

We have repeatedly called virtues "traits." They are qualities or features of persons that affect our conduct, taken in a many-faceted sense: they affect our actions, our behavior where it's less than outright action, our perceptions of our situations, our desires, our impulses, our emotions and feelings, and our deliberations about what to do and how to size up what we've done and how we've behaved. We have said that these traits are temporally extended dispositions: they aren't to be identified with any of their "outputs" (actions, emotions, perceptions, and so forth), but are in some sense the origin and explanation of the outputs. Gilbert Ryle (1949) illustrates the notion of a disposition with the brittleness of glass. Its brittleness is a disposition to shatter under certain conditions (say, when it's hit with a certain force by a metal hammer). The shattering is the output; the brittleness is the readiness or disposition to shatter, given the specific conditions (the hammer-blow). The brittleness can be explained by the physical state of the glass—presumably, its molecular structure, its temperature (that it's cool enough to be rigid), and so forth. This physical story specifies the kind of disposition it is.

Now, what kind of disposition is a virtue? We might be inclined to say that it's a state of our brains, a neurological disposition. That's no doubt true, but for a discussion of ethics, it's not specific enough. Our digestive processes are governed by neurological dispositions: the brain in a healthy state detects inputs of nourishment and automatically sets in motion digestive events in the stomach and other digestive organs, the activity of the heart increases, and so on. It satisfies very nicely a stimulus-response model, just as the brittleness of glass does. But if virtues are neurological dispositions, they aren't *that* kind. Neither digestion nor brittleness is personal and intelligent: they yield their output automatically and mechanically, given the stimulus conditions. But the virtues are personal (qualities of whole persons, not just bodily processes) and intelligent (not just automatic responses).

Habit

A sub-tradition within virtue ethics holds that virtues are habits. In the English translation of the works of Saint Thomas Aquinas, Thomas's word '*habitus*,' by which he intends an equivalent of Aristotle's word '*hexis*,' is translated as 'habit.' 'Habit' is not a very good translation of the Latin and Greek terms, but habits do seem to be qualities of whole persons. We attribute habits to people, not to their parts. In a moment I will try to locate them with respect to intelligence. Let's consider whether virtues are habits.

N. T. Wright illustrates the kind of disposition that virtues are by the amazing story of Chesley Sullenberger's safe landing of US Airways

Flight 1549 when, soon after departing LaGuardia Airport, the engines were disabled by running into a flock of Canada geese. The plane was over densely populated territory with a full load of people, and Sullenberger and his co-pilot had limited time for the plane to glide down. They were unsure that they could get the plane as far as a nearby small airport before it hit the ground, and didn't dare try to set it on the New Jersey Turnpike. So they decided to try landing in the Hudson River. Success would require masterful judgment and skill.

> In the two or three minutes they had before landing, Sullenberger and his copilot had to do the following vital things. . . . They had to shut down the engines. They had to set the right speed so that the plane could glide as long as possible without power. . . . They had to get the nose of the plane down to maintain speed. They had to disconnect the autopilot and override the flight management system. They had to activate the "ditch" system, which seals vents and valves, to make the plane as waterproof as possible once it hit the water. Most important of all, they had to fly and then glide the plane in a fast left-hand turn so that it could come down facing south, going with the flow of the river. And—having already turned off the engines—they had to do this using only the battery-operated systems and the emergency generator. Then they had to straighten the plane up from the tilt of the sharp-left turn so that, on landing, the plane would be exactly level from side to side. Finally, they had to get the nose back up again, but not too far up, and land straight and flat on the water.[10]

Wright notes that people have called what the pilots did that day a miracle, but he prefers to call it "the power of right habits" and "character."[11]

But note that if someone were to ask, "How in the world did they manage to do it?" it would be odd to answer, "They landed that plane by habit." They weren't in the habit of landing passenger planes on the Hudson! Speaking of petitionary prayer, John Calvin comments on people who do it mechanically.

[10] Wright, *After You Believe*, 19–20.
[11] Wright, *After You Believe*, 20.

And although they admit it to be a necessary remedy for their ills, because it would be fatal to lack the help of God which they are beseeching, still it appears that they perform this duty from habit, because their hearts are meanwhile cold, and they do not ponder what they ask.[12]

Notice Calvin's association of habit with coldness of heart and absence of attention. Habit is the mode in which you act with mindless indifference without paying attention to what you're doing. When you have done something purely by habit, it is hard to remember what you have done (or even whether you've done it!) because you weren't paying attention.

Habits' mindlessness is what makes them important. If we had to think through or attend to everything we do, down to the gritty details, we would be less capable of complex actions than we are. With habits we can do complex actions while paying attention to only certain aspects of them—namely, not to the parts that are habitual. Many of the micro-actions that Sullenberger performed in landing the plane safely were no doubt performed by habit, for example, the specific muscular contractions involved in working the steering mechanisms of the plane, the quick automatic inferences he made from a reckoning of where the plane was in relation to the river and the muscular movements by which he adjusted the rate of descent or the angle of the plane. These muscular contractions are what we might call behaviors, in distinction from full-fledged actions. Much of our behavior in this sense is habitual. But in the overall *action* of landing Flight 1549, Sullenberger is engaged, mind and heart, throughout his amazing performance, with the complexities of timing, the physics of gliding, the specific mechanics of the plane, the psychological maintenance of calm among the passengers, all with an eye on the goal of a safe landing. His action is filled with judgment and even deliberation, though the deliberation must have been pretty quick. His overall performance, though it depends on many micro-automatic behaviors, is highly intelligent, passionate, goal-focused, and attentive. These features make it a good

---

[12] John Calvin, *Institutes of the Christian Religion*, trans. Ford Lewis Battles, ed. John T. McNeill (Philadelphia: The Westminster Press), 856.

analogy for virtue. It is nothing like the inattentive rote praying by "habit" of which Calvin complains.

On a scale of automaticity/personal intelligence, habit is somewhere between a process like digestion and a virtue. A well-engrained habit allows you, as we say, to "do it in your sleep," yet with attention and effort we can intentionally manage our habits, breaking, deepening, or fine-tuning them. A habit is more automatic and less intelligent than a virtue, but it's more subject to intelligent, personal direction than a mere process. You can't deliberately regulate the process of digestion in the way that you can your habits. But mere habits can't be virtues. Virtues are better categorized as habitus.

Habitus

Aristotle's word that is typically translated "habituate" is *ethizesthai*, from the word *ēthos* which means "custom." *Ethizesthai*—the process of becoming accustomed—is how habitus, and in particular the virtues, are acquired. By repeatedly acting justly, you become accustomed to do so. But as far as English goes, I think you can become "accustomed" to acting ethically without becoming wise. Acting justly is part of your routine, and you do so with a certain amount of intelligence, but as to a deep impression of its importance, a passionate commitment to it, and resourcefulness about how to bring justice about, custom isn't adequate. So I think Aristotle must have in mind a developmental process that's not quite captured by thinking in terms of acquiring a custom. We will go a bit deeper into this question of "habituation" in Chapter 10, "A Reciprocity Between Acting and Understanding," in our discussion of acquiring wisdom through acting.

Think of a pianist, an expert performer of Beethoven's works. She understands Beethoven in all his diversity of expression. Her performances consistently reflect the varying moods of the compositions and are beautiful in technical execution. She "brings out" the lyricism in the lyrical passages, the anger in the angry passages, the tender sadness in the melancholic passages, and so forth. Her performance of each section of a piece reflects her sensitivity to its overall structure, her sense of its whole. If someone were to ask, marveling about a performance, How does she do it?, it would be muddle-headed to answer, "She does it by habit," but just right to say, "She has a wonderful *habitus*." She is skilled, sensitive, and intelligently flexible in her understanding and powers of execution of Beethoven's works.

Habits can be deployed in acts of improvisation, but they aren't improvisatory; they can be parts or aspects of *habitus*, but they aren't *habitus*. Habits are the "mechanical" parts of *habitus*, but *habitus* are not mechanical. They are personal, intelligent, and goal-directed.

In being *habitus* (*hexeis* in Aristotle's vocabulary), virtues are intelligent dispositions, ways of being attentive to and wisely improvising responses to situations. Their outputs are therefore not automatic but intentional, informed by attention, sensitive to the particularities of situation, and creditable to the agent. At moments, no doubt, the agent is carried along on the tide of his gentleness, affected without intention by his compassion, and effortless in his self-control, but even then, it will be typical that these automaticities are under the direction of an attentive will for the good.

Skill

Sullenberger's excellence as a pilot is better termed skill than habit. Skills are abilities that are intelligent and deployed with attention. In employing a skill, the practitioner improvises and may even brilliantly adapt to circumstances. So skills, too, are better termed *habitus* than habits. Skills depend on habits, but they aren't habits. They're rational in a way that habits aren't. Being abilities, skills can be deployed for a variety of reasons. And this implies that not all virtues are skills (though plausibly, all virtues involve or presuppose skills). The reasons for the actions that express some virtues are "built in" to the virtues in such a way that, as Augustine says, "no one can make bad use" of them.[13] For example, you can't "use" justice or kindness for evil. If you intend evil, then it's not justice or kindness you're "using."

---

[13] Augustine, *Of Free Will* ii.19, quoted in Aquinas, *Summa Theologiae* I-II, 55.4, objection 1.

We might be tempted to say that such virtues are intelligent about the ends of life, whereas skills are intelligent only about the means. But skills have their own ends. The end of lock-picking is to get locks open without the key, the end of hitting a baseball is to make it go far in a chosen direction, and the end of self-control is mastery of one's impulses, emotions, and habits. These skills have ends, but their ends are not the goal of human life. Skills presuppose a limited kind of wisdom, but the life of virtue presupposes wisdom about the goals of our life. An essential element of such wisdom is caring about those ends. Caring goes beyond skill and is a different kind of psychological reality.

But consider this: A skill is an *ability* to do *something*. It's a power with a purpose. As a power, it doesn't imply wanting to do the thing, but in practice, it requires aiming to do the thing, which aiming normally requires wanting to do it, at least provisionally. Apart from the gun that's pointed at your head, you may not want to pick the lock, but given the gun, you want to do it. Apart from its actual aiming, a skill remains inert, merely a potency, not actualized in practice. Yet skills are essentially *to be practiced*. Skills are highly diverse and particularized to specific goals. There is the purpose internal to the skill, and there are the purposes to which the deployment of the skill is instrumental. Whether a skill is deployed in the interest of virtue (that is, of the good) depends on something outside the skill, namely, the goal for which it is deployed. Skills can be deployed for many purposes other than the good.

Our examples of habitus so far are examples of skills. Sullenberger's expertise as a pilot is a skill, but it's not quite a virtue. A pilot might use the same skills that Sullenberger displayed in saving the lives of the passengers on Flight 1549 just to make money or become famous or even to do something horrific like crash his plane into a building full of people. Sullenberger himself, it turns out, is a man of virtue, as shown by his concern for the passengers. Saving them while keeping people on the ground safe was overwhelmingly the guiding reason of his effort. After the plane was in the water, he walked up and down the aisle a couple of times to make sure everybody was off before leaving the sinking plane himself. And once in the life raft, he took off his shirt and gave it to a passenger who was suffering from the

January cold.[14] But his expertise is separable from his generosity, his sense of duty and compassion.

Similarly, our Beethoven performer's habitus is a skill, though I think a Christian will think it may be more than a skill because of its sensitivity to beauty. Beauty, for the Christian as for the Platonist, is closely associated with the Good, and the Good is a stand-in for and expression of God. If the Good is a stand-in for God, Beauty is a stand-in for the Good (see Plato's *Phaedrus*), and so a habitus like that of the Beethoven performer is not quite a mere skill, but more like a virtue (an aesthetic virtue?). We are cast into ambivalence about calling such a virtue "moral" by the petty character of some good musicians and by reports of Nazis who combined extraordinarily cruel inhumanity with high artistic taste.

For the Stoics, virtue is a skill, a know-how about life, an expertise at living.[15] So the goal of this skill *is* the good (as the Stoic conceives it). The Stoics' hyper-wariness about emotions, combined with their claim that virtue is skill at the living of life, puts them in a bind. If you have no emotions about the good, then you don't care about it. But if you don't care about the good, then your skill about life will never be implemented. So if Stoic virtue is skill at living life and the practice of skills requires their use *for* some *purpose*, then Stoic virtue, requiring, as it does, a concern for what the skill is directed at, can't be apatheia (emotionlessness).

The shortcoming of skill as an answer to the question, What kind of dispositions are virtues? is that mere skills are indifferent relatively to the moral good, while virtues—at least, moral virtues and Christian virtues—are by their nature aimed at the good (God's will and the well-being of creation, especially the human part of it). The virtue of compassion, for example, cannot be exemplified for any reason other than the relief or prevention of suffering. Self-control is a self-management skill and so are virtues of the same ilk, such as patience, perseverance, and courage. These virtues seem in principle divorceable from the good. They can be advantageous for thieves and murderers, in contrast

---

[14] Wright, *After You Believe*, 19.
[15] Christopher Gill, "What Is Stoic Virtue?," https://modernstoicism.com/what-is-stoic-virtue-by-chris-gill/.

with justice and compassion which, to say the obvious, discourage thievery and murder. But if we add the qualifier "Christian" to their names, speaking of Christian self-control, and so forth, we lock them into connection with love, faith, and hope, so that they do after all, if indirectly, imply an orientation to the good. Christian self-control is a moral virtue by way of its service to love of God and neighbor.

The virtue of self-control, considered just in itself, is more like being a good lock-picker than like being an honest person. The thief can be just as self-controlled in his thieving as the truthful person is in his truth-telling. Self-control does indeed have a goal: the control of emotions, impulses, habits, and so forth. But its grammar leaves open what further goal such control serves, in particular whether that further goal is a good one. This is why self-control is a different kind of virtue from truthfulness; it aims at a good (control), but not necessarily any part of the ultimate good. Ideally, self-control is in the service of justice, compassion, generosity, forgivingness, and so forth. I think the reason self-control nevertheless counts as a virtue is that it is a skill so intimately tied up with being an integrated person. It serves a goal that is integral, if subordinate, to the goal of which the virtues of caring are central. In the highest integration of persons, self-mastery, self-possession, is an essential dimension of the virtues of caring for the good.

Self-control, then, is a skill. But even virtues that are not just skills involve skills as elements. The compassionate person, because he cares about others' well-being, needs to have at least basic skills in avoiding others' suffering and soothing it when it occurs. The just person, because she cares that justice prevail and realizes that justice now can sometimes increase injustice in the future, needs the skill to anticipate adroitly the consequences of present actions.

Conclusion

We've considered two questions that bear on the rationality or intelligence of Christian virtues: How are the virtues related to formulated rules for the moral life, in particular, God's commandments? and What kind of disposition is a virtue?

I've proposed that God's intention in promulgating commandments is the formation of a people composed of persons with traits that fit them to be God's people, functional members of God's kingdom. These traits are the Christian virtues of faith, hope, love, compassion, wisdom, generosity, forgivingness, humility, patience, gratitude, and so forth. The second question calls for locating the psychology of virtues with respect to the dispositions of habit, skill, and habitus. I have claimed that while virtues presuppose and "contain" habits and skills, they are not just habits or skills or any combination thereof but are kinds of habitus. Skills too are habitus, that is, intelligent dispositions whose display in action involves intention and attention, but the substantive virtues are a special kind of habitus that is centered in caring about the good: God above all, then human neighbors, and the rest of God's creation. In the next chapter we will examine two further questions related to rationality and intelligence: What is the criterion by which we distinguish habitus that are virtues from ones that aren't? and What is the role of philosophical ethics in the life of Christian virtue?

9

The Golden Mean and the Pursuit of Wisdom

Introduction

We're considering four questions that touch on the concept of a virtue as a rational norm. In Chapter 8 we looked at rules, and in particular the commandments of the Jewish law, and we examined the notions of habit, skill, and habitus as possible categories in which to understand the concept of a virtue.

In this chapter we'll consider two more questions. The first is about Aristotle's famous idea that what gives a trait the status of a virtue is its falling in the middle of a continuum on whose extreme ends are vices. Even Aristotle seems to admit that this idea doesn't work. A better way is based on the idea of a moral framework that I introduced in Chapter 5. It helps to clarify Aristotle's idea that virtues are dispositions to get actions, passions, and judgments "right." I think Aristotle is right about this, but he mistakenly thinks it is further elaboration of the idea of a mean. Second, we will then finish the chapter by returning to the theme of the proper nature of moral philosophy that we began discussing in Chapter 5. I will argue that Christian virtue ethics, which is distinctly philosophical and, I think, a paradigm of moral philosophy, is an activity that can and should nurture its practitioners in an ethical kind of understanding that has traditionally been called wisdom and entails the other virtues. Moral philosophy is an effort to acquire an understanding of our life that gets actions, passions, and judgments morally right. Such understanding is a virtue and presupposes the whole range of virtues; so moral philosophy is in the end an effort, by philosophical means, to become mature, more rational, human beings. It's a formative exploration of the norms for being human.

Virtue Ethics. Robert Campbell Roberts, Oxford University Press.
© Robert Campbell Roberts 2026. DOI: 10.1093/9780197848005.003.0012

What Gives a Trait the Status of a Virtue?

The Question

What makes courage a virtue? What makes cowardice a vice? Why couldn't they exchange places, courage being a vice and cowardice a virtue? After all, courage can get you killed and cowardice can save you some trouble, maybe even your life. Justice can get you in trouble and injustice can get you out of it (as a recent president of the United States has repeatedly shown). A number of traits or qualities of persons get the title of virtues, and another set are designated as vices. But what sorts these lists into virtues and vices? Consider these moral qualities:

greed, justice, courage, arrogance, self-indulgence, cowardice, patience, vengefulness, respect for others, compassion, cruelty, forgivingness, kindness, humility, vanity, contemptuousness, generosity.

The list could go on. These qualities are all moral ones, in the sense that they have moral bearing, for good or evil. It is hard enough to say what marks off qualities that belong to this category from traits or qualities that are non-moral, such as being six feet tall, having darkish skin, being male or female, and so forth. But, sticking with moral qualities for the moment, how do we sort them into two lists, the virtues and the vices? Anyone can do it, but what's the principle?

Gentleness: Aristotle's Doctrine of the Mean

Aristotle's conception of "moral" (*ēthikos*) is broader than ours. For example, "quick wit" (being a good conversationalist) is a moral quality. But I think he shares with Christianity the broad idea that "moral" qualities are the essentially human ones. In moral thought, being rich or powerful or beautiful or strong doesn't make you more of a human being, but being loving, humble, just, and courageous does. We say of someone with deep wisdom or unusual kindness or courage, "Now there's a *real* human being!" "He's a mensch!" And of somebody of corresponding shortcomings we might say, "He's arrogated a lot of power to himself, but he's not much of a human being." True, Christians believe we're all completely human insofar as we are all of the species of beings who are potentially moral or immoral, and for that reason must be equally respected, whether or not we're virtuous. But in the virtues we actualize that potential. And in that sense, person can differ from person in the degree of their humanity.

Oddly, one of Aristotle's most widely adopted teachings is his proposed answer to the question of how we sort traits into virtues and vices: To be a virtue is to be at or near a mean between two extremes, an extreme of defect (too little) and an extreme of excess (too much) with respect to emotions and actions (NE 1106b36ff).[1] Courage is at the mean of fear and confidence, between the extremes of cowardice (too much fear and not enough confidence) and rashness (too much confidence and not enough fear). Liberality is at the mean of giving things away, between the extremes of stinginess (giving away too little) and the extreme of profligacy (giving away too much). And so forth.

The virtue of gentleness (*praotēs*) can serve as an illustration and test case. The continuum on which gentleness is at the mean is the emotion of anger. The gentle person would be one who is disposed to a mean amount of anger, neither too much nor too little. The answer to the questions, How much is too much, and How much is too little? is: the mean is not too much and the mean is not too little. The right amount is the mean—the middle point on the continuum. The mean is a quantitative measure, and Aristotle's answer, insofar as it is a doctrine of *the mean*, is a quantitative answer.

It's true that anger can be quantified, at least roughly, in several dimensions: intensity on a behavioral scale (that is, its degree of motivational power—what you will *do* out of anger), intensity on a feeling scale (how strong it feels and perhaps how much it distracts your attention from other matters), duration (how long it tends to last),

---

[1] When it comes to the all-important virtue of practical wisdom, which governs the whole moral life, Aristotle doesn't propose that it consists in being neither too intelligent nor too obtuse morally, but morally intelligent to a medium degree. No, to be practically wise is to be maximally morally intelligent!

frequency (how often you tend to be angry), and perhaps by other measures (say, blood pressure).

Aristotle sees that, for two reasons, the quantitative mean won't do. First, some virtues, including gentleness, don't fall exactly at the mid-point of the continuum. Aristotle notes that, even if you restrict the question to quantifiable aspects of anger, it seems that gentleness falls a little toward the defect end of the continuum (1125b26–1126a3). A gentle person, though he has a tendency to get angry in some circumstances, is marked more by his tendency not to get angry. Second, anger is not to be measured only by quantitative criteria, but also by qualitative ones. He notes that a person's gentleness must be defined by his tendency to get angry at the right persons, at the right time, and for the right reason (1125a31–2), as well as to have the right amount of anger. A person whose anger fell consistently in the mean with respect to quantity, but who often got angry for the wrong reason and toward the wrong people and on the wrong occasions wouldn't count as gentle. So, in a second attempt to identify the criterion, Aristotle defines a virtue as getting various relevant things, both quantitative and non-quantitative, "right": gentleness is the disposition to be angry in the right amount, but also at the right person, at the right time, and for the right reason. Yet he treats this standard as a further clarification of his doctrine of the mean. The getting-it-right criterion is certainly correct; though it is empty (it doesn't answer the question about what the norm is: What *is* right?). The substantive question is, what *is* "right" and what makes it so? But, though Aristotle is surely right that gentleness involves getting your anger "right," this isn't an explication of the doctrine of the mean. Aiming your anger at the *right* person on the *right* occasion and for the *right* reason isn't a matter of achieving a correct or medium quantity of anything.

In noting that the gentle person tends toward the defect end of the anger-continuum, Aristotle obviously can't be appealing to the criterion of the mean. He is in fact appealing to his understanding of the concept of gentleness, and this understanding is an aspect of his sensitivity to the moral framework within which he's thinking. A moral framework, as we've seen (Chapter 5), is a body of ethical thought, largely implicit among the wise, but which can be made explicit on reflection and discussion and roughly approximated in a body of laws.

At one point, realizing that the get-it-right criterion doesn't tell us what "right" is, and is thus empty as a criterion for distinguishing virtues from other traits, Aristotle advises the reader to consult reason as the man of practical wisdom judges what is reasonable (1107a1–2): he'll know what is "right." Since the wise man's thinking something is right isn't what makes it right, he could in principle give us the rationale for thinking, say, that a certain instance of anger was right and another was not. More generally, Aristotle, as a wise man, could have given us the rationale for his judgment that gentleness falls on the defective side of the mean with respect to those aspects of anger that come in quantities. To do that, he would have consulted his understanding of the moral life.

What might that rationale be? One possibility is that perfect alignment at the mean of anger would be less healthy for social relations within the polis (say, in contexts of marriage, collegiality, or legislation) or outside the polis (negotiations with representatives of neighboring city-states) than an alignment somewhat to the left of the mean. For the criteria of rightness that aren't quantitative at all, he might appeal to the concept of truth: anger would be true when directed at the person who did the wrong, and not deflected at the dog or the children. And truth in anger is plausibly important for social and other reasons (it is unjust to be angry at someone who's done nothing to offend). In other words, Aristotle's concepts of citizen and polis and an ideal of civic life would control the concept of gentleness more than would the concept of the mean. They would have overriding authority where they disagree with the mean and, where the concept of a mean has no application (in the non-quantitative dimensions of what is "right"), they would have a different kind of authority.

I'm arguing that in propounding the doctrine of the mean, Aristotle doesn't know what he's doing. Not only does the doctrine not work, but Aristotle seems to realize that and correct for it by a criterion that he doesn't quite clearly recognize. And that criterion is the moral culture to which he belongs and the moral framework that guides his thinking. (True, he prefaces many of his normative statements with phrases like "seems to be" and "is thought to be," thus seeming to consult his moral culture.) Let us now take a look at the Christian version of gentleness and see how its parameters are set by Christian theology—the Christian view of the world, the Christian moral framework.

Christian Gentleness

I noted in Chapter 7 that several of the Christian virtues—generosity, compassion, gratitude, forgivingness—are variants of *agapē*, a moral attitude unknown to Aristotle. Gentleness is one of these. If compassion is *agapē* for someone who is *suffering*, and gratitude is *agapē* for someone who has *given you a gift*, and forgivingness is *agapē* for people who *have injured you*, then gentleness is *agapē* for people who are *fragile*. It involves the loving construal of the other as potentially injured by your response, and it is a carefulness to avoid such injury. You might think of it as anticipatory compassion. *Agapē* requires gentleness because the people to be loved are fragile, like a bruised reed or a smoldering wick (Matt 12:20, Is 42:3–4). The fragility can be of various kinds. It could be physical fragility, the fragility of a baby or an old person or a sick person. It could be moral fragility, that of a person's self-esteem or susceptibility to temptation. It could be a person's susceptibility to be offended and to get angry, or to be afraid. The gentle person anticipates such effects of his actions, and inclines to avoid them if possible. Forgiveness will express gentleness in case the fragility results from transgression. In the interest of treating with gentleness someone in the congregation who has transgressed, Paul encourages the leaders (Gal 6:1) to adopt an attitude of humble penitence, lest they themselves be tempted (the temptation might be to be angry with the transgressor). In being gentle, they bear the burden of the transgressor's transgression, rather than dissociating themselves from him in anger. Gentleness is a virtue with wide application because all of us, or nearly all of us, are fragile in one way or another.

The two Greek words that are translated "gentle" are *praüs* and *epieikes*. For example, in Matthew 11:29 Jesus says, "I am gentle (*praüs*) and humble in heart." I Peter 2:18 says, "Slaves, accept the authority of your masters with all deference, not only those who are kind and gentle (*epieikesin*) but also those who are harsh." *Epieikeia* is sometimes translated "equity," in which case it suggests considerateness, flexibility, or sensitivity to context in matters of justice, and a default preference for clemency. It would be opposed to the harsh side of legalism.

As we saw in the case of Aristotelian gentleness, *praotēs* (note the slightly different spellings in the Aristotelian and New Testament texts) is especially associated with anger. Anger is a paradigm kind of harshness. It is harsh in two ways, both of which are in tension with *agapē*. First, it tends to be expressed in kinds of punishment or retribution, all the way from a dirty look to murder. Anywhere along this continuum, punishments are bad experiences, and angry people tend to dole them out, more or less intentionally. Anger prompts you to be harsh, and if you are strongly disposed to anger, you will be a harsh, not a gentle, person. Second, and relatedly, anger is alienating: it erects an emotional barrier between the angry person and the one she is angry with. Harsh people tend to put others off.

The gentle person is sensitive to the adversities of anger and other forms of harshness, and especially to people's susceptibility to be hurt by these. That susceptibility is what I'm calling fragility. As part of urging the churches to be slow to anger, the apostle James says, "In the gentleness of wisdom, let [wise persons'] works show their excellent manner of life" (James 3:13, my translation). The wisdom that gentleness exhibits is the awareness of the other's fragility and the ways the fragile one's response to harshness is likely to cause social disharmony and related adversities. Gentleness is a preference for peace.

Why is the gentle person so careful about the other's fragility? If she's a Christian, her central reason for caution is that this fragile being is a being of awesome and glorious value, despite his irritating ways and maybe even his deserving an angry response. Behind her understanding of herself and the other is the fact that both are beloved of God, forgiven through Christ, and destined in common for the royal priesthood. Furthermore, in seeing the other in this way she's aware that she's looking over God's shoulder, as it were, and seeing the other with the eyes of the Spirit who guides her vision. In Galatians 5:23, Paul mentions gentleness as among the fruit of the Holy Spirit.

I don't say that *agapē* is the Christian's only motive in treating persons gently. For example, if you're interviewing for a job, you may be cautious about the interviewer's fragility because you know that if you treat her roughly, you're less likely to get the job. Or we may treat each other gently because we want to remain friends. Or we may just want to keep peace in the church. Any of these reasons may be based, in our spirituality, on our love of God and our consequent love of the neighbor. Our desire for the job may go back to our love of God's kingdom, as our concern for friendship might, or peace in the church. But if these other motives are not based in *agapē*, our love will not have the distinctively Christian character. It might be analogous or preparatory to Christian love, but it won't be specifically Christian. Secular persons can certainly learn to be gentle, and their reasons may be various: to make money, to be socially accepted, to further political aims; and among these secular reasons may be moral reasons: respect for the other as a human being, a concern not to cause unnecessary distress. But Christians have theological reasons; that's what makes their gentleness distinctive.

Several virtues, including the variants of *agapē*, are adaptations to kinds of situations. Compassion doesn't always apply, because we aren't always confronted with suffering; forgivingness doesn't always apply, because we interact with people who haven't injured us. And the same is true with gentleness: the situations that we face may present no danger of injuring anybody's fragility, and thus not call for gentleness. But sometimes, even when people's fragility makes them prone to injury, the gentle person may opt for the ungentle response. In Matthew 11:29 Jesus tells us that he is gentle in character. But he is not always gentle in behavior. He calls the scribes and Pharisees "hypocrites" to their faces (Matt 15:7); he drives the sellers rather violently from the Temple (Luke 19:45–46); he pronounces woes on unrepentant cities in which he had preached to no avail (Matt 11:20–24). The fragility consideration can be overruled by other considerations. For example, the fragile person may need to be awakened to a fault (perhaps the very fault of his fragility), and so the gentle person may need to forgo gentle behavior for the sake of the other and wound him (slightly). But for the gentle person, hesitance to wound is the default position. The important thing is to practice *agapē* in every case and to be ready with the gentle response when it's called for.

This account of the Christian virtue of gentleness illustrates how the rational structure of a Christian virtue (its "normativity" or virtue-status) derives from the moral framework to which it belongs. I think this is true of Aristotelian virtues, Stoic virtues, Epicurean virtues, Confucian virtues, and any other kind of virtues there may be. In the case of Christian gentleness, it derives more particularly from the love that Christians attribute to God and Christ and the Holy Spirit and which we human beings, as bearing the image of God, are to reflect; the Christian expectation that we will one day be fully effective glorious members of a royal priesthood of God; and some generally observable facts such as that we are fragile, dependent beings and that our social life thrives on peace and love.

Ethical Theories Again

In Chapter 1 we noted that modern ethical philosophy, in the form of ethical theories, sought to discover and secure the "foundation" of ethics independently of any ethical tradition or historical moral framework. The project of modern ethical theory arose from a worry about moral pluralism and the feeling that it implied either relativism or skepticism. Moral traditions must be transcended, it was thought, because they are the "plurality" in pluralism. This problem was to be solved by fixing on some uncontroversial element of general ethics (practical reason, happiness, social harmony, moral sentiments) and then constructing the rest of the system of ethical thought on that element as the foundation.

These theories also offered answers to the question of this section, the question about how we sort traits into virtues, vices, and traits that are neither virtues nor vices: Virtues are traits that are implied by practical reason (Kant), or tend to the happiness of their possessor and his fellows (Mill), or make for social harmony (Hobbes), or are approved by moral sentiments (Smith, Hume). As far as I know, not until the twentieth century, with the advent of "pure" virtue ethics (see Chapter 3), was it suggested that the concept of virtue might be the foundation of all ethical concepts. All these rationales are legitimate elements of morality; the problem with theories, I propose, is their foundationalist form. Troubles arise when you try to make one of these elements *the* foundation of ethics.

If the search for the foundation of ethics arose from a worry about moral pluralism and the feeling that it implied either moral relativism or moral skepticism, it seems to me that Christian ethics refutes this implication by its existence. Christians are not moral relativists or skeptics, yet the premises of Christian ethics, that God has promised our glorification in a new creation, that he has fulfilled this promise proleptically in Jesus the King, and that the Holy Spirit of Jesus bears his fruit in the variants of our *agapē*, our self-control, and our humility, are so peculiar and particular as to keep it from crossing our mind that anybody should be privy to these truths independently of any tradition. These fundamental truths are universal in their universal application, but they are not universal in the sense of being available to all apart from the Christian revelation.

Christian Virtue Ethics as a Branch of Philosophy

Two Kinds of Philosophy

Let me distinguish two kinds of philosophy. In one kind, the goal has the form of some conclusion or thesis. The aim is to convince the audience or reader of some controversial proposal. It is to change the audience from a stance of skepticism or no opinion about the proposal to a stance of assenting to it, or at least of coming closer to assent. The means of changing the audience in this way is argument, and the goal is a verdict. This can also be thought of as problem-solving. Then the goal is an answer or solution to the problem. Philosophers of this sort speak of "philosophical problems," and their work consists of arguments. In a second kind of philosophy, there will also be arguments along the way, but the goal is not so much to change the audience from unbelief to belief or to solve a problem as it is to deepen the audience's (and one's own) understanding. Philosophy of this kind consists in exploring and contemplation. It is to bring about insight and appreciation of some important matter, and only incidentally to bring about assent and conviction or resolution.

As I read it, Aristotle's *Nicomachean Ethics* and pretty much all of ancient philosophical ethics belongs to this second kind. The difference between the two kinds of philosophy is a matter of emphasis, focus, tone, and ultimate goal; they both involve argument and they both involve understanding. Just as the kind of philosophy that aims at understanding makes use of arguments along the way, the kind of philosophy that aims at conclusions no doubt enhances, along the way, understanding of various matters. Arguments, if they are good, do tend to increase understanding. They display connections among premises, and between premises and conclusion. Appreciation of connections is conceptual understanding.

"Pure" virtue ethics (see Chapter 3) belongs to the first kind of philosophy and consists of arguments to the conclusion that virtue(s) can supply the foundation that supports all the other ethical concepts. It proposes a solution to the problem of finding a foundation for morality that is independent of contestable tradition. I propose that Christian virtue ethics, like ancient pagan virtue ethics, belongs to the second kind of philosophy, and aims, not so much to convince, as to engender wisdom, which is a kind of understanding that implies the whole range of virtues (see Chapter 10). To understand a virtue is to know how it "works" and to see its goodness, its attractiveness, and so to appreciate it and desire it for oneself and those one loves. Philosophy at its best is an agent of character change in the direction of human happiness. The goal of virtue ethics is success in life—fundamental human success, success at being human.

Philosophical Questions about the Virtues

Contemporary analytic philosophy tends to exemplify the first of these kinds, though it needn't do so. Analysis can as well be deployed in the interest of understanding as in the interest of convincing people of truths. It seems to me that, to be good, philosophy needs to be careful and adequately (though not obsessively) detailed, and thus analytical. 'Analysis' comes from a Greek word that means to loosen, to take apart. Taking apart an internal combustion engine is a potent exercise in learning how it works: you identify the components, see how they fit together, and come to see the contribution that each component makes to the whole functioning when the engine is all together in working condition. In your imagination, you go back and forth between examining the individual parts and noting the role that each part's shape contributes to its "fit" with adjacent parts, and thinking about the contribution that each makes when the engine is running. You think about how each part pushes or slides on its neighboring parts and how they exploit one another, to draw in resources from the environment and expel their wastes into the environment. The ultimate goal of analysis is not to pick the parts apart, but to understand how they contribute to the functioning of the whole engine.

The object of analysis in Christian virtue ethics, as I see it, is Christian character. We focus attention on its parts, namely the virtues, and on the parts or aspects of these parts, namely the dispositions to feel (emotions and desires), to think (to understand and deliberate), and to act. We take apart the idea of character so as to put it back together again. This helps us understand it, to know what it is and how it works. In doing this, we take apart the concepts of the distinct virtues (truthfulness, justice, compassion, and so forth) so as to put *them* back together. And maybe we take apart the parts of the virtues—the powers of emotion, action, thinking, and whatever else goes into virtue, to put *them* back together again. Let's now change the metaphor to honor the fact that living a life is a human activity, as Aristotle notes, rather than the running of a mechanism like a car engine, though both are dynamic and fall under the general concept *functioning*. An engine runs well or badly, depending on the condition of its parts; people practice life well or badly, depending on their character, what they're "made of," the dispositional components of their character.

I adopt my preferred metaphor from Wittgenstein: the activity of speaking a language. When we speak a language properly, we're active. We make the language function as it should by using the words, which belong to functional parts of speech, in such a way that they fit properly with one another, playing their complementary roles in a way that enables us to make sense in using the language. Our activity of speaking the language follows the rules of the language's grammar. Similarly, the activity of living has a grammar, and it is the grammar of the virtues, the rules for the roles of the virtues in the internal structure of character. In virtue ethics we trace the grammar of the good life, and therefore the grammar of character.

If we think of virtues as components of character, and themselves as being composed of dispositions to think, feel, and act, we can probe their nature with questions about their functions and their functional relations to one another. Here are some of the main kinds of questions that analytic Christian virtue ethics uses to take apart the concept of character and the virtue concepts and put it and them back together again:

1) Assuming that virtues are interrelated and interdependent, what makes for their differentiation from one another, their individuation: what makes them each worthy of a name of their own ('wisdom,' 'generosity,' 'self-control,' and so forth)?

2) Are there different kinds of traits, or are all virtues of one kind? And if they are of more than one kind, what are the kinds of traits? Is wisdom a different kind of trait from generosity? Is generosity a different kind than self-control? If so, what makes for the differences?

3) What patterns of thinking are characteristic of each of the particular virtues (justice, generosity, courage, and so forth)?

4) What are the components of virtues? I'm proposing that they are personal/mental dispositions to think, understand, deliberate, judge, feel emotions, have desires, and exercise abilities.

5) How do these components interact? For example, how does thinking (deliberating, judging, understanding) depend on caring, and caring depend on thinking?

6) How do the particular virtues interact with one another in the person of overall good character? For example, how does justice affect generosity, or courage affect generosity and justice and humility, and vice versa? How does this or that virtue *support* other virtues and how is it supported by other virtues? For example, how does courage support love, or love courage?

7) Are there virtues that pervade and encompass the whole character of the good person? If so, how do they do this? I shall argue that wisdom and humility have this kind of quality.

8) How are the Christian (Buddhist, Confucian, Stoic, Aristotelian) virtues (justice, generosity, humility, for example) similar to and different from their counterparts in other frameworks?

9) What are the psychological constituents of the virtues (see Chapter 6), and in what way are they dispositional, that is, traits of a *person* rather than discrete events in a person's life (see the second half of Chapter 8)?

10) How does this or that virtue contribute to or constitute human flourishing?

11) How is the trait an expression of essential human nature? Or: how does it exemplify or fulfill essential human nature?

Since our goal in doing virtue ethics is not so much to conclude this or that thesis about ethics or the virtues as to understand how our concepts work together, we endeavor to achieve what Wittgenstein calls "perspicuous representations." The answers to these questions are embedded in the practices of the moral life, in one or another moral outlook. Philosophy's task is to bring to light the truths that, in a sense, the moral practitioner already knows. But in producing perspicuous representations of the moral life and personality, philosophy may enhance our knowledge and deepen our fitness to put it into practice.

I think we can see that these philosophical questions are not ones to which the New Testament offers direct answers. The New Testament is not a set of philosophical essays, but its stories (in the gospels) and pastoral discourse (in the letters of Paul, Peter, and James and the author of Hebrews) lend themselves to philosophical questions about the ethical and psychological thought they represent, and philosophical answers to those questions can be teased out of the writings.

One such question is, What is it to *live* as a full-fledged *human being*? The New Testament shows that living a mature human life, a life worthy of a human being, requires development of good character—such virtues as faith, hope, love, patience, humility, and the like. But good character has to be learned. Many of our fellow creatures have to learn things to become mature, functioning members of their species. Predators need to learn hunting skills, condors need to learn to fly, monkeys need to learn to navigate the treetops. In some cases, they learn these skills from their elders, in others they learn them just by trying out their equipment, so to speak. But it seems that most of what other animal species need to learn to be mature members of their kinds are *skills*.

Human beings are different in this way: we need to learn, not only skills, but more fundamentally, *understanding of who we are* and *love of what is really good*. If a person thinks that the meaning of his life is maximizing his power over others, or his material possessions, or the pleasures of leisure, or the mastery of certain technical skills, he will fail as a human being, no matter how exquisitely skilled he may become. He may succeed at grabbing power, money, passing pleasures, or being the best ski jumper in the world, but at being human he will flop.

The acquisition of the virtues, as we saw in Chapter 6, is only partly a matter of skills, and those skills are largely ones you apply to yourself. Furthermore, mature people apply them in the interest of becoming better persons or retaining their integrity. The more central or spiritual virtues are not a matter of skill, but of what and how you *think* and what you *care about*. In this, we human beings are much more prone than the other animals to get derailed and go off in wrong directions. This is why Socrates said that the unexamined life is not worth living (*Apology* 38b–c). It's why Plato made it a requirement for being a city leader that a person spend years in philosophical conversation (*Republic* 7). It's why Aristotle wrote his *Nicomachean Ethics*. It's why the ancients more generally tended to think of philosophy as necessary for becoming really human. And it's why it is good, in a rather fundamental way, for people to practice virtue ethics.

Let's think for a moment about Socrates's famous comment that the unexamined life is not worth living. This can sound harsh. A Christian would not want to think, "Giorgio is unreflective about his life, so let's just consider him human junk, not worth having around." Such contempt for a human being is contrary to the Holy Spirit and isn't a corollary of Socrates's thought. But we might well think, of a heedless playboy, "he is of great worth, created in God's image, but sadly negligent of the great gift: his way of living is not up to his real worth." A better translation of Socrates's remark might be, "an uninspected life is not a life worthy of a human being," or "not a truly human life." Socrates is saying that a person who doesn't think about himself critically, alert day after day as to whether he's living a worthy human life, is failing to realize his human potential. "Unexamined" means "not disciplined in the way of human excellence and depth." The examination Socrates has in mind is a "judgment," a moral examination, a personal inventory as the twelve-step philosophy says; it is a *self*-examination, driven by the aspiration to be a real human being. It's a continual asking, How am I doing, *as a human being*? And this is essential to virtue ethics.

Being fully human isn't a purely biological process, a state that emerges automatically through the genetic character of the organism plus a lot of cooperation from the environment. Becoming human requires each individual to think about good and evil, virtue and vice, happiness and misery, and to make a moral inventory of herself in those terms. Self-reflection, self-evaluation, self-criticism, and self-correction are essential to human development. This self-activity will emerge naturally with a little cooperation from the individual, as virtue ethics feeds the understanding of a person's humanity.

Virtue ethics aims ultimately at the kind of understanding that makes a person a real human being. By contrast, philosophy that is aimed at conclusions requires little if any *self*-reflection. On that understanding, doing good ethics requires personal detachment and you achieve the necessary detachment only by renouncing the application of the concepts to yourself. Keep yourself out of the picture! Be objective! Be disinterested! Such detached ethics requires cleverness and some basic knowledge about ethics. But philosophy as virtue ethics requires that your reflection be, at least partly, critical reflection about yourself. Being human is an ideal, an aspiration, and not to understand this and take up the challenge is itself a form of failure at the human project. If philosophy is the love and pursuit of wisdom (your *own* wisdom, presumably), then such ethical detachment isn't philosophy.

An Activity, Not a Theory

Christian virtue ethics, as I propose we understand it, isn't a theory. It's an activity. It's what Alasdair MacIntyre calls a practice. The good that is internal to it is the understanding of our life, where such understanding is located not just in the "intellect," but in the heart. When I say it's not a theory, I don't deny that, along the way, as we practice virtue ethics, we make assertions and enter into debates and form beliefs and acquire understanding about virtues and vices and about the good life. If the activity is to help us acquire the virtues, all of that is crucial! The activity of virtue ethics includes explaining some things, but its driving purpose is personal transformation, and that requires active personal participation. It is, after all, *philoso*phy! It has the human, essentially worthwhile aim of happiness and character construction: the nurture of real human beings. What could be more important than that? Without that, as Aristotle says, there's no point in doing it (NE 2.2, 1103b26–29). Without the passion to become wise and virtuous, "ethics" is piddling for smart people.

Our present inquiry doesn't aim ultimately at contemplation. But it does involve contemplation in an important penultimate way. Philosophy of the kind that Christian virtue ethics exemplifies is contemplative, if we contrast contemplation, as appreciative, loving attention with achieving satisfactory conclusions from true premises and flawless logic. I think Aristotle's opposition between knowing what virtue is and becoming good is limited to a certain kind of knowing. By contrast, the kind of knowledge that saves you, according to the Bible, involves "setting your mind on the things of the Spirit" and thus having your mind and character derived from the Spirit and the Spirit's "things." This is the intimate kind of knowledge that involves being of one mind with the Spirit of God. "And this is eternal life, that they may know you, the only true God, and Jesus Christ whom you have sent" (John 17:3).

Christian virtue ethics has the character of an inquiry, an attempt to answer some questions, but it's personally "interested," comparable with an inquiry into something you want to buy or make: inquiry with a practical end. Christian virtue ethics is a special branch of the generic human program of becoming human, and its specialty involves the practice of philosophy—the loving, eager pursuit of wisdom. It is encompassed by parentheses, bordered by a moral framework. It isn't an entirely open inquiry, as though the answer to the question, "What is the good life?" might be "fulfillment of the will to power" or "maximal physical pleasure." Instead, it considers the place of power and pleasure in a Christian light. It doesn't purport to be to everybody's taste, though it satisfies a concern for what everybody yearns for. Still, Christian virtue ethics is not just for Christians.

It can be practiced in a subjunctive mood, by people who are not committed to the Christian way of life. In that case, the inquiry does happen outside the parentheses, and looks *into* them, so to speak. This is possible because many non-Christians are attracted to such virtues as compassion, gentleness, forgiveness, generosity, forbearance, and patience.

Setting Your Mind on the Virtues

The apostle Paul says,

> For those who live (*ontes*, exist) according to the flesh set their minds on (*phronousin*) the things of the flesh, but those who live according to the Spirit set their minds on the things of the Spirit. The fleshly mindset (*phronēma*) is death, but the spiritual mindset is life and peace. For this reason, the fleshly mindset is hostile to God. (Romans 8:5–7a, my translation)

Paul here distinguishes the setting of your mind (*phronein*) on the things of the Spirit from the resultant disposition or orientation of your mind (*phronēma*), the mindset. The difference between the setting of the mind and the mindset, to my way of thinking, is the difference between the *action* of setting your mind on something and the ongoing character that your mind and heart acquire if you habitually set your mind on those things in that way.

A principle is that setting the mind on something, if it becomes a regular act, results (probably gradually) in a change in the character of the mind—a mindset. The mind takes on the character of what it's "set" on, or the way it's set on it. And a further principle is that the mindset will be virtuous or vicious depending on the ethical status (goodness, badness, triviality, neutrality) of what it's set on. Thus, if the mindset results from setting the mind on things like the coming kingdom of God, the spiritual beauty of the neighbor, the glory of God, the virtues of a saint, the ways you can use your money to promote human thriving, and the gospel of Jesus Christ, it will be the mindset of the Christian virtues.[2] Consider two people who illustrate what Paul has in mind.

Abe is preoccupied with comparing his own status with that of others, whom he sees as his rivals (even though some of them are his "friends"). He habitually asks himself, "Am I as smart as Steve? Is my success in life the equal of Carl's? Am I as popular as Greg, as good-looking as Burt, as talented as Sylvia?" This rivalrous, comparative thinking about others in relation to himself wears a groove in his perception so that it becomes habitual and second nature to him. Through setting his mind, again and again, on these things in this way, he has acquired a mindset. And it is the mindset of envy (when he sees himself as losing the contest) and invidious pride (when he sees himself as the "winner"). Paul would call this mindset "fleshly."

Burt, by contrast, makes a point of looking for the strengths in people. He keeps an eye out for marks of Steve's generosity, Carl's compassion, Greg's loyalty, Sylvia's temperance. He praises people behind their backs, both to himself and to others. And he not only catches glimpses of these qualities in people. He delights in seeing them, he's touched with admiration. People's excellences make him glad. These people are not extraordinary moral exemplars, heroes or saints, but they sometimes glimmer with virtue. Burt got onto this practice after reading Iris Murdoch's *The Sovereignty of Good* (Routledge, 1971), where she commends a similar moral-mental exercise. He's just learning the practice, so he has to *pay* attention to notice and appreciate these good qualities. He has to exert some effort. These payments of attention wear a groove in the soul. They establish a pattern of thought and concern in Burt's mind which, over time, makes looking, thinking, and perceiving in their terms a second nature, an integrated quality of his mind.

---

[2] The person who sets his mind on his stock portfolio (and the like) as intrinsically good has *an* understanding that shapes his character, but it's not a correct understanding of what is ultimately good and what makes, or would make, his life good, and it won't be virtuous from a Christian perspective.

Two Requirements for Setting the Mind

What is it to set the mind on something, and what does it take for that setting of the mind to form a mindset? Well, each such character—one who "exists" according to the flesh and one who "exists" according to the Spirit—does so by *thinking* about something in some *terms* or categories. The categories (concepts) will be fleshly or spiritual. Abe thinks about himself and the others in terms of *comparison, competition,* and *rivalry;* while Burt thinks about others in terms of the *excellences by which they reflect the Holy Spirit.* To do such setting-the-mind-on, they have to have the categories in terms of which they think about the others. Abe has to have the concepts of self and rival and of the self as deriving its positive or negative value from its success or failure in the competition, and Burt has to have the concepts of the virtues that he identifies in the others. You can't set your mind on something of which you have no idea, no concept. That's the first requirement.

A concept is an object-gripper. It enables you to get a (mental) grip on something. In the activity of virtue ethics, we attempt to get a grip on the virtues by way of deepening and sharpening our concepts of them. But the kind of setting-the-mind that Paul has in mind is not just getting a grip on the object, but getting a special *kind* of grip on the object in which it gets a grip on you. This person-forming kind of grip requires that you care about the object in some way that is special to the concepts involved. The caring is the formative power of the grip. In one sense, Burt has all the concepts that Abe has (he knows what a rival is, for example), but they function differently in shaping and targeting his concerns. Abe's envy requires not only that he know what a rival is and thus understand what competition and comparison are, but that he characteristically *care* about winning competitions with *his* rivals as a way of getting and maintaining his self-importance. His grasp of the concepts of *comparison, rival, win,* and so forth won't amount to a mindset (*phronēma*) in Paul's sense of the word—in this case, an envious mindset—unless the concepts have for him this special emotional significance and personal attraction. Abe has to care about getting social status by besting his rivals, rejoicing when he succeeds and resenting when he doesn't.

In a similar way, virtue ethics requires an understanding of the virtues—a grasp of the virtue concepts—that's infused with caring about them. A person with a full understanding of the concepts of generosity, forgivingness, patience, and so forth is one who not only can identify instances in the people around her but tends to admire them for it and to be sorry when she sees corresponding vices in people. Her concepts of the virtues are not just categorical slots for character traits but ways of grasping manners and modes of personal loveliness, of perceiving occasions of joy and complexions of beauty. Her concepts of the vices are not just categorical slots for other character traits but ways of gripping and being gripped by ugly stains, blemishes, and disfigurements of persons. If it lacks this emotive import of the moral character traits, the virtue ethicist's understanding of the concepts of the virtues and vices, for all its technical precision, falls short of *philo*sophical understanding. This fact about philosophical understanding may be subject to the framework-relativity of virtue concepts. For example, if a virtue ethicist is working within a concertedly Nietzschean ethical framework, her emotional understanding of gentleness and compassion might be toned with disgust rather than admiration, thus placing the traits in, or bordering on, the territory of the vices. In that case, her understanding of and attention to the gentleness and compassion won't tend to form the corresponding mindsets in her, but contrary ones.

Virtue ethics is the project of getting a grip on the virtues by having robust, clean concepts of them. To have a grip on the virtues is to understand them, and to understand them with good appreciation of their nature as human excellences is wisdom. Philosophy is one way to get such a grip. It's not the only way: Plato meets Socrates, and Plato thereby begins to grasp (understand) an excellent way of living. Then he starts doing philosophy as a way of strengthening his grip by understanding Socrates better.

Our pre-philosophical concept of a virtue—let alone the concepts of the particular virtues—isn't perfectly clear in itself. Our concept isn't yet robust, crisp, and clean. It needs to be examined, explored, and thus understood; its features need to be displayed to view; they need to be highlighted. We highlight them by trying the fit of categories for them, and by comparing them, both in likeness and unlikeness, with other concepts. In earlier chapters we've explored how concepts of virtues belong to ethical conceptual frameworks. We've explored their relation to concepts of human happiness. We've looked at their broad psychological constituents (concerns, thoughts, powers, incorporation of other minds) and their relationships with moral rules. We've tried their fit into such categories as habit, skill, and habitus. All this conceptual exploration aims to cultivate, by philosophy, a clearer understanding of the notion of a virtue. The aim is that you and I—particular participants in the activity of philosophy—might have a clearer understanding of this concept which is so central to our existence as human beings, and so might become wiser, better formed human beings.

Take the example of gentleness that we briefly explored earlier in this chapter. We all initially have some rough idea what gentleness is. But philosophy will make it more precise. We compared gentleness with compassion, gratitude, and forgivingness. We said that in their Christian versions, these virtues are all forms of *agapē* (that is the broad category in which they belong), but they differ in the kind of consideration (in the case of gentleness, the other's fragility) to which the loving person is responding with *agapē*. We also compared Christian gentleness, which is motivated by *agapē*, with other kinds of gentleness, which take the other's fragility into consideration for other reasons (e.g., self-interest or friendship). And we said that Christians, too, often have these other reasons for gentleness, in addition to their neighbor-love (*agapē*). This kind of exploration, and the features of the virtue that it highlights, are what we have called the "grammar" of the virtue. It sharpens our focus. It's like tuning in a radio signal or focusing a telescope or microscope. You can recognize something in a blur, but as you tune in the focus you can tell better what you're looking at. Clarity can be distinguished from presentation. Having a clear view is one thing, but having something "in view" at all is also crucial. Presentation corresponds to attention (calling to mind), while clarity corresponds to attention's precision and accuracy. Philosophy can serve both these purposes, and thus promote understanding of the virtues.

So we start with an intuitive understanding of the concept of a virtue—say, wisdom, humility, or gentleness—and by philosophy we grip it more firmly, present it to ourselves more explicitly, "see" it more accurately, more perspicuously. It was something like this process of starting with what you know and deepening your knowledge through reflection that Socrates (or Plato) had in mind when they spoke of philosophy as recollection (*Meno*). It's the deepening awareness and appreciation, the articulation of detail, of something we already know, the "bringing out" of something that's already in our possession by raising questions and trying and sorting out answers. We all have some understanding of gentleness, its conceptual grammar and its value in life, but by refining our concept of it our understanding improves, and this may be an increase in wisdom. That is how philosophy works when it's aimed at understanding. So the first requirement for setting your mind on the virtues is to possess the concept of a virtue, and we have seen that having a concept is understanding and is a matter of degree: we improve our concepts by practicing philosophy.

And there is a second requirement. We have already touched on it, when we talked about the objects getting a grip on us. No doubt both Abe and Burt have each other's concepts. Abe may have the concepts of the virtues (he's not ignorant of what gentleness, humility, and wisdom are), and Burt certainly understands the concepts of rivalry that underlie envy. In fact, both of them may have applied philosophy to these concepts, and so possess sharpened, improved versions of them. The difference between them is not that they *have* different concepts, or even the clarity of their concepts, but that they *use* very different concepts for setting their minds on themselves and others. They experience others differently because they use different categories to think about others. If each has the other's concepts, what accounts for their using such different concepts?

The difference is in what they care about. Our cares are shaped by concepts. They are the specific cares they are by being about what they're about, and they manage to be about what they're about by way of the concepts. Burt's love of the spiritual qualities of his neighbors is the particular love that it is by way of the concepts of the spiritual qualities: the ideas of *generosity*, *compassion*, *loyalty*, *temperance*, and so forth, as human excellences. Burt knows what a rival is, all right, but the terms of rivalry don't shape his concerns. He doesn't care in that way. He cares about human excellence and the excellence of the humans in his orbit, and so the concepts of excellence—the concepts of the virtues—come naturally into his attention, his focus, and his usage. Abe, by contrast, "naturally" thinks about himself and others in the "terms" of rivalry and comparison because that's how he cares about himself and others; it's in the terms of rivalry, winning, being better than so-and-so, and so forth, that people matter to him.

Setting your mind on, as Paul uses the expression, is a special kind of attention. A contrasting case is that of the eighth grader who knows how to do her math assignment, but cares about it only instrumentally. She wants to get it "out of the way," so she turns her attention to it as soon as she gets home from school. She has the concepts she needs and she recruits them for the task, completes the assignment, and gets on to what she really wants to do. She gives her attention to her math assignments, but this attention isn't what Paul calls *phronein*; it doesn't have much effect on the formation of her heart as the heart of a mathematician. If we were to assign a concern-based concept to her math assignment, it might be *hurdle*: to be a hurdle is to be a matter of concern: something to be got over.

We human beings have this power of intentionally turning our attention to something, and it doesn't have to be anything we greatly love (though I suppose we have to have *some* reason for intentionally turning our attention). By contrast, what Paul calls setting your mind on (*phronein*) is loving attention, an attention with your heart in it. It's attention to what really concerns you. Abe's quiet rivalries preoccupy him; they matter deeply to him. He attends to them with caring attention. The same is true of Burt's interest in his neighbors' virtues: their moral glimmering intrinsically delights him. He loves the beauty of human reality that he detects in people.

We've sketched Abe and Burt in starkly contrasting terms. But in reality each of them is more complex. Though envious, Abe isn't completely insensitive to others' virtues, and Burt's heart is not pure as the driven snow. I think that for most people, the concepts of virtues and vices are emotionally loaded. To confront a virtue and to designate it as such is to be touched with admiration and desire; to confront a vice is to be touched with repugnance. Because of these latent passions in the hearts of most of us, most people are "moved," at least a little bit, by perspicuous representations of virtues and vices, and thus by well-done virtue ethics. So I think virtue ethics has not only the power to "edify" Burt—to build him up morally—but also to throw a caution into Abe, to create in him an uneasiness with himself that may lead to moral change.

Conclusion

Becoming real as a human being is or should be a central concern of a human life. Everybody wants to be *some*body, a particular individual. We pursue this goal in different ways, and with varying degrees of accuracy. It is a concern for what everybody actually wants and yearns for. Philosophy just puts a point on this basic human passion. Nothing can be more important to a human life than getting this right. That's why "the unexamined life is not worth living." In asking this question of yourself, the answer you arrive at is "personal," but you are really asking on behalf of humanity generally. The task of virtue ethics is to refine our concepts of the virtues to enhance the accuracy of our attention to the virtues themselves and thus to our own humanity, and to commend them to ourselves and others so that our attention may grow wholehearted. Philosophy, in this conception, is "contemplative." It is analytic, accuracy-seeking, "self-interested" attention to concepts with the intent of understanding what they are about.

The last two chapters have addressed four questions that bear on the rationality of virtues: How are the virtues related to commandments? What kind of dispositions are virtues—habits, skills, habitus? What makes a disposition a virtue? and What is the nature and task of Christian virtue ethics as a branch of philosophy?

In the final two chapters of the book, we will illustrate Christian virtue ethics by exploring two important Christian virtues: wisdom and humility. We will see that within the Christian moral framework they are interconnected with a wide variety of other virtues, and that it is the whole network of these traits that constitutes their "grammar."

10
Wisdom

Introduction: Why Be Wise?

A brother-in-law of mine who served God faithfully for fifty or so years as a physician in Canada and Africa read my book on Kierkegaard.[1] With just a hint of protest he told me the story of a recent children's sermon in which his pastor spoke in the simplest terms. The pastor complimented the children on having responded to his call to come forward to listen to God's word, and he spoke that word by telling them that Jesus loves them. Now John didn't say that Kierkegaard (or perhaps Roberts) makes things more complicated than they need to be, but that seemed to be the point of the illustration. Why make the moral psychology of Christianity so hard? Why do Christian virtue ethics? Why infuse the Christian life with philosophy? Isn't the blessed truth so simple that an uneducated child can understand it?

The answer, it seems to me, is, "That depends on what you mean by 'understand.'" Understanding is subject to a criterion of adequacy. What's adequate understanding in a child may not be adequate for an educated adult. And wisdom is a kind of understanding that we attribute to children only by hyperbole: What a wise child! we say, with a wink. But adults want a richer, more robust understanding, one that harbors the answers to more questions, one that really merits the adjective "wise."

I suppose that Christian virtue ethics is not for everybody. Decidedly, your salvation doesn't depend on it. But you may want a kind of understanding that satisfies a grown-up, inquiring mind, one that is typical of an intellectually mature person. And not only intellectual maturity is at stake here, but more generally spiritual maturity. The fact that wisdom is among the Christian virtues, and indeed

---

[1] Roberts, *Recovering Christian Character*.

Virtue Ethics. Robert Campbell Roberts, Oxford University Press.
© Robert Campbell Roberts 2026. DOI: 10.1093/9780197848005.003.0013

pervades all the other virtues, suggests that anybody seriously interested in being a Christian grown-up will want to deepen the understanding that goes with faith: to grow in wisdom. The fact that John keeps reading my books suggests to me that he finds a sharpened understanding worthwhile.

In this chapter we'll look at the Christian virtue of wisdom, addressing three philosophical questions about it. First, where does it fit among the various kinds of knowledge? What is it to know what only a wise person can know? I'll propose that wisdom is a kind of understanding (not so much a matter of information) and that what wisdom understands is God, creation, oneself, and other people, all in relation to one another. Since various frameworks prescribe different understandings of the "world," Christian wisdom will differ from alternative "wisdoms," as Paul notes in I Corinthians 1–2. Second, we are talking here, not about "theoretical" wisdom but about "practical" wisdom. It's a kind of knowing that is related to action and living an ethical life. So we must ask, how is "practice" (action) related to this kind of knowledge? What kinds of actions are in question, and how do they affect wisdom and flow from wisdom? I'll propose that both mental and overt actions are shaped and motivated by wisdom and that these actions have a moral and spiritual character. Wisdom and its actions are reciprocally causal: the actions deepen the wisdom and the wisdom begets the actions. Third, how is wisdom related to such other virtues as generosity, compassion, forgivingness, patience, self-control, gratitude, courage, perseverance, and humility? I shall argue that each of these other virtues is an expression of wisdom, and that each has its own special department within the larger wisdom of the Christian life. Wisdom is the "intelligence" of the virtues that we talked about in Chapters 8 and 9. Each of the virtues is wise in its own way and each is a facet of wisdom.

Wisdom Among the Kinds of Knowledge

Three Kinds of Knowledge

Wisdom is a special kind of knowledge, so to understand it we need to specify just what kind it is. It will be helpful to survey briefly the various kinds of knowledge. That will put wisdom in perspective for us.

Mere factual knowledge comes in propositions like *Lincoln was the first Republican president, Water is H_2O,* and *A bird is perched on the branch outside my window.* Most philosophers think that to know such a proposition, three conditions have to be met. You have to believe it, it has to be true, and you either have to have some good reason for thinking it's true or it has to come into your mind by some normal process (like seeing the bird on the branch with your own eyes or getting the information from a reliable source such as your brother-in-law who sees the bird with his own eyes).

Another kind of knowledge is called "acquaintance." It is knowledge that you have by some kind of direct access. For example, if you know that the bird is on the branch only by your brother-in-law telling you so, then you don't know it by acquaintance, but you do if you see it for yourself. Simple mathematical truths are by acquaintance for most people: for example, you can just "see" that $3 + 2 = 5$. Some knowledge seems to *have to* be by acquaintance: for example, the knowledge of what coffee tastes like, or what the color red looks like, or how it feels to be in the presence of God. You can know there's a bird outside your window without seeing it for yourself, but you can't know what coffee tastes like without tasting some. People can try to tell you what the experience is like, but as to knowing, there's no substitute for experiencing it yourself.

A third kind of knowledge is understanding. It is a matter of putting things in categories, thus associating them with things that are in the same category and distinguishing them from things that are in different categories, and grasping other connections among things (causal connections, thematic connections, analogies, grammatical connections, functional dependencies). For example, to understand the proposition that Lincoln was the first Republican president, you have to *connect* Lincoln and the presidency with some facts about what Republicans stood for in the 1860s (it's definitely not what Republicans stand for in the 2020s). If you don't make any such connections, you don't understand the proposition—even if you "know" it in the sense that it's true and you believe it and have it on good authority that it's true.

But now we might think that, even if we don't understand *much* about what it means that Lincoln was a Republican, we do know that it was a political party (that is, we understand the concept in a general way) and we know that Lincoln was a man and a president, so we connect 'Lincoln' with these two ideas, and so forth. If we didn't understand this much, we wouldn't be able to think the proposition is true or have a good reason to think so. To know that Lincoln was the first Republican president, we have to be able to understand the sentence *Lincoln was the first Republican president*, and thus to connect 'Lincoln,' 'was,' 'first,' 'Republican,' and 'president' in such a way that this string of words makes grammatical sense as a sentence. So some minimal understanding is required even for simple factual knowledge.

In fact, even acquaintance with facts has to be understanding. For example, to be acquainted with the fact that the bird is on the branch by seeing it sitting there, your seeing has to be organized by the concepts of 'bird,' 'on,' and 'branch.' That is, you have to recognize one of the items as a *bird* (it's not a car or a grapefruit, but a bird), one of the items as a *branch* (which is a part of a tree, which is different from a river or a muffin) and the relation of *on* (which is different from the relation of *under* or *brother-in-law*), and you have to construct your perception out of these elements. For the contrasting case, think of a newborn infant who looks at the bird on the branch and recognizes neither the one nor the other nor the relationship of *on* between them, but has just a buzz of visual sensory "data." The child has to *learn to see*, and she does this by dividing her world into categories like *bird* and *branch* and *on*, sticking things visually in these categories, and relating them to one another. All of this is understanding. Even the simplest observations require understanding.

Wisdom and Pluralism About What Matters

Wisdom, I take it, is a special kind of understanding. The relationship of which it is the grasp is that of *relative importance for living*. For example, a kind of wisdom that prevails in certain cultures both historically and now is that a person's honor trumps everything else in importance. Retaining your honor is more important than retaining your life or health or wealth or daughters. This outlook also, of course, has views on *what* is honorable and dishonorable. For example, it might be that if someone has insulted you, your honor depends on fighting a duel with that person: it makes sense to risk your life (and the other's) for your honor so conceived. Among some Muslims, sexual deviancy by a daughter brings such dishonor on the whole family that she must be killed to restore the family's honor. The honor of the family is more important than the life of the daughter. According to one kind of economic wisdom, maximizing your wealth is the first and highest priority. Everything else—family life, other people's prosperity, rare animal species, the health of the physical environment—is of secondary importance and can be sacrificed for profit. Jesus summarizes biblical wisdom when he says, "But strive first for the kingdom of God and his righteousness, and all these things will be given to you as well" (Matt 6:33). It is expressed also in the first commandment: "I am the LORD your God . . . you shall have no other gods before me" (Exod 20:2–3). God's kingdom and its norms are the most important things in a human life, to which all else can be properly sacrificed.

Now you may respond by saying that putting personal or family honor above your own or other people's lives is not wisdom, but folly. And that so-called economic wisdom is, if possible, an even more outrageous folly.

You speak, perhaps, from the perspective of biblical wisdom. Both of these other "wisdoms" are folly by the standard of putting God and his righteousness first. Your objection is well taken but let me cite biblical precedent for the way I am speaking. The apostle James comments, "if you have bitter envy and selfish ambition in your hearts, do not be boastful and false to the truth. Such wisdom does not come down from above, but is earthly, unspiritual, devilish" (James 3:14–15). According to one kind of wisdom it is wise to take bankruptcy as a way of avoiding debts and "starting over," though this causes losses and suffering for people who trusted you. According to one kind of wisdom it is wise to say that the election you lost was rigged and that in reality you won it, though you know this isn't true. Such wisdom is the logos of bitter envy and selfish ambition. In a similar vein, Paul says,

> When I came to you, brothers and sisters, I did not come proclaiming
> the mystery of God to you in lofty words or wisdom. For I decided
> to know nothing among you except Jesus Christ, and him crucified.
> And I came to you in weakness and in fear and in much trembling.

> My speech and my proclamation were not with plausible words of
> wisdom, but with a demonstration of the Spirit and of power, so that
> your faith might rest not on human wisdom but on the power of
> God. (I Cor 2:1–5)

In their use of 'wisdom,' James and Paul are recognizing the situation of
pluralism that we discussed in Chapter 1. To speak of human wisdom
in such a way as to contrast it with Christian thought about Jesus and
his kingdom is to put the word in double quotation marks, as it were.
It is to speak of "wisdom," as in contrast with wisdom. In Chapter 1
we noted that while the plurality of "wisdoms" must be acknowledged,
acknowledging them needn't lead to relativism or skepticism, because
a person may well believe that the concept of wisdom to which he
adheres is wisdom itself, true wisdom. Paul goes on:

> Yet among the mature we do speak wisdom, though it is not a wisdom
> of this age or of the rulers of this age, who are doomed to perish. But
> we speak God's wisdom, secret and hidden, which God decreed be-
> fore the ages for our glory. (I Cor 2:6–7)

Here God's wisdom is more than just a priority of importance. It
includes information about God's plan to implement such a priority
by perfecting his people as stewards of his kingdom. For us to have
God's wisdom—real wisdom, and not just one of the wisdoms (that
is, follies) of the world—is for us to know the mind of the Lord by
"having" his mind (I Cor 2:16). In knowing this, we know the true
order of importances and we know that God has destined us in his love
to live them out in service to him in the age to come. The privilege of
serving him in this way, and thus of flourishing ourselves, is what Paul
calls our "glory." By way of our role in God's kingdom, we are to be glorious creatures.

In fact, we are already glorified to the extent that we have the mind
of Christ. Paul's word for 'mind' is *nous*, which in translations of
Aristotle is rendered 'intellect.' But that translation wouldn't do here,
any more than it would for Romans 12.2: Be transformed by the renewal of your *intellect*? We have the *intellect* of Christ? I don't think so.
The shortcoming of the word 'intellect' in translating Paul's thought

is that it leaves the "heart" out of "mind." '*Nous*' in Paul's usage usually implies an orientation of desire, concern, passion, and so forth. So it's very similar to "heart"—*kardia*—which is not just a seat of feelings, but also of thoughts, some true and some false. Wisdom is a kind of knowledge, all right, but to be wise is not just to be "intellectually" developed—even if what you know "intellectually" is the right priorities in living and choosing. Such a heartless intellect is not wise. Wisdom is knowledge infused and oriented by love. A love that is wise is a properly measured love: first, of God and his kingdom, including the constituents of his kingdom (people and other creatures), second, of "goods" that are indifferent with respect to God's kingdom (comforts, conveniences, luxuries, tranquility, abundances, power, good reputation), and opposition to (hatred of) everything that is contrary to God and his kingdom. To have such a measured loving-hating understanding is to have the mind of Christ.

Wisdom as a Deep Knowledge

Of things that matter to our humanity, wisdom is a fuller and more accurate kind of knowledge than mere factual knowledge or mere understanding. Consider a theologian who has an extensive and detailed understanding of the doctrine of God. She knows the history of all the major questions concerning the nature of God, and how these questions have related to one another and how they've been answered by various important theologians. She understands the ways philosophy has contributed to the development and articulations of these questions. She grasps how the doctrines of God's existence and nature are related to the biological and astronomical sciences. She loves the questions and appreciates the subtlety of the answers that have been given to them, and she takes pleasure in discussing them. She has lots of understanding. But as to caring about God himself and his kingdom she is quite indifferent. So despite all her extensive understanding of the concept of God, she isn't wise. Still, her failure to be wise is a failure of understanding: there's something about God that she personally fails to "get," and it is his greatness, his awesomeness, his transcendent beauty, his exquisite wonderfulness, his glory, and the enormous blessing he is to us. But to fail to get that is surely an abysmal failure to understand God. Paul both expresses his own wisdom and prays for the wisdom of his readers:

> I pray that the God of our Lord Jesus Christ, the Father of glory, may give you a spirit of wisdom and revelation as you come to know him, so that, with the eyes of your heart enlightened, you may know what is the hope to which he has called you, what are the riches of his glorious inheritance among the saints, and what is the immeasurable greatness of his power for us who believe. (Eph 1:17–19a; see also Col 1:25–28)

The word that is translated 'revelation' is *apokalupsis,* which means literally "unhiding" or "unveiling." We can distinguish two concepts of revelation: the event in which God reveals himself in Christ, and the event of enlightenment or insight in which a person ethically receives that revelation. The first is not a mental event and doesn't depend on our character. It is a world-historical one, an objective change in what can be known. The second is a kind of understanding, knowledge of Christ and of God, and depends on our being ethically formed in such a way as to be able to have the experience. It comes in a flash of insight, an event in one's mind and heart of seeing and feeling the truth and appreciating the significance of the objective revelation. This is the moment in which the disciple "gets" the gospel message. It's an instance of being touched by wisdom.

I suggested earlier (Chapter 6) that a spirit is a living character. Thus a person's spirit is his character as he lives it daily, and the Holy Spirit is the living presence of Christ's character among us. The fruit of the Holy Spirit is *his* traits as they become *our* traits; thus Christ bears in our spirits the fruit of his Spirit. Wisdom, as the knowledge of the proper order of goods, is one of the traits bestowed on us by our life in Christ. It is our sense of priorities. A person who has this wisdom will be disposed to think and act in accordance with the immeasurable greatness of God as it relativizes the greatness of everything else. In Paul's words, the "light" shed on our hope is perceived by the "eyes" of a wise heart. She experiences "revelation" when she turns her attention to that hope. So this understanding is manifested in experiences of vivid insight: in jubilation about God's greatness and about her hope in him. She *sees* that greatness with the eyes of her heart. This is understanding as acquaintance. Thus wisdom, as the height of understanding of oneself and the universe, is evident both in the mundane undramatic choices of daily existence and in moments of vivid experience of what matters most.

Christian Wisdom as "Practical"

Aristotle distinguishes practical from theoretical wisdom. Theoretical wisdom is about truths that can't be otherwise than they are. Think of the "necessary" truths of mathematics and logic; for Aristotle, the truths of physics, including theology, were similarly necessary. For him the notion of practical theology would have been puzzling. Practical wisdom, by contrast, is about what can very well be otherwise than it is, namely human action. Actions can be done or not done, done well or badly, virtuously or viciously; and practical wisdom is the knowledge by which a person acts well, as befits a rational being who is seeking to live his life well. Christian wisdom, while being knowledge of God and Christ in their "immeasurable greatness" and importance, is also practical in forming, infusing, and motivating the actions, perceptions, feelings, and deliberations of everyday life.

The apostles make knowing, thinking, and perceiving crucial to Christian living. The knowledge in question is knowledge of what has happened to humanity (and the rest of creation) in Christ Jesus, but it is also knowledge of how to live, *given* what God in Christ has done to us human beings. To the Colossians Paul says, "we have not ceased praying for you and asking that you may be filled with the knowledge of God's will in all spiritual wisdom and understanding" (Col 1:9; see also 3.10; Phil 1.9; Eph 1.17–18). Peter greets his readers by saying, "May grace and peace be yours in abundance in the knowledge of God and of Jesus our Lord. His divine power has given us everything needed for life and godliness, through the knowledge of him who called us by his own glory and virtue" (II Pet 1:2–3).[2] He then goes on to urge his readers to be diligent in adding virtue and virtues (knowledge, patience, self-control, piety, love of fellow Christians, and neighbor-love) to their faith, "For if these things are yours and are increasing among you, they keep you from being ineffective and un-fruitful in the knowledge of our Lord Jesus Christ" (II Pet 1:8).

It's a little bit odd that Peter lists knowledge among the virtues that are to prevent our knowledge from being "fruitless," though he uses a slightly different word (*gnōsis*) for the knowledge that does the preventing than for the knowledge (*epignōsis*) that is thereby prevented from being fruitless. The latter is the knowledge of Christ; perhaps the former is some supplementary knowledge, such as the knowledge of how to make oneself self-controlled or patient, and how to get along with fellow Christians and neighbors. Such mundane how-to knowl-edge differs from knowledge of the Lord, and it is also clearly handy in making one's knowledge of the Lord count in everyday life. This is a way in which general human psychology can contribute to Christian living and Christian wisdom.

Through a plethora of concepts and metaphors, Paul seeks to im-press on his readers that the light, understanding, knowledge, word, and wisdom of the Christian gospel is to be expressed in actions, in living, in "existing" (Rom 8:5).[3] Here are some of the main ones, with just a selection of where they can be found. "Walk" (Rom 8:4, Gal 5:16, Eph 2:10), "yield" (as to a master; Rom 6:13), "let rule" (Col. 3:15), "let dwell" (Col 3:16), "put on," "take off," "put away" (Rom 12:13–14, Eph 4:22–24, Col 3:12–13a, 14), "kill" (Rom 8:13, Col 3:5). Practitioners of virtue ethics are not just dreamy speculators, spinners of theories, members of graduate seminars, ivory tower intellectuals—they are to walk in the Spirit, yield their members to Christ as his "slaves," let his peace rule in their hearts, let his word dwell in their very personalities;

<hr>

[2] Where I have written 'virtue,' the NRSV has 'goodness.' But the word in question is *aretē*. And for reasons that I gave earlier in discussions of the fruit of the Spirit, I think 'virtue' is perfectly fitting in reference to the Holy Spirit.

[3] It is interesting that the language of "existing," which gave unfortunate rise to the language of existentialism, and which seems at first look to be innovative on the part of Søren Kierkegaard (see *Concluding Unscientific Postscript*, trans. Howard and Edna Hong [Princeton: Princeton University Press, 1992] and many of his other works), ap-parently derives from Paul.

they are to kill the yukky old geezer in them and strip themselves naked of the ragged stinking clothes of sin and dress themselves up in Christ's generosity, compassion, humility, patience, self-restraint, and gratitude to the Father.

A Reciprocity Between Acting and Understanding

The wiser you get, the better you act, and the better you act, the wiser you get. Because the wisdom in question is practical, this is a causal, and not merely logical, reciprocity. We start with some understanding of right action, and by acting on it we come to a deeper understanding of right action. Or we start with some action, approximately right, and by reflecting about it using what wisdom we have to assess it and ruminate on it, we become better able to act well. The reciprocity of acting and thinking, starting from either of these points of departure, results in an increase of virtue. The practical corollaries of this truth are (1) the life of moral action must be infused with high quality moral reflection; and (2) the life of moral reflection must be infused with moral action. The "practical" person who dives into action while impatient about careful moral reflection is neither more nor less foolish than one who reflects endlessly about moral questions but is loathe to rise on his legs and act. Both will suffer from arrested development in virtues.

In William Lee Miller's wonderful book, *President Lincoln: The Duty of a Statesman*, he stresses that Abraham Lincoln, faced with the daunting and risky tasks associated with honoring his oath to preserve the union of the United States against the forces of secession, relentlessly subjected his own actions to critical attention. Miller compares the thoughtfully philosophical Lincoln with his predecessor in the presidency, James Buchanan, who was reputedly one of the best "prepared" persons in history, by the number and variety of leadership positions he had held, to take on the role of president.

> But simply holding lesser offices is not all one needs in order to prepare for supreme national leadership. A fool or knave can rise through many eminent positions and still be a fool or knave. A thoughtful person can gain wisdom from the daily round of

ordinary life; a superficial person can learn little from commanding armies or being king. It depends upon what happens in the depths of one's mind and inner being while one fills those roles, whether high or low. Had all those places he had filled left a deposit of profound understanding in James Buchanan?[4]

This reciprocity has implications for the practice of virtue ethics. Virtue ethics is primarily a reflective activity: contemplating the virtues, thinking about their interrelations, their excellence and implications for human happiness, their relations to actions, emotions, perceptions, and judgments, their belonging within moral frameworks, and so forth. One implication, then, is that the practitioner of virtue ethics needs to keep in mind that her reflections are not self-sufficient, but are essentially connected to the life of practice. She must remind herself constantly that virtue ethics is not an end in itself but is properly in the service of living well, having a good and happy life, encouraging healthy institutions, being a good citizen and family member and friend, living bravely and generously, compassionately and truthfully. The other implication is that virtue ethics, properly practiced, can make an important contribution to the humanity of our lives. It supplies a special kind of reflection and begets a special kind of understanding. Thus it can enrich our moral practice by supplementing the on-the-fly thoughtfulness of the life of virtue. By its careful attention to psychological detail, it can deepen the wisdom with which we act.

Becoming "Accustomed" to Act Virtuously

Aristotle says we acquire virtues by repeatedly performing the actions to which they dispose us. We thus become "accustomed" ("habituated") to perform them, and this custom (habit) becomes the virtue. I argued

---

[4] William Lee Miller, *President Lincoln: The Duty of a Statesman* (New York: Vintage Books, 2009), 8. Some reviewers fault Miller for "hagiography" because of the slight attention he gives to Lincoln's shortcomings and mistakes. This is a historian's criticism, and as such may be well taken. But the book is so richly insightful and illustrative of Lincoln's excellences, which even Miller's critics acknowledge, that for the virtue ethicist the book is a treasury.

in Chapter 8 that 'habit' isn't a very good word for the kind of disposition that a virtue is, because it suggests a thoughtlessness, a rote or automatic quality that falls short of the intelligence that we attribute in attributing a virtue to a person. But Aristotle also says that in the early stages of this process the learner doesn't perform the actions as a virtuous person would; and he suggests that the repeated actions of justice or liberality or temperance[5] bring about a change in attitude or understanding of what the agent is doing. If the actions in question are acts of justice, this change of attitude would be mostly about the justness of the situations in which the actions are taken and what to do about it. It would be an improvement of the agent's understanding of the complexities of justice, and it would also likely be an increased concern for justice, a sense of its importance and urgency. These two improvements would be growth in wisdom as it relates to justice. The person becomes more just by becoming wiser, and wiser by becoming more just. If the actions in question are acts of temperance, then the change in attitude will be toward "the pleasures of touch" and what to do about them. For example, the new attitude might be that satisfying my appetite for food or sex is less important than other considerations such as justice, faithfulness to friends, and peace in my community. Such changes of "mind" bring the moral learner closer to virtue until, at last, he has become fully just, liberal, or temperate. Thus, what is at first merely repetition of behaviors characteristic of justice, temperance, and liberality comes to transform the individual's outlook—his understanding, his tastes, his dispositions of emotional response.

My point is that the bodily and social engagement is crucial to the transformation of the outlook; a person's outlook wouldn't change in the same way or to the same degree by merely thinking about the virtue, or even discussing the virtues with others. Aristotle seems to be counting on the repetition of "virtuous" action to bring about this attitudinal change that we can now name as an increase in wisdom. Surely the moral learner can also profit, along the way of his "habituation," from some instruction on the rationale for just and temperate behavior, though Aristotle doesn't say so. Such instruction would convey

---

[5] Such early "temperance" (*sophrōsunē*) must actually be self-control (*enkrateia*).

the wisdom that permeates these virtues. This would be the purpose of the instruction contained in *Nicomachean Ethics*. See book II. The apostle Paul seems to appeal to a similar psychological process when he says,

> I appeal to you therefore, brothers and sisters, by the mercies of God, to present your bodies as a living sacrifice, holy and acceptable to God, which is your spiritual worship. Do not be conformed to this world, but be transformed by the renewing of your minds, so that you may discern what is the will of God—what is good and acceptable and perfect. (Rom 12:1–2)

Whereas Aristotle seems just to assume that the learner of virtue will somehow pick up the rationale for the behavior to which he is becoming "accustomed," for Paul, the rationale is elaborate and controversial. The antecedent of Paul's 'therefore' is his discussion in Romans 1–11 of his understanding of the "history of salvation": the creation and corruption of humanity, God's provision of Israel and the divine law communicated to Israel as God's shepherding all of humanity back to himself, of his provision of Jesus Christ, God's own son, as God's loving "answer" to humanity's perdition, and the expectation of the renewal of the creation in him. This understanding is to be incorporated into our living, our existence, where it will make us wise by forming us in faith, hope, love, patience, gratitude, and humility. How do we go about incorporating this history so that our mind (our *nous*, our understanding) is renewed and becomes wise and insightful into God's will?—We do it by *acting on it*, by getting our *bodies* going in sacrificial service to the God who has done these glorious things on our behalf.

Thus, Aristotle and Paul presuppose an understanding of human moral development according to which moral understanding and moral action are reciprocal. To become wise, you must act well; and to become the sort of person who reliably acts well, you must think well (wisely). This chicken-and-egg order of causal priority can seem to create a conundrum if construed in abstract or absolute terms. Thus, if we're utterly bereft of understanding we can't act well enough to increase our understanding, and if we absolutely can't act well, we can't increase our understanding to become better at acting. But the truth is that we start out early in life with both some understanding and some ability to act. So the challenge is one of bootstrapping: to use the understanding we have to gain more by acting well; and to use the virtue we have to gain more by deepening our understanding. In Romans 12 Paul urges us to the former strategy; and in Romans 8 to the latter. Both are exhortations to action in a broad sense. To set your mind on (*phronein*) the things of the Spirit (several of which Paul points out in Romans 1–11) is a primarily mental action, though it may be implemented by a bodily offering (say, attending a weekly study of Romans); and serving at the soup kitchen is primarily a bodily offering, though it may have been triggered by thinking with gratitude (*eucharistia*) about the abundance of food in your freezer.

The mention of giving thanks as a kind of setting your mind on things of the Spirit alerts us that Paul has a variety of concepts of mental actions that can be naturally regarded as ways of exercising wisdom and thus increasing it. By rendering thanks to God for the great benefits we've received from his hand we set our minds on those benefits with emotional appreciation: we apprehend them as the *bene*fits they are. Similarly, when we accept Paul's urging always to rejoice (1 Thess 5:16–18), we discipline ourselves in the wisdom of seeing with the eyes of our heart the great goodness of God's provisions. In Philippians 4:8, Paul gives a string of kinds of excellent things and recommends that his readers "think about" (*logizesthai*) them. I don't think Paul is denying a place in the life of wisdom for being distressed at injustice, corruption, sleaziness, debauchery, fraud, cruelty, and the like. His several lists of vices and works of the flesh belie such a suggestion. But due appreciation of the badness of evil derives from an appreciation of what is good, making attention to the good the primary basis of wisdom.

The mental action of discerning (*dokimazein*) that Paul refers to in Romans 12:2 and in many other places has a rather different place in the formation of virtues and practice of wisdom. To discern is to test, to examine, to think critically about—say, some proposal or possible judgment about good and evil. It is to discriminate good from evil, or perhaps good from better or less good. If practiced well, it is the sharpness of wisdom, the ability to cut through deception and immature impressions. It's an ability we wouldn't expect children to have much of, or to be engendered by the children's sermon we referred to at the beginning of this chapter. But we would hope that the adult sermon that followed would both exhibit discernment and help the congregation acquire it.

Yes, virtue ethics approaches the acquisition of wisdom at some distance from practice: it is a conceptual, meditative, contemplative activity. It isn't the acquisition of wisdom that consists, itself, in laying one's body on the line for Christ. Yet, though at a distance, Christian virtue ethics keeps constantly in mind the practical character of the wisdom that it strives for. That is essential to virtue ethics being a discipline intended to deepen the practitioners' Christian wisdom. Christian virtue ethics conscientiously resists descending into pure "theory."

Wisdom and the Other Virtues

What Wisdom Understands

The apostle James asks, 'Who is wise and understanding among you? Let him show his works in wisdom's gentleness by his beautiful way of living' (Jas 3:13).[6] James's phrase "wisdom's gentleness" can be taken as a model of wisdom's relation to the other virtues. Thus, we would have wisdom's love, wisdom's humility, wisdom's generosity, wisdom's forbearance, wisdom's gratitude, wisdom's hope, wisdom's faith, wisdom's forgivingness, wisdom's courage, and so on.[7] Our moral understanding bears on each of the virtues and connects them. Practical wisdom implies all these dispositions (and more) in the person who possesses it. We can see, I think, why Socrates (in Plato's *Protagoras*) once proposed that really there is just one virtue, and it's wisdom. This one virtue would have a variety of facets, to which we give names like 'honesty', 'forbearance', and so forth. We could say that the particular virtues are different applications of wisdom.

---

[6]   The first sentence follows the NRSV. The second is my translation. The NRSV reads, "Show by your good life that your works are done with gentleness born of wisdom."
[7]   See Philippians 1:9–11.

We can think of the phrase 'wisdom's gentleness' as having two dimensions. First, it's the wisdom of *being* gentle: the appreciation of the importance of gentleness for having a good life and contributing to the good life of your associates. Wisdom is the caring understanding of something, in this case, gentleness. The wise person understands the importance of *his* or *her* being gentle, honest, compassionate, humble, patient, generous, courageous, and so forth. Someone who appreciated the importance of other people having the virtues but was easily willing to forgo the pleasure of having them himself might have a lot of understanding, but without being wise. This first aspect of wisdom is also, among other things, the appreciation of the virtue's place in the array of virtues, and thus it is a surveying or comprehensive view of the good life. For example, gentleness is often a way of being loving and compassionate; it may also be a way of being fair (just). And it may require self-control and perseverance (e.g., when you're dealing with an exasperating person). And humility may contribute to your success in being gentle. The understanding of these connections will make available to you a compelling rationale for wanting to be gentle and to have the related virtues. This understanding of the interconnections of gentleness with the other virtues will be a matter of degree; you can have some wisdom without having "complete" wisdom.

The second dimension is that wisdom is the understanding internal to the virtue in question, and thus the understanding, not *of the virtue*, but of contexts in which the virtue needs to be exemplified and of the importance of acting virtuously in those contexts. You can (just barely) conceive of a person who knew what was best to do in the relevant situations—and thus knew what all the virtues are wise about—but didn't have words for the virtues and thus was unable to evaluate the virtues as such. You could call the first kind of understanding objective inasmuch as it makes the virtue its object, and the second subjective inasmuch as it is the subject's understanding of the situations in which he acts virtuously. In exploring both the value of the particular virtues in human living and their internal logic, virtue ethics explores both of these perspectives of wisdom. Let us now illustrate them by looking briefly at three Christian virtues: gentleness, honesty, and patience.

Gentleness

In Chapter 7 we identified Christian gentleness as a variant of *agapē* (love of neighbor). The neighbor has, or may have, any number of aspects that are relevant to loving her. She may be powerful and impressive, disgusting and ugly, attractive and loveable, tempting, a malefactor, a benefactor, or fragile and vulnerable, to name a few possible qualities. The gentle person, as such, is sensitive to the last of these qualities. You will care about the neighbor, and so will be alert to and perceptive of her vulnerability to be hurt, afraid, or offended. To the extent that your gentleness is Christian, and thus a kind of *agapē*, you will be concerned *for the neighbor's sake* about the neighbor's potential for such disruption, rather than, say, because that fragility might drive away a customer or bring down on you the neighbor's wrath. This is how you, as a gentle person, "see" or think of the fragile persons in your midst. It is the part of your wisdom that belongs to your gentleness.

But if you're a little bit reflective—or *very* reflective, as you will be if you practice virtue ethics—you will not only think *with* wisdom's gentleness about your neighbor; you will also think wisely *about* gentleness. You will know, for example, that gentleness is a way of loving your neighbor and so belongs to that greater good that is the love of neighbor. You will also appreciate the special contribution that gentleness makes to the kingdom of love by short-circuiting the alienating potential that lies in fragility when it confronts the emotional roughness of anger and resentment. And perhaps you will appreciate that gentleness partakes of both generosity and compassion, and profits from self-control. You'll also see that, though gentleness is always a virtue and never to be eschewed, its "output" isn't to be recommended in every situation. It's in the nature of a virtue to *possess* it across all situations; but it's also in its nature not to be "applicable" in every situation (with the exceptions of faith, hope, and love).

Honesty

For our contemporaries, honesty is one of the first traits that come to mind when we're asked to give examples of virtues. But it's not a classical or biblical category.[8] Nevertheless, I think we can make out a virtue that would go by the name of Christian honesty.

The contemporary concept of honesty seems to blend justice (fairness) and truthfulness. If you're honest, you play fair, keep your promises, and tell the truth. In keeping your promises, you play fair by making them come true. But honesty isn't just a matter of behaving in these ways, because you might do so for reasons that differ from the reasons for which honest people would do them. If, for example, you play fair just because you don't want to be caught cheating, you wouldn't be *acting* honestly, even though you behave that way. The honest person sees and feels a deeper importance in acting honestly and behaves honestly *because* doing so has that importance. This is the wisdom of honesty, or the honesty of wisdom.

Similarly, if you tell a person the truth just because you want to protect your reputation as a truth-teller, then you aren't exemplifying the *virtue* of truthfulness or honesty. Your reputation can't be the deepest importance of truth-telling. There must be some reason that a reputation for it has become something to be cherished, and that reason would be the deeper one, the one closer to the bedrock motive defining the virtue. Truth is the right connection between what is said or thought, and the way things are. It's the condition of the situation being as the claim or the thought "says" it is. Telling the truth to one another is the way to give the other access to that connection and telling her something contrary to the truth is thus a way of misleading her, making her negotiation of reality more difficult and less effective than it would be if you told her the truth. (Admittedly, she may not want to hear the truth, and may prefer to be misled or kept in the dark for the sake of short-term emotional comfort.) Telling others the truth is a basic way of respecting them and helping them. This is the deeper

---

[8] The word occurs three times in the NRSV of the New Testament, each time translating a different Greek word: Luke 8:15 (*kalos*), Luke 20:20 (*dikaios*), and Ephesians 4:28 (*agathos*). In older English, 'honest' seems to be a generic word meaning something like morally upright or even just respectable. But Rosalind Hursthouse, in her introductory book on virtue ethics, devotes to honesty one of her most sustained accounts of a single virtue (*On Virtue Ethics*, 10–12). Honesty has perhaps received more attention from empirical psychologists than any other virtue. See the summaries of the studies in Christian Miller's books. For an account of our contemporary conception of honesty, see Roberts and West, "The Virtue of Honesty," 97–126.

reason for telling the truth and is the motive of wisdom's truthfulness. It's part of the rationale for classifying honesty as a virtue.

This brings us back to justice. Fundamental to the virtue of justice is respect for the ones to whom justice is to be done. Telling people the truth is a fundamental way to express respect. Truthfulness to others is a kind of justice. So it seems that truthfulness is important for two reasons: truth is the right connection of thoughts and claims to reality, and telling the truth to others is a fundamental way to respect them as persons. The honest person, then, is one who plays fair, keeps his promises, and tells the truth as he sees it *out of respect for reality and for persons as persons*. This is the thinking or orientation of the mind of the honest person; it's his wisdom insofar as it belongs to honesty.

So far, we've described a real virtue of honesty, but not a distinctively Christian one. To be peculiarly Christian, the reason for respecting reality and persons must set Christian honesty apart from mere virtuous honesty. It must draw on the Christian understanding of reality and persons. If God is the ultimate reality, the origin of all reality ("truth"), then to respect reality is to respect it as what God is and has made, or as what has been corrupted from what God has made. To know or tell the truth about the corruption is also to tell the truth about reality; but it's to see that reality as out of joint with what God made. To be truthful about corruption is to see it in its deviance from a standard of creation. To respect persons in a distinctively Christian way is to respect them as ones God has made in his own image. So to respect people is to respect God, and to respect God is to respect people. By their association with God, people take on a weight of glory that they don't have "on their own." Christian honesty is playing fair with people, including being truthful with them, because the world is God's and people are created in his image. This is Christian wisdom's honesty or Christian honesty's wisdom.

Patience

Patience is one of the traits that I have called "virtues of willpower."[9] In this book I'm calling them the "enkratic virtues." They include

---

[9] Robert Roberts and Ryan West, "Virtues of Willpower and Self-Possession," in *The Virtues of Endurance*, ed. Nathan King (Oxford: Oxford University Press, 2025), 33–59; "Will Power and the Virtues," *Philosophical Review* 93 (1984): 227–247.

self-control, perseverance, and courage in addition to patience. Unlike honesty and gentleness, these virtues are not defined by any kind of motive or reason. To manifest them, we must, of course, be motivated, but no particular kind of motive is intrinsic to the virtue. You can be self-controlled, persevering, courageous, or patient for just about any kind of reason—moral, immoral, and morally indifferent. For example, you might patiently wait for the kingdom of God, or practice patience in an effort to undermine democracy, or as part of your discipline to become a skilled poker player.

Patience is an ability to manage your impulses with respect to time. In particular, it's the ability to wait tranquilly as processes or events take time to unfold. The resistant force against which patience is practiced is an emotion that we call impatience. Impatience is an unpleasant anxiety, a frustration of the desire that waiting be over, an agitation in which you vainly wish you could hurry up the process. It is often marked by pacing and fidgeting, actions that you know to be fruitless in cutting down the time, yet provide a certain satisfaction, or at least a mitigation of the distress of impatience.

Patience, when actively practiced, is a skill at managing impatience. Since impatience is an emotion and mental state of a person, this skill is self-directed. To practice patience is to work on yourself, to manage yourself as one who is subject to impatience. One strategy of patience is to keep in mind that patience is needed, that good things often take time. If you're working on a long-term project and find yourself impatiently cutting corners out of anxiety to finish it, you can practice patience by reminding yourself of the gratification you'll have by doing a good job and the inevitability that it will take time and carefulness to do a good job. If you're waiting for someone else to do her part, you can remind yourself that she's under the same constraints and that impatience is fruitless. You can redirect your concern to other things that need attention while you wait, rather than waste your mind on barren fretting. If what you await is something good and pleasant, you can learn to enjoy the present moment as enriched by the prospect of what you're waiting for. If it's threatening (like a possible medical diagnosis), you can quiet your impatience by taking a very long view, for example, that of Bertrand Russell, who noted that in 200 years his little private anxieties would be swamped in oblivion. The understanding, skill, and resourcefulness with which you counter impatience are a learned know-how that is the wisdom of patience.

Like other skills, self-management of impatience can become second nature and so with long usage may be practiced almost without effort. We might say that it hardly needs to be *practiced* any more. In that case, patience's wisdom has been deeply appropriated and has become a reliable disposition, not just a practice but genuinely a virtue.

So far, we have mostly described patience in general terms and, though it's a virtue, it is neither distinctively Christian nor is it even necessarily moral, since it can be motivated by and used for a variety of purposes—Christian, moral, morally neutral, and even immoral. But some patience has a distinctly Christian character. How so? We have spoken of what patience is used for, and we have spoken of the resources that the patient person uses for managing his or her impatience. Both of these may distinguish Christian from non-Christian patience. You may deploy your patience in the interest of peace in the church, of love for your neighbor, and for God's sake. It may serve your worship and your spiritual growth. But also, particular strategies for managing impatience may derive from the Christian outlook. You may quell your impatience by remembering the patient faithfulness of God and the perspective of eternity. The prominent place of hope in the Christian outlook on the world is a resource that makes it especially fruitful for the development of patience. When you recruit your hope as a way of quieting your impatience, you are trading on the Christian wisdom of patience or the wisdom of Christian patience.

Conclusion

I've argued that Christian wisdom is a kind of knowledge, more specifically a kind of understanding, and even more specifically an understanding of what matters most and what matters less. It is a proper sense of priorities in human life. Christian wisdom also includes looking forward to a renewal of creation in which the proper order of priorities will prevail among its participants. Wisdom is "practical," being both manifested and learned in action. It is embedded, in one way or another, in all the virtues. The other virtues can be thought of as practical expressions of wisdom.

11
Humility

Introduction

I have chosen wisdom and humility as examples of virtues to illustrate the practice of Christian virtue ethics. Following the model of classical ancient virtue ethics, the choice of wisdom is a no-brainer: Virtue ethics *is* the conceptual exploration of wisdom, and the purpose of philosophy, as the loving pursuit of wisdom, is above all to make its practitioners wise. I have argued that wisdom is as central to the Christian virtues as it is to the classical ones, though the content of Christian wisdom is not quite the same. In contrast, by classical standards humility is an odd choice of illustration. I choose it for two reasons.

First, though this book is an introduction to virtue ethics in general, I have made Christian virtue ethics the central example, the illustrative case. In a pro-pluralist vein, I have stressed peculiarities that distinguish one moral outlook from another. Humility is a virtue that sets Christianity in contrast with Aristotle as an intellectual descendent of Homer. In the New Testament humility comes into prominence as a character ideal. This virtue, which was ignored, if not shunned, in classical ethics, is a major node in the Christian moral framework.

Second, humility is like wisdom in that both virtues penetrate deeply and pervasively, though in different ways, into the life of virtue. Both have widespread implications in moral psychology. They touch all the other virtues. I shall argue that humility is a special (and especially important) kind of purity of heart, one in which the heart is free from the polluting concern for what I shall call "self-importance." This purity will be a mark of all the virtues that center on caring about something good: love and worship of God, compassion to those who suffer, generosity to the neighbor, forgiveness of the offender, penitence for one's sins, and so forth, as well as such general goods as beauty, excellence

Virtue Ethics. Robert Campbell Roberts, Oxford University Press.
© Robert Campbell Roberts 2026. DOI: 10.1093/9780197848005.003.0014

in craftsmanship, and scientific or humanistic knowledge. Intellectual humility frees the love of understanding, knowledge, and truth from the pollution and impediment of self-importance.[1]

Humility and Classical Virtue Ethics

Humility is not named as a virtue in classical virtue ethics, but Socrates exemplifies a kind of humility. In Socrates, humility is perhaps more in the service of knowledge than of love, though it is also in the service of Athens and those who are willing to discuss life with Socrates. Benjamin Franklin, in his program of self-education in the virtues, affixes to the concept of humility a precept that "fully expresses" it: "Imitate Jesus and Socrates." The reason to think Socrates exemplifies humility is that he, the brilliant and original philosopher, refuses to have disciples, claims to be ignorant, and insists that his role is not to originate ideas, but only to draw them out of others. He is but a humble midwife of ideas, fruitless in himself but able to extract truth from other souls (*Theaetetus*). Having disciples, having knowledge, and being original in coming up with ideas are, for many people of intellectual ambitions, points of pride, even comparative invidious pride and thus self-importance. But Socrates explicitly forgoes them all. His love of knowledge is unmingled with selfish motives. It's a purity of motivation.

Humility has a number of properties or consequences that justify calling it a virtue. Franklin notes that, having put on at least the appearance of humility,

I soon found the advantage of this change in my manner; the conversations I engag'd in went on more pleasantly. The modest way in which I propos'd my opinions procur'd them a readier reception and less contradiction; I had less mortification when I was found to

---

[1] See my chapter (with Jay Wood) on humility in *Intellectual Virtues: An Essay in Regulative Epistemology* (Oxford: Oxford University Press, 2007) and "Understanding, Humility, and the Vices of Pride," in *The Routledge Handbook of Virtue Epistemology*, ed. Heather Battaly (New York: Routledge, 2019), 363–375.

be in the wrong, and I more easily prevail'd with others to give up
their mistakes and join with me when I happened to be in the right.[2]

But in Christian thought, humility's chief "advantage" is that it
protects the soul for love of God and fellow human beings. As doing so,
it promotes the social harmony and fruitfulness that the Bible calls life
and peace. In an uncanny anticipation of Christianity, Plato explicitly
commends a virtue of humility in a passage in *Laws* (4.716a–b). As in
the Christian conception, the larger good that humility serves, as a sort
of prophylactic, is *dikaiosunē*—justice, relational "rightness" with God
and human beings. A character called "the Athenian" speaks:

ATHENIAN. Now, then, our address should go like this: "Men, according to the ancient story, there is a god who holds in his hands the
beginning and end and middle of all things, and straight he marches
in the cycle of nature. Justice, who takes vengeance on those who
abandon the divine law, never leaves his side. The man who means
to live in happiness latches onto her [justice] and follows her with
meekness (well-ordered, *kekosmēmenos*) and humility (*tapeinos*).
But he who bursts with pride (*megalauchia*) puffed up by wealth or
honors or by physical beauty when young and foolish, whose soul
is afire with the arrogant belief that so far from needing someone to
control and lead him, he can play the leader to others—there's a man
whom God has deserted. And in his desolation he collects others like
himself, and in his soaring frenzy he causes universal chaos. Many
people think he cuts a fine figure, but before long he pays to justice
no trifling penalty and brings himself, his home and state to rack and
ruin. Thus it is ordained. What action, then, should a sensible man
take, and what should his outlook be? What must he avoid doing or
thinking?"

   CLINIAS. This much is obvious: every man must resolve to belong
to those who follow in the company of God.

---

[2] Benjamin Franklin, *The Autobiography of Benjamin Franklin* (1771–1790),
chapter 9. https://www.gutenberg.org/files/20203/20203-h/20203-h.htm#IX.

Though the concept of humility as a virtue seems to have taken firm root in the human imagination first in the New Testament, this passage makes it clear that the Christian revelation is not strictly required for the concept to emerge. All that is required is the insight that pride of the kind the Athenian describes here—indulgence of the desire for self-aggrandizement—muddies the commitment to the good of such "others" as home and state, so that they can be let go to rack and ruin for the sake of one's personal importance. In general, the vices of pride weaken and corrupt and jeopardize, and in the extreme case obliterate, commitment to the good in its various manifestations, including the virtue of justice. In the New Testament, the good in question is the rescue of the world from sin, and as Andrew Pinsent points out, the virtue that humility allows is the "extravagant" (246) one of Christ's love.[3]

The concern for self-aggrandizement takes various more specific forms, which are implied by a variety of Greek and English vice-terms. Some of the English terms are 'conceit,' 'envy' (the "positive" counterpart of which is 'invidious pride'), 'grandiosity,' 'domination,' 'self-righteousness,' 'arrogance,' 'presumption,' 'snobbery,' 'vanity,' and 'pretentiousness.' Another important vice, whose name is not, however, canonical in English, I call 'hyper-autonomy': the concern to be the only or ultimate agent of your actions. These vices have in common a concern for what I call *self-importance*. Self-importance differs from the kind of personal importance that is conferred by being loved. It is healthy and ethically legitimate to want to be important *to* somebody, and ultimately, important to God. But this kind of importance differs from the importance that people feel they get, or

---

[3] This passage in *Laws* is one of several uncanny anticipations of Christianity in Plato's writings. Another is a passage in *Republic*. Glaucon is expounding arguments to the effect that it's not good for you to be just, but only to appear so. The person who is thoroughly and purely just from the heart in all his motives and actions "will have to endure the lash, the rack, chains, the branding-iron in his eyes, and finally, after every extremity of suffering, he will be crucified (*anaschinduleuthēsetai*), and so will learn his lesson that not to be but to seem just is what we ought to desire" (361e; the translation is by Paul Shorey in the Loeb Classical Library. He notes, in a footnote, that the word he translates "crucified" is more strictly "impaled"). And a third anticipation is the very existence of Socrates as a man and as a thinker. For the reference to the passage in *Laws* I am grateful to Andrew Pinsent in his paper "Humility" in Michael Austin, and Douglas Geivett, eds., *Being Good: Christian Virtues for Everyday Life* (Grand Rapids: Eerdmans, 2012).

might get, from having more privileges than other people (arrogance or presumption), or by domineering over other people (domination), or by being admired and adulated by other people (vanity), or by being morally better than other people (self-righteousness), or by out-competing some important people in some area of supposed excellence such as beauty, wealth, influence, and the like (envy and invidious pride), or by belonging to some elite group (snobbery). These vices have in common the concern for self-importance (which has a strong comparing or competing aspect) but differ from one another in how self-importance is envisioned or achieved.

Humility and the Unanimity of the Church

The vices of pride threaten the single-mindedness of the church. "Let us not become conceited, competing against (*prokaloumenoi*—calling out, provoking) one another, envying one another" (Gal 5:26). After listing the ninefold fruit of the Holy Spirit in verses 22 and 23, Paul ends the chapter with these words about conceit, competition, and envy— two of the vices of pride, along with their structural essence: competition for self-importance. People who construe themselves as on the losing end of invidious pride or conceit or arrogance do tend to feel themselves hostilely "called out" or "put down," and, if not helplessly shamed, perhaps inclined to "rise up" in opposition. These attitudes are alienating. People who challenge others in this sense are not engaged in friendly competition, though they may fake it, but in malignant competition, the competition characteristic of envy and invidious pride. Other vices in the same class are self-righteousness (Luke 8:9– 14), vanity (Matt 6:1–6), arrogance (I Cor 4:19–5:2, 13:4), snobbery (James 2:1–7), envy and invidious pride[4] (Phil 1:15–18, James 3:13– 18), and domination (Mark 10:35–45; Luke 9:46–48). The harmfulness of these vices, combined with the universal and stubborn human penchant for them, suggests the importance of the virtue of humility, in which the concern for self-importance and the vices that are variants

---

[4] Invidious pride is joy in being more important than some select other, just as envy is pain in being less important than some select other.

of this concern are reduced or eliminated. The varieties of fruit of the Holy Spirit are all threatened with corruption by the vices of pride, and therefore supported by humility.

Note the repetition of "one another" in the Galatians passage. The vices of pride are intrinsically social. We envy *others*; we arrogate privileges from *others*; we dominate *others*; in self-righteousness we compare ourselves with *others*; in vanity we display ourselves before *others*; in servility[5] we suck up to *others*; snobbery is self-association *with certain others* for self-importance and self-dissociation *from certain others* for the same reason; and so forth. Self-importance is essentially *comparative with others* and *competitive against others*. Compare self-importance with the kind of importance we feel ourselves to have in knowing that someone loves us. If the love we feel ourselves to be the objects of, and our receiving of it, is pure, then we will not be interested in whether we are *more* loved than someone else or than other people generally. Thus, humility in the New Testament, as an "emptiness" of the vices of pride is, in its negative or indirect way, a relational virtue, not just a matter of "accepting our limitations," as people often suppose and say. It is a freedom from a social bondage or pathology. The bondage in question is to self-importance with its many social syndromes; and the freedom to which humility liberates us *from* that bondage is the freedom *to* the love of God and fellow humans, as well as to other good things such as truth and beauty and knowledge.

Paul encourages the Philippians, "Only, live your life in a manner worthy of the gospel of Christ, so that, whether I come and see you or am absent and hear about you, I will know that you are standing firm in *one spirit*, striving side by side *with one mind* for the faith of the gospel" (1:27, italics added). Paul is supposing that, if people are

---

[5] Servility may not be thought a vice of pride, but rather a vice of "humility"—insufficient self-respect. *As servile*, the servile person doesn't feel "proud," but "humble." This is not to deny that servility can be a device of self-promotion (see Mark Leibovich, *Thank You for Your Servitude* [New York: Penguin Press, 2022]). In that kind of case, it is a device of the vices of pride. But this much seems obvious: as a relational vice, servility is a device for exploiting the arrogance, conceit, vanity, domination, and so forth, of the other. It is grounded in a cynical exploitative understanding of the other's vices of vanity and domination. To be on the receiving end of servility can be uncomfortable for the person who not only sees that he is being exploited, but that the attempted exploitation presupposes his vice.

living in a manner worthy of the gospel of Christ, they will be of one spirit and one mind. If they are self-conceited, vying with one another for importance, and envying one another, their minds are assaulting one another and they're not living their life in a manner worthy of the gospel of Christ.

Paul goes on to speak of God's graciousness in that gospel, including the privilege of suffering with Christ, and concludes by repeating, in different words, the "one mind" standard for living worthily of the great benefits of the gospel: "If then there is any encouragement in Christ, any consolation from love, any sharing in the Spirit, any compassion and sympathy, make my joy complete: thinking the same way, having the same love, being in full harmony of souls and thinking the same thing" (Phil 2:1–2). And he reprises, again changing the vocabulary, the mention of what fragments the mind and soul of the church: "Do nothing from selfish ambition or conceit [strife or vainglory], but in humility regard others as better than yourselves" (Phil 2:3). The word 'competition' could be used to get at the meaning of *eritheia* (strife). *Eritheia* isn't friendly competition, but the nasty kind of rivalry that involves pleasure in the other's diminishment, whether in the resentful "losing" mode of envy or in the joyful "winning" mode of invidious pride. *Kenodoxia* means literally "empty glory" (vainglory) or "empty appearance." In an older English, a conceit is an imagining; thus a conceited person imagines himself to be something he isn't. *Dokeō* has this sense. Thus, *kenodoxia* is an empty "conceit" of oneself.

In verse 3 of Philippians 2, Paul goes on to identify the virtue that is contrary to selfish ambition, conceit, malignant competition, and envy (also domination and self-righteousness): "in humility regard others as better than yourselves. . . . Let the same mind be in you that was in Christ Jesus, who, though he was in the form of God, did not regard equality with God as something to be exploited, but emptied himself, taking the form of a slave, being born in human likeness. And being found in human form, he humbled himself and became obedient to the point of death—even death on a cross" (Phil 2:3b, 5–8). Humility is the mindset of people in whom the one-mindedness of the church is manifested. Their lack of the vices of pride leaves space in their hearts for "the same love" of one another and of God, the delights of encouragement in Christ, the consolations of love, sharing in the Spirit, compassion and sympathy.

Paul compares the humility that church members need if they are to be of one mind with the humility that Christ showed in becoming incarnate for our sake. In both cases, humility is accessory to love, and in both cases the act that expresses humility—the self-humbling—is a matter of emptying oneself of something. What the Christian empties herself of is analogous to what Christ emptied himself of, but they differ. We empty ourselves of the vices of envy, domination, and so forth, while Christ emptied himself of a rightful claim to the perquisites of deity. The result of an emptying (the act of self-humbling) is an emptiness, a void, an absence; and a partial emptying is a reduction.

It is arguable that Christ's self-emptying doesn't include all the perquisites of deity. For example, in the Sermon on the Mount (Matt 7:28–29), Christ seems to retain divine moral authority. Similarly, when he forgives the sins of the paralytic (Mark 2:1–12). Analogously, but also differently, when we empty ourselves of envy, arrogance, and the like, the evacuation is almost never complete. But whereas the limits of Christ's self-emptying are perfectly consistent with his act of love in the incarnation, the limits on our self-emptying compromise our love and mark an impurity in our character. When the writer of Hebrews says that Jesus "learned obedience," presumably he was also learning humility; but he wasn't emptying himself of the vices of pride. Maybe he was forfeiting, for the Father and for humankind, the ordinary goods of a human life—an amply long life, bodily comforts, the joy of parenthood, the support of friends, the respect of fellow human beings. But when, by contrast, we humble ourselves, we are often going against the grain of our arrogance, our pretentiousness, our urge to dominate others, our self-righteousness, thus "dying to self." The self in the sinner case is the false self; in the case of Christ, it is part of the true human self. But in both cases, humility is an emptiness accessory to love. The act of self-humbling is an expression of the trait of humility or an act by which the trait is acquired. In particular acts of humbling yourself you acquire more of the character trait of humility.

Let's consider some of the vices of pride as they arise in New Testament texts, and the virtue of humility that corresponds to them.

The Vices of Pride

Vanity

Beware of practicing your piety before others in order to be seen by them; for then you have no reward from your Father in heaven. So whenever you give alms, do not sound a trumpet before you, as the hypocrites do in the synagogues and in the streets, so that they may be praised by others. Truly I tell you, they have received their reward. But when you give alms, do not let your left hand know what your right hand is doing, so that your alms may be done in secret; and your Father who sees in secret will reward you. And whenever you pray, do not be like the hypocrites; for they love to stand and pray in the synagogues and at the street corners, so that they may be seen by others. Truly I tell you, they have received their reward. But whenever you pray, go into your room and shut the door and pray to your Father who is in secret; and your Father who sees in secret will reward you. (Matt 6:1–6)

Almsgiving is supposed to be an expression of generosity or compassion, thus of *agapē*. It is to be *for the sake of the other*. Only if it has this intentionality will it express the virtue. Prayer is to communicate praise and express loving trust and dependency on God. Only so will it be real prayer, and thus express faith and love. The satisfactions of faith in God and love of God and neighbor will be the "rewards" that Jesus speaks of. If these acts are done only for show, they are "hypocritical"— not what they pretend to be, and the essential reward will have been forfeited for something fake. Such actions are "vain" in the sense of lacking their proper point. The root problem and the source of vanity's tenacity is the order of what a person cares about. But this is a matter not just of our actions, but of our character, the orientation of mind from which our actions spring. Many of us care far too much about being praised and highly regarded by our fellow human beings, and far too little about actually helping others and having a relationship with God. That is, we are short on love of neighbor and God, and long on love of approval and admiration and praise by our fellow human beings.

Vanity is a faking, a distraction, and a way of being unserious about what we're doing. Sometimes it doesn't matter much; if we play piano for show rather than for the excellence of the music, we may play just about as well as if we were doing it with a more essential motive (although maybe not). But where we're performing actions characteristic of a virtue, as in the case of giving alms, doing it for show can evacuate the action of its purported meaning. To the extent that alms are given for show, they don't express generosity or compassion. And this is because here the motive is essential. But even in the case of playing the piano, the vain person has a misplaced joy: he enjoys the adulating attention, and to that extent turns his attention away from, or dilutes his appreciation of, the beauty of the music. He's distracted.[6]

Concerns that are fixtures of character are recalcitrant. A "hypocrite" may try unhypocritically to revise the order of his cares, but they have a way of returning to their former equilibrium. Just when we think we've had a bit of success at re-ordering them, we find the lower priority ones sneaking back into their former high positions. Jesus offers a bit of very practical advice on how to combat this recalcitrance. When you give alms, don't pay any attention to the fact that *you* are giving alms; just focus on the other's need and the relief or joy that the other experiences because of them: don't focus on the almsgiving, but on its real purpose. And when you pray, don't even give your vanity a chance of satisfaction. Do it where you can't be seen (and don't tell anybody about it). This will give it a better chance of being an authentic act of devotion and trust. And if you keep up this discipline of non-attention and non-display for a long time, the vanity of your character and the vain order of your cares may actually diminish and you become a more humble and faithful and loving person. You grow in humility by starving your vanity. Consider another piece of "advice" from Jesus on increasing your humility:

When he noticed how the guests chose the places of honor, he told them a parable. "When you are invited by someone to a wedding banquet, do not sit down at the place of honor, in case someone

---

[6] See Laura Frances Callahan, "Intellectual Humility: A No-Distraction Account," *Philosophy and Phenomenological Research* 108 (2024): 330–337.

more distinguished than you has been invited by your host; and the host who invited both of you may come and say to you, 'Give this person your place,' and then in disgrace you start to take the lowest place. But when you are invited, go and sit down at the lowest place, so that when your host comes, he may say to you, 'Friend, move up higher'; then you will be honored in the presence of all who sit at the table with you. For all who exalt themselves will be humbled, and those who humble themselves will be exalted." (Luke 14:7–11, altered)

This parable can sound like a send-up. Seeking the place of honor, says Jesus, is a risky way to get honor. If you want honor without danger of shame, better advice is to take the lower place. That not only protects you against being dishonored by being sent down (which is painful if you're an honor-seeker), but if your host should send you up, you get to be paraded to the higher place in front of everybody. A wonderful opportunity to feed your vanity! Faking humility is the better recipe if you're hungry for honor! To say the least, this worldly advice, taken straightforwardly, is not in the spirit of Jesus's self-emptying (Phil 2), or of his criticisms of the Pharisees' enthusiasm for honor, but rather in the competitive spirit that Paul so often challenges as destructive of love and church fellowship. So what shall we make of it?

—Well, it's a parable. So the point may not be the flat-footed worldly one that I've just read off its surface. For one thing, it does, rather humorously and by way of analogy, make the deeply biblical point that the humble will be exalted and the exalted humbled. 'Exalt' is ambiguous. To be morally exalted is to be an excellent or virtuous specimen of humanity—to be loving, just, compassionate, and truthful to the core—and humility as purity of heart is certainly that. That's the exaltation proper to humility. To be honored by your fellow humans is another kind of exaltation, and to make much of this second kind of exaltation is contrary to humility and all the virtues that depend on it. It is in fact to be "humbled" in the sense of being degraded and diminished as a person. To read the parable as a send-up is to read it as teetering playfully between these two concepts of "exalt." John 5:44: "How can you believe when you accept glory from one another and do not seek the glory that comes from the one who alone is God?"

Domination

James and John, the sons of Zebedee, bring their mom along to ask Jesus for a special privilege: to be seated at his right and left hand when he comes into his kingdom (Matt 20:20–28). Jesus responds that these positions of authority are conditional on being someone who is willing and able to suffer for the kingdom in the way that he is about to suffer. The brothers declare, presumptuously, that they are persons of such character. But they don't know what they're saying. It's the Father's business to prepare people for such authority.

When the other disciples hear about James's and John's power-play, they take it personally and resent it. They're provoked, *prokaloumenoi.* Jesus takes the occasion to have a little talk with the disciples about the exercise of power and authority, and what it is to be "great," since that's what they seem to want. He tells them that out there in the secular world being great is thought to come with being a ruler who lords it over others and can tyrannize them. Greatness is the power of the bully. But this is fake greatness. Real greatness comes from serving *others*, seeking *their* good, subordinating your private interests to the real interests of others. "Whoever wishes to be great among you must be your servant, and whoever wishes to be first among you must be your slave; just as the Son of Man came not to be served but to serve, and to give his life a ransom for many" (Matt 20:26–28). This is the wisdom in which the Father prepares those who love him. And if you're wise and so understand true greatness and desire *that*, you'll have the virtue of humility.

In their arrogance, James and John suffer from the vice of domination. The reaction of the other disciples suggests that they too aren't entirely free of this vice: they too see the attractions of self-importance by way of power over others, and don't like being elbowed into subordinate seating in the coming kingdom. Were all to empty themselves of this concern as Jesus was empty of it, they would be free to love one another as Jesus loves them. They would be great with the greatness of Jesus.

Self-Righteousness

Here is another parable of Jesus:

> Two men went up to the temple to pray, one a Pharisee and the other
> a tax collector. The Pharisee, standing by himself, was praying thus,
> "God, I thank you that I am not like other people: thieves, rogues,
> adulterers, or even like this tax collector. I fast twice a week; I give a
> tenth of all my income." But the tax collector, standing far off, would
> not even look up to heaven, but was beating his breast and saying,
> "God, be merciful to me, a sinner!" I tell you, this man went down to
> his home justified rather than the other; for all who exalt themselves
> will be humbled, but those who humble themselves will be exalted.
> (Luke 18:10–14)

The Pharisee exalts himself, in his own estimation, by joyfully
contemplating his moral superiority to the penitent tax collector. The
"advantage" of superiority to one's fellow human beings pervades the
concerns of the vices of pride. Envy, for example, exploits comparison
of a wide variety of kinds: beauty, wealth, privilege, power, skill, intelligence, and so forth. People can envy one another for all these kinds of
"superiority." Self-righteousness, by contrast, specializes in moral superiority. And because moral qualities are closer to being the essential
human qualities than the "accidents" of beauty, wealth, and so forth, it
seems particularly nasty: an offense against the very core of the other's
human identity and worth.

The Pharisee's joy is invidious: a species of schadenfreude. The
tax collector in question humbles himself, in his own estimation, by
reflecting on his sins—by presenting himself in the exposure of his
faults before the holy God. Jesus makes a judgment about which of
these is showing his true human dignity: it's the tax collector who is
exalted in his humanity. By contrast, the Pharisee who prides himself on his moral superiority to the tax collector, thus glorifying himself by vilifying his fellow worshiper, degrades himself as a human
being. Again, the offense in vicious pride is against *agapē* and its
variants: kindness, generosity, compassion, forgivingness, forbearance. And the beauty in humility—the utter lack of interest in building

oneself up by comparison with one's fellow human beings—is that it opens the heart for the virtues of neighbor-love, and thus for faith, hope, and love for God, the qualities of a true human being.

Snobbery

Part of the innate corruption in the current edition of the human race is the tendency to malignant tribalism. We tend to think of human beings as divided into two classes: Us, who are the good people, the normal people, the clean people, the respectable people, the real people, the important people, on the one hand; and the Others, on the other hand, who are a little weird, different, of questionable habits and intelligence and morals, of deviant opinions, not quite clean, a little disreputable, eaters of unwholesome and yukky things, not quite fully human, and not nearly as important as we are. This mindset sometimes crowds out the Holy Spirit in the church:

> My brothers and sisters, do you with your acts of favoritism really believe in our glorious Lord Jesus Christ? For if a person with gold rings and in fine clothes comes into your assembly, and if a poor person in dirty clothes also comes in, and if you take notice of the one wearing the fine clothes and say, "Have a seat here, please," while to the one who is poor you say, "Stand there," or, "Sit at my feet," have you not made distinctions among yourselves, and become judges with evil thoughts? (James 2:1–4)

The Christian brothers and sisters whom the apostle James challenges in this text are perhaps "middle class," respectable people, and they are a little put off by an invasion of their nice meeting by people who don't quite "fit." But the "glorious Lord Jesus Christ" had and has a different idea. His very glory reveals, among other things, that the poor person in dirty clothes is as beautiful a soul as anybody and is worthy of honor and a hearty welcome. James pointedly includes the poor person as belonging to the meeting: in treating her as second-class, "have you not made distinctions among *yourselves*?" In the light of Christ's glory, anyone who willingly comes belongs. A failure to see that is a darkness of the heart where Christ's glory should be shedding light.

Snobbery is a false sense of your superiority and a love of that supposed superiority, but it has a "we" focus rather than an individual one. You feel superior *because of* belonging to a certain elite, and you feel superior *to* people who are outside that elite. You look *down* from a social position at persons who are below it. As I say, this attitude is widespread among human beings, maybe even universal, but sometimes it is canonized in social-moral assumptions. For example, in the Greek attitude toward "barbarians" and the Ivy League attitude toward the unwashed multitude at the state universities. There is also an aspirational snobbery, a sense of your inferiority because you *don't* belong to the idealized elite; and this may have an active side in efforts to join the elite by "climbing" up into it.

Snobbery is a nasty kind of pride and division, and humility, insofar as it is opposed to snobbery, is manifested in the Christian virtues: love and justice. Generosity and compassion, gentleness and kindness, bespeak it (see the parable of the good Samaritan). I say snobbery is nasty, but isn't this wrong? Isn't classism ("favoritism," as James calls it) just normal human conduct? Many Princetonians and Greeks wear their snobbery with perfect comfort; it fits them like soft, deliciously cozy old clothes. It doesn't *feel* nasty. On the contrary, it feels good. The comparing contemplation of those barbarians and state university people is uplifting and pleasant.

But no: it's nasty. The Holy Spirit of the glorious Jesus makes this clear. Feeling comfortable in our snobbery is a glitch in our Christian character, a gap in our *agapē*, an incursion of pagan pride into our soul. We should strive for perfect humility, the eradication of snobbery, the purity of our Christian heart.

Arrogance or Conceit

After a greeting and words of encouragement, Paul opens I Corinthians by addressing the divisions in the church. The church at Corinth is suffering from factional conflict: the Paul-faction versus the

Apollos-faction versus the Peter-faction, and even the Christ-faction! (I Cor 1:12). Then Paul "digresses" until Chapter 3 into a discussion of pagan and Christian wisdom to which we referred in Chapter 10. In Chapters 3 and 4 Paul returns to the discussion of divisions. The divisions among the Corinthians have resulted from being guided implicitly by pagan wisdom, and from failure to incorporate and exemplify Christian wisdom. Apparently, the members of these factions are taking their loyalties as a matter of competing prestige. To some, attaching themselves to the wise and profound Paul seems to give them special importance, while to others, attaching themselves to the golden-tongued Apollos seems to give them a similar advantage. According to Paul, this isn't just a matter of ideological preference or loyalty, but bears on the adherents' sense of their own importance:

> I have applied all this to Apollos and myself for your benefit, brothers and sisters, so that you may learn through us the meaning of the saying, "Nothing beyond what is written," so that none of you will be puffed up in favor of one against another. (I Cor 4:6)

I take it that "what is written" refers to the wisdom of the prophets and apostles (Paul being a chief example), and that he takes the Corinthian factionalists to have gone beyond that in adopting a pagan way of thinking about prestige. The pagan way of thinking that Paul has more particularly in mind is that excellences like Paul's theological profundity and Apollos's eloquence are properly points of personal distinction for their possessors and their possessors' hangers-on. But by Christian standards that's pagan foolishness, not wisdom. Their excellences are not for personal ego-inflation. Paul and Apollos are instruments for promoting the kingdom of God: they want to be thought of as humble "assistants of Christ and stewards of the mysteries of God" (I Cor 4:1).

My dictionary says that *phusioûsthai* (NRSV "be puffed up") can be translated 'conceited' or 'arrogant.' In either case, Paul's redundant expressions "one above another" and "against the other" stress the competitive, interpersonal character of this foolishness. In English, conceit and arrogance are different vices of pride. Roughly, conceit is having too high an opinion of your importance (due to some supposed particular superiority, such as wealth, beauty, wisdom, or eloquence), where the importance in question is self-importance. Arrogance, by contrast, is impertinence or presumption. It's an implicit or explicit claim to entitlement or privilege, where (usually) the claim is illegitimate and its purpose is self-importance. An illegitimate claim to entitlement or privilege is not necessarily arrogant, though it may appear so to by-standers; it can be based on an innocent mistake. For example, a person might have been led to believe that the office he holds carries the privilege of free lunches, while in fact it doesn't. When he then insists on a free lunch because of his office, this isn't arrogance; he's just misinformed. The self-importance can be either conceited, in which the case the presumptuous claim presupposes that the arrogant person has that importance and is justified in the claim by his importance; or aspirational, in which the presumptuous claim is a way of creating or establishing his self-importance. Arrogance is compatible with low self-esteem. It is possible for a person to have an arrogant attitude (and in this sense be arrogant or express arrogance) even if he has the entitlement that he claims, if it has for him the significance of bolstering or expressing his self-importance. For the Christian, at least, the purpose of entitlements and privileges is not the self-importance of the person who has those privileges, but the "cause" that the entitlements serve. For example, Paul insists on his authority as an apostle, but this is not arrogant as long as his insistence on it is for the purpose of serving Jesus and his church.

In verse 7 Paul interrogates the supposed justification for the factionalists' conceit and/or arrogance: "For who sees anything different in you?" This "difference" would be some distinguishing excellence or entitlement that would justify the implicit claims of superiority, authority, or right in conceit and arrogance. "What do you have that you did not receive? And if you received it, why do you boast as if it were not a gift?" That is, what justifies your high opinion of yourselves? Other people, looking on, don't see any real superiority in you. If, say, you're priding yourselves on your adherence to Paul rather than Apollos, does this adherence actually make you wiser or more virtuous than those with whom you're comparing yourself? And if you do have any such superior wisdom or virtue because of your adherence to Paul, this is a gift that God has given you, not an excellence for which you can take credit. So: stop glorying in your superiority! The word 'humility' doesn't occur in I Corinthians 1–4, but it's clearly the virtue that's called for. All this strife for ascendancy needs to be dropped to make room for the unanimity of the Spirit, the mutuality of good will, Christian gentleness and kindness and generosity and forbearance.

Humility as Purity and Freedom

The concern for self-importance that marks the vices of pride is, from the point of view of God's kingdom project, a pollution, a distraction, and a bondage. So humility, which drives out the concern for self-importance, making room for spiritual health, unanimity of the community, and the virtues of love, is a kind of purity of heart, a firmness of attention, and a liberation.

Purity is subject to the prepositions 'in' and 'of.' All purity is purity in something—say, water, gold, cotton, love, justice. It's never just free-standing purity. Where there's purity, there's always *something* that's pure. Also, purities are relative to pollutions. When something is claimed to be pure, it's always proper to ask, "pure *of* or *from what*?" If you have in mind bacterial pollution in water, then water can be pure even if it has some dissolved alkalis in it. If you have in mind artificial fibers that might be mixed into cotton, your jeans can be pure cotton even if they're a little dirty. A person's heart might be pure of greed even though it's polluted with white supremacy: she's not at all out to make money, but just to make the world safe for white people. The virtue of humility is a specific purity, a purity of heart. Most people's hearts are polluted with concern for self-importance: we are to some extent vain, domineering, arrogant and conceited like the Corinthians, and envious. We are short on the purity of heart that is humility. And here, when we speak of the heart, we are speaking of our love of neighbor and of God and his kingdom. Our love of these beautiful and good things is not pure but compromised by our concern for self-importance. The more we grow in humility, the purer is our love.

The ideal of Christian formation is that in all that we do—in our work, in our families, in our play, in our fellowship with others, in our politics—we be oriented by God's kingdom and his righteousness. That requires paying attention to it. The concern for self-importance distracts us from it. So in rooting out the concern for self-importance, humility makes it possible for our attention to be more steadily fixed on what really matters.

In the Christian moral framework, the concern for self-importance that is basic to envy, domination, conceit, arrogance, and vanity is a mighty impediment to living well, to happiness and human fulfillment. It disrupts peace in the community and causes personal misery. It's a barrier to reaching our essential human goal. The vices of pride are shackles. Humility, then, is a state of liberation, a freedom of the soul.

Paganism Again: The Concept of Hubris

I've expounded the Christian virtue of humility as contrary to the vices of pride and have said that ancient Greek paganism didn't have a canonical virtue of humility. This combination of positions invites a question about the very Greek concept of hubris. Hubris is certainly a kind of pride, so wouldn't a person who exhibits little or no hubris, or struggles against his hubris, exhibit or at least be reaching for a virtue of humility, even in the absence of a name for it?

Hubris, as the Greeks understand it, is uppitiness or arrogance in attempted violation of the limits of human finitude. It is the disposition to trespass on the gods' territory. The gods are not very generous with their territory. In fact, they're defensive in a way suggestive of the vices of pride. They are touchy about human competition for their prerogatives. The concept of hubris belongs to a context of envy and vengeance, namely the gods' envy and their vengeance on any humans who dare to compete for their special entitlements. The gods get angry with uppity humans and bring about their downfall. Humility doesn't get much attention as a theme in Greek thought, but to the extent that we can think of a virtue that is contrary to hubris, it would be a cautiousness not to overstep human limitations. It would be motivated by a fear of the gods' tendency to get nasty when envious. Its maxim would be: Watch out for the gods' envy! Don't get too big for your mortal britches! Be careful not to make the gods jealous!

The contrast with God as presented in the New Testament couldn't be starker. God wants to share his territory with us humans. He is himself humble and generous. He humbles himself to exalt us, to glorify us, to share his divinity with us. He gladly dwells among us and in us, and gives us his Spirit, bearing in us his Spirit's fruit, imprinting traces of his character on us. To the extent that we exemplify the virtue of humility, we resemble the character of God.

Conclusion: What Is Humility Made Of?

In Chapter 6 we addressed the question of the kind of dispositions that virtues are. We said that the substantive virtues, such as justice, generosity, truthfulness, and compassion are "made of" thoughts and concerns—thoughts dynamized by concerns and loves, concerns sculpted by an understanding of their objects. Wisdom is the understanding that goes with each of the substantive virtues and the overarching understanding of life that makes for the whole array of such virtues. And we said that the enkratic virtues, such as self-control, patience, courage, and perseverance are constituted primarily by abilities (capacities, powers, skills) of self-management—the management of concerns, desires, impulses, emotions, perceptions, and habits. Each such ability also presupposes some self-understanding as deployable in a know-how of self-management.

To which class of virtues does humility belong? What kind of disposition or personal quality is humility? Is it a concerned way of thinking about self, world, and others? Is it a self-management skill? I have said that it is a purity of love, generosity, compassion, justice, truthfulness, and whatever other substantive virtues of the heart there are. The pollution of which it is a purity is the concern at the center of the vices of pride: the concern for the kind of pseudo-importance that I have called self-importance. I have said that it is a freedom from such vices as envy, domination, arrogance, and vanity, and from the moral distraction that they embody. All three of these characterizations are negative or privative: *lack* of pollution, *exemption* from distraction, *freedom* from bondage. Tradition distinguishes humility as a distinct virtue. It is not identical with generosity, truthfulness, justice, or whatever. And it can characterize other things than these Christian virtues: a commitment to a craft or a political ideal, Socrates's quest for knowledge. I conclude that humility is an especially important kind of absence, namely, the absence of the vices of pride. It has the status of a distinct virtue and is not simply identical with any of the interests of which it can be the purity, because the vices of pride are endemic among human beings and are such a dire and insidious threat to our happiness and goodness.

Postscript

I've argued for a practice of philosophical ethics that focuses on the virtues and whose main purpose is to improve the wisdom, and by implication, more generally the virtues, of its practitioners: Its purpose is to aid in the formation of better functioning, more complete, and happy human beings. Truths about the virtues are learned along the way, but if the activity succeeds as philosophy, such truths will not be idling, "academic" insights, but embodied in a distinctly ethical kind of understanding that engages the practitioner's emotions, purposes, and actions. The practice centers on sorting out the concepts of the virtues, but in doing so, involves exploring a range of psychological concepts such as judgment, emotion, intention, concern, perception, and action. I take it that Elizabeth Anscombe had something like this in mind when she spoke of a "philosophy of psychology."

A subtext of this book has been that virtue ethics in its modern edition hasn't lived up to its potential. The Christian tradition, in its practice of regular reflection on the Christian life and its psychological constitution, with the explicit purpose of encouragement in the formation of Christian character, has something to teach philosophers who reflect about virtues and vices. Regardless of what ethical tradition and outlook a philosopher regards as correct, the mere fact that it's an *ethical* outlook would seem to imply some conception of the ethically well-formed person, a serious concern to understand how virtues and vices work, and the expediency of an effort to help ourselves and others, through philosophical reflection on the ethical concepts, to become persons who exemplify the ideals

Virtue Ethics. Robert Campbell Roberts, Oxford University Press.
© Robert Campbell Roberts 2026. DOI: 10.1093/9780197848005.003.0015

of that outlook. Such an orientation and purpose in philosophizing hearkens back not only to the ancient Greek ethicists but also to the Mosaic law, the wisdom tradition of ancient Israel, and the theology of the church in its best moments.[1]

[1] See Ellen Charry, *By the Renewing of Your Minds: The Pastoral Function of Christian Theology* (Oxford: Oxford University Press, 1999); and Ellen N. T. Wright discusses "in Christ" and "Christ in us" extensively across many works, particularly focusing on the theme of **new creation** and the believer's participation in Christ's resurrected life, with key insights found in books like *Simply Jesus*, *Surprised by Hope*, and his commentaries on the Pauline epistles (like *Paul and the Faithfulness of God*, part of the *Christian Origins and the Question of God* series), where he emphasizes being a foretaste of the renewed creation Charry, *God and the Art of Happiness* (Grand Rapids: Eerdmans, 2010).

Bibliography

Adams, Robert (1999). *Finite and Infinite Goods: A Framework for Ethics*. Oxford: Oxford University Press.

Adams, Robert (1987). "Pure Love." In *The Virtue of Faith and Other Essays in Philosophical Theology*. New York: Oxford University Press, 174–192.

Adams, Robert (2009). *A Theory of Virtue: Excellence in Being for the Good*. Oxford: Oxford University Press.

Anscombe, Elizabeth (1958). "Modern Moral Philosophy." *Philosophy 33*: 1–19.

Aquinas, Saint Thomas (1948). "*Summa Theologiae*." Translated by the Fathers of the English Dominican Province. 5 vols. Westminster, MD: Benziger Brothers.

Arendt, Hannah (1959). *The Human Condition: A Study of the Central Conditions Facing Modern Man*. Garden City, NY: Doubleday.

Aristotle (1932). *Politics*. Translated by H. Rackham in Loeb Classical Library. vol. 264. Cambridge, MA.

Aristotle (1935). *Eudemian Ethics*. Translated by H. Rackham in Loeb Classical Library. vol. 285. Cambridge, MA.

Aristotle (1980). *Nicomachean Ethics*. Translated by David Ross, revised by J. L. Ackrill and J. O. Urmson. Oxford: Oxford University Press.

Austin, Michael, and Douglas Geivett, editors (2012). *Being Good: Christian Virtues for Everyday Life*. Grand Rapids: Eerdmans.

Battaly, Heather, editor (2019). *The Routledge Handbook of Virtue Epistemology*. New York: Routledge.

Baumeister, Roy, and Kathleen Vohs (2016). *Handbook of Self-Regulation: Research, Theory, and Applications*. New York: Guilford Press.

Benedict, Ruth (1934). "Anthropology and the Abnormal." *The Journal of General Psychology 10*: 59–80.

Besser-Jones, Lorraine, and Michael Slote, editors (2015). *The Routledge Companion to Virtue Ethics*. New York: Routledge.

Book of Common Prayer (1928). New York: The Church Pension Fund. https://www.bcponline.org.

Callahan, Laura Frances (2024). "Intellectual Humility: A No-Distraction Account." *Philosophy and Phenomenological Research 108*: 330–337.

Calvin, John (1960). *Institutes of the Christian Religion*. Translated by Ford Lewis Battles, edited by John T. McNeill. Philadelphia: The Westminster Press.

Camus, Albert (1988). *The Stranger*. New York: Vintage.

Card, Claudia (1988). "Gratitude and Obligation." *American Philosophical Quarterly 25*: 115–127.

Charry, Ellen (1999). *By the Renewing of Your Minds: The Pastoral Function of Christian Theology*. Oxford: Oxford University Press.

Charry, Ellen (2010). *God and the Art of Happiness*. Grand Rapids: Eerdmans.

Crisp, Roger, and Michael Slote, editors (1997). *Virtue Ethics.* Oxford: Oxford University Press.

DeYoung, Rebecca Konyndyk (2021). "What Are You Guarding? Virtuous Anger and Lifelong Practice." In Adam Pelser and Scott Cleveland, editors, *Faith and Virtue Formation: Christian Philosophy in Aid of Becoming Good.* Oxford: Oxford University Press, 20–47.

Evans, C. Stephen (2004). *Kierkegaard's Ethic of Love: Divine Commands and Moral Obligations.* Oxford: Oxford University Press.

Feynman, Richard (1985). *You Must Be Joking, Mr. Feynman,* as told to Ralph Leighton, editor. Edward Hutchings. New York: W. W. Norton.

Flanagan, Owen, and Amélie Oksenberg Rorty, editors (1993). *Identity, Character, and Morality: Essays in Moral Psychology.* Cambridge, MA: MIT Press.

Franklin, Benjamin (1771–1790). *The Autobiography of Benjamin Franklin.* https://www.gutenberg.org/files/20203/20203-h/20203-h.htm#IX.

Frede, Dorothea (2003). "Stoic Determinism." In Brad Inwood, editor, *Cambridge Companion to the Stoics.* Cambridge: Cambridge University Press, 179–205.

Furtak, Rick Anthony (2005). *Wisdom in Love: Kierkegaard and the Quest for Emotional Integrity.* Notre Dame, IN: University of Notre Dame Press.

Garcia, Jorge (2015). "Roles and Virtues." In Lorraine Besser-Jones and Michael Slote, editors, *The Routledge Companion to Virtue Ethics.* New York: Routledge, 415–423.

Gauthier, David (1986). *Morals by Agreement.* Oxford: Clarendon Press.

Gill, Christopher. "What Is Stoic Virtue?" https://modernstoicism.com/what-is-stoic-virtue-by-chris-gill/.

Hadot, Pierre (1995). *Philosophy as a Way of Life.* Translated by Michael Chase. Oxford: Blackwell.

Hadot, Pierre (2004). *What Is Ancient Philosophy?* Translated by Michael Chase. Cambridge, MA: Harvard University Press.

Hare, John (2009). *God and Morality: A Philosophical History.* Hoboken: Wiley-Blackwell.

Herdt, Jennifer (2008). *Putting on Virtue: The Legacy of the Splendid Vices.* Chicago: University of Chicago Press.

Hobbes, Thomas (1651). *Leviathan.* https://www.gutenberg.org/ebooks/3207.

Hume, David (1888). *Treatise of Human Nature,* L. A. Selby-Bigge, editor. Oxford: Oxford University Press. https://davidhume.org/texts/t/3/3/full.

Hursthouse, Rosalind (1999). *On Virtue Ethics.* Oxford: Oxford University Press.

Inwood, Brad, editor (2003). *Cambridge Companion to the Stoics.* Cambridge: Cambridge University Press.

Irwin, Terence (1999). "Splendid Vices? Augustine For and Against Pagan Virtues." *Medieval Philosophy and Theology 8:* 105–127.

Kant, Immanuel (1996). "Groundwork of the Metaphysics of Morals and Critique of Practical Reason." In Mary J. Gregor, editor, *The Cambridge Edition of the Works of Immanuel Kant: Practical Philosophy.* Cambridge: Cambridge University Press, 41–108 and 133–271.

Kawall, Jason (2009). "In Defense of the Primacy of the Virtues." *Journal of Ethics and Social Philosophy 3:* DOI: 10.26556/jesp.v3i2.32.

Kierkegaard, Søren (1980). *The Sickness unto Death.* Translated by Howard and Edna Hong. Princeton: Princeton University Press.

Kierkegaard, Søren (1992). *Concluding Unscientific Postscript.* Translated by Howard and Edna Hong. Princeton: Princeton University Press.

King, Nathan, editor (2025). *The Virtues of Endurance.* Oxford: Oxford University Press.

Kristjánsson, Kristján (2017). *Aristotelian Character Education.* London: Routledge.

Leibovich, Mark (2022). *Thank You for Your Servitude.* New York: Penguin Press.

MacIntyre, Alasdair (2007; first edition 1981). *After Virtue: A Study in Moral Theory.* Notre Dame, IN: University of Notre Dame Press.

MacIntyre, Alasdair (1999). *Dependent Rational Animals: Why Human Beings Need the Virtues.* Peru, Illinois. Open Court.

MacIntyre, Alasdair (2016). *Ethics in the Conflicts of Modernity: An Essay on Desire, Practical Reasoning, and Narrative.* Cambridge: Cambridge University Press.

Mill, John Stuart (1863). *Utilitarianism.* https://www.gutenberg.org/cache/epub/11224/pg11224-images.html.

Mill, John Stuart (1873). *Autobiography.* https://www.gutenberg.org/cache/epub/10378/pg10378-images.html.

Miller, Christian (2013). *Moral Character: An Empirical Theory.* Oxford: Oxford University Press.

Miller, Christian, and Ryan West, editors (2020). *Integrity, Honesty, and Truth Seeking.* New York: Oxford University Press.

Miller, William Lee (2009). *President Lincoln: The Duty of a Statesman.* New York: Vintage Books.

Nussbaum, Martha (1994). *The Therapy of Desire: Theory and Practice in Hellenistic Ethics* Princeton: Princeton University Press.

Nussbaum, Martha (2001). *Upheavals of Thought: The Intelligence of Emotions.* Princeton: Princeton University Press.

Pelser, Adam, and Scott Cleveland, editors (2021). *Faith and Virtue Formation: Christian Philosophy in Aid of Becoming Good.* Oxford: Oxford University Press.

Pinsent, Andrew (2012). "Humility." In Michael Austin and Douglas Geivett, editors, *Being Good: Christian Virtues for Everyday Life.* Grand Rapids: Eerdmans, 242–262.

Plantinga, Alvin (1981). "Is Belief in God Properly Basic?" *Noûs* 15: 41–51.

Plantinga, Alvin (1984). "Advice to Christian Philosophers." *Faith and Philosophy* 1: 253–271. https://place.asburyseminary.edu/cgi/viewcontent.cgi?article=1019&context=faithandphilosophy.

Plato: Complete Works (1997). John M. Cooper and D. S. Hutchinson, editors. Indianapolis: Hackett.

Porter, Steve, and Brandon Rickabaugh (2021). "The Sanctifying Work of the Holy Spirit in Virtue Formation." In Adam Pelser and Scott Cleveland, editors, *Faith and Virtue Formation: Christian Philosophy in Aid of Becoming Good.* Oxford: Oxford University Press, 123–145.

Roberts, Robert (1984). "Will Power and the Virtues." *Philosophical Review* 93: 227–247.

Roberts, Robert (2003). *Emotions: An Essay in Aid of Moral Psychology.* Cambridge: Cambridge University Press.

Roberts, Robert (2007, 2008). "Situationism and the New Testament Psychology of the Heart." In David Lyle Jeffrey, editor, *The Bible and the University*. Paternoster Press (2008) and Grand Rapids: Zondervan (2007), 139–160.

Roberts, Robert (2013). *Emotions in the Moral Life*. Cambridge: Cambridge University Press.

Roberts, Robert (2019). "Review of Zagzebski, *Exemplarist Moral Theory*." *Australasian Journal of Philosophy 97*: 205–207.

Roberts, Robert (2022). *Recovering Christian Character*. Grand Rapids: Wm. B. Eerdmans.

Roberts, Robert (2025). *Virtue Ethics in Christian Perspective*. Eugene: Cascade.

Roberts, Robert (2025). *Attention to Virtues: An Affective Grammar*. Cambridge: Cambridge University Press.

Roberts, Robert, and Ryan West (2025). "Virtues of Willpower and Self-Possession." In Nathan King, editor, *The Virtues of Endurance*. Oxford: Oxford University Press, 33–59.

Roberts, Robert, and W. Jay Wood (2007). *Intellectual Virtues: An Essay in Regulative Epistemology*. Oxford: Oxford University Press.

Roberts, Robert, and W. Jay Wood (2019). "Understanding, Humility, and the Vices of Pride." In Heather Battaly, editor, *The Routledge Handbook of Virtue Epistemology*. New York: Routledge, 363–375.

Roberts, Robert, and Ryan West (2020). "The Virtue of Honesty: A Conceptual Exploration." In C. Miller and R. West, editors, *Integrity, Honesty, and Truth Seeking*. Oxford: Oxford University Press, 97–126.

Robinson, Marilynne (2013). *When I Was a Child, I Read Books*. New York: Farrar, Straus, and Giroux.

Russell, Daniel (2011). *Practical Intelligence and the Virtues*. Oxford: Oxford University Press.

Sartre, Jean-Paul (2023). "*The Stranger* Explained." In Ronald Aronson and Adrian van den Hoven, editors, *We Have Only This Life to Live*. New York: New York Review Books, 16–43.

Schneewind, J. B. (1990). "The Misfortunes of Virtue." *Ethics 101*: 42–63.

Seneca (1995). *Seneca: Moral and Political Essays*. Edited and translated by John M. Cooper and J. F. Procopé. Cambridge: Cambridge University Press.

Seneca. *Of Benefits*. Translation by Roger L'Estrange. https://www.gutenberg.org/files/56075/56075-h/56075-h.htm.

Slote, Michael (1997). "Agent-Based Virtue Ethics." In Roger Crisp and Michael Slote, editors, *Virtue Ethics*. Oxford: Oxford University Press, 239–262.

Slote, Michael (2001). *Morals from Motives*. New York: Oxford University Press.

Smith, Adam (1759). *The Theory of Moral Sentiments*. https://www.ibiblio.org/ml/libri/s/SmithA_MoralSentiments_p.pdf.

Sorabji, Richard (2000). *Emotions and Peace of Mind*. Oxford: Oxford University Press.

Stocker, Michael (1976). "The Schizophrenia of Modern Ethical Theories." *Journal of Philosophy 73*: 453–466.

Thaddeus, Monk (2012). *Our Thoughts Determine Our Lives, The Life and Teachings of Monk Thaddeus of Vitovnica*. Compiled by the St. Herman of Alaska Brotherhood, translated by Ana Smiljanic. Platina, CA: St. Herman of Alaska Brotherhood Press.

Williams, Bernard (1972). *Morality: An Introduction to Ethics*. San Francisco: Harper and Row.

Williams, Bernard (1986). *Ethics and the Limits of Philosophy*. Cambridge, MA: Harvard University Press.

Wright, N. T. (2012). *After You Believe*. San Francisco: HarperCollins.

Zagzebski, Linda (1996). *Virtues of the Mind: An Inquiry into the Nature of Virtue and the Ethical Foundations of Knowledge*. Cambridge: Cambridge University Press.

Zagzebski, Linda (2018). *Exemplarist Moral Theory*. Cambridge: Cambridge University Press.

Index

For the benefit of digital users, indexed terms that span two pages (e.g., 52–53) may, on occasion, appear on only one of those pages.

abilities (capacities, powers), 17, 58–59, 63, 93–94, 131–32, 133, 140–41, 145–50, 152, 155–56, 160, 163–66, 170–73, 197–98, 214, 240–42, 247, 268

actions, 59–63, 68, 94, 96, 100, 121–22, 124, 131–32, 149, 149n.9, 228, 237–42
  and commandments, 183–87
  and getting into another's mind, 151–55
  and passion, 173
  relation of the believer's to God's, 173–77

Adams, Robert M., 57n.10, 132n.1

admiration, 54–55, 142, 169, 175–76, 189, 220, 225–26, 257

agapē (love), 157, 166–70, 177–78, 207–10, 223, 244, 257, 262–63

agency, 34–35, 63, 99, 101, 150, 157, 171, 252–53

alienation from one's work, 39–40

analysis, philosophical, 83–86, 212–13

anger, 17–20, 83–89, 95, 97, 117–18, 204–6, 208, 244

Anscombe, Elizabeth, 2, 3–4, 30–34, 40, 182

apatheia, 27–28, 78–89, 114, 116–17, 118, 199

Aquinas, Thomas, 5, 34, 44, 45–46, 47–48, 55, 88, 118n.4, 122, 193

Aristotle, 2, 4, 34, 35–36, 44–48, 53, 55, 63, 72–73, 89, 98–102, 110, 113–22, 125–27, 129, 138–39, 218
  on friendship, 161–62
  on justice, 121, 161
  on pleasure, 135
  on self-control, 160–61
  on shame, 160–61
  on virtues, 160–62

arrogance, 142, 253–54, 263–66

attention, 54n.4, 73–74, 76–77, 84, 89–90, 121–22, 136–37, 145–47, 154–55, 165–66, 170, 184, 195–96, 201, 213, 218, 219–20, 221–26, 237, 238, 241, 258, 266–67

Benedict, Ruth, 12–13

biology, moral (metaphysical), 5, 36–37, 45–48, 114–18

Calvin, John, 194–96

capacities (abilities, powers), 17, 58–59, 63, 93–94, 131–32, 133, 140–41, 145–50, 152, 155–56, 160, 163–66, 170–73, 197–98, 214, 240–42, 247, 268

character, 17–19, 30–31, 40–41, 42–43, 52–54, 63, 72–73, 74, 75, 78, 83, 84, 88–89, 90, 93, 97, 100–1, 102–3, 107–8, 110–11, 112–14, 116–17, 123, 130, 131, 132–33, 135–36, 139–40, 179, 183–84, 187, 190–91, 213–14, 219–20, 222, 234–35, 257, 258, 267–68
  concerns as traits of, 134–36
  and laws, 183–87
  mental powers as traits of, 145–47
  others' minds as entering into, 149–55
  Stoic, 116–17
  thought as forming, 136–45, 146

Charry, Ellen, 30n.2, 271n.1

chastity, 147, 184, 185, 187

commandment, 60, 167, 181–87